The Fight to Save American Freedoms

WAS NOVEMBER 3, 2020, AMERICA'S RUSH TO REPEAT THE DARKEST FAILURES OF WORLD HISTORY?

Stanley Duncan

NEWMAN SPRINGS PUBLISHING
320 Broad Street
Red Bank, NJ 07701

First originally published by Newman Springs Publishing 2021

ISBN 978-1-63881-831-1 (Paperback)
ISBN 978-1-63881-832-8 (Hardcover)
ISBN 978-1-63881-833-5 (Digital)

Printed in the United States of America

Contents

Sounds the alarm to all American patriots—The impact of the 2020 election—A nation at risk—Explanation of why we must look back into our distant history in order to appreciate the wonderful protections this nation affords all Americans.

The United States of America had not been born, but it would be the answer for combating the life of despair suffered by Europeans for centuries! Protestants fight Catholics—Radical religious changes and challenges—Millions die—Centuries of persecution in Europe—Religious, political, and social injustice—The power of religious fervor—What happened when divergent religious doctrines in medieval Europe competed to win souls into their church?

The monarch who used religion to support his personal agenda—Rules for thee, but not for me!—Rule by divine right—Defying the Catholic Pope in Rome—How to start, own, and rule your personal church from the throne!—More religious turmoil and persecution—Bloody Mary I and Elizabeth I were their father's daughters and ruled over "Unmerry Old England"—A great turning point in world history, 1588, English defeat of the Spanish armada—English men and women yearned to "Breathe Free!"—Identifying the causes and effects of historical events! Once born, the United States of America and all patriots would abhor the actions of all monarchs!

Readers' patriotic pride, respect, and appreciation will be rekindled as you read this chapter! Identifying additional causes and effects of historical events!—Escaping persecutions of the English monarchy—A leap of faith into the darkness of the American wilderness—Compare and contrast colonists' successful struggle to survive the real life challenges of human existence with the false narrative of modern government handouts that doom us all because socialism is a failure that cannot stand up to the scrutiny of natural law—Hacking out a home and sustenance in the wilderness—Reviewing the injustices and persecutions of autocratic rule—Planting the seeds for unalienable rights of free speech, free press, and freedom of religion—Separation of church and state—Foundational documents—American institutions—Thirteen English colonies of North America—Development of colonial philosophy and attitudes that were defiant of the tyranny and persecutions of the autocratic rule of England!

A closer look at colonial philosophy and attitudes that were defiant of the tyranny and persecutions of the autocratic rule of England—A discussion of what is in the First Amendment for all Americans—Why the "radical left" is determined to destroy the First Amendment—Why patriots must protect, at all costs, the First Amendment—The "unholy alliance" of the "radical left" with the liberal press and big tech's social media platforms.

Britain's 1775 attempt at gun control—Second Amendment rights are part of the American psyche—Yes, Americans do cling to their guns and Bible—Destroying the hypocrisy of gun control by the "Radical Left"—What is the real reason the "Radicals/Neo-Marxists" want your guns?—A brief history of conflicts between King George III and the thirteen British colonies—Discussion of Amendments III, IV, and VI—Why the election of 2022 is vital.

Read about the real accounts of valor demonstrated time and again throughout our history and you will want to stand and shout, "I am proud to be an American!"—Be an example for our youth, stand and place a hand on your heart when you hear the "Star-Spangled Banner" being played—True stories of sacrifice and heroism that will make you appreciate every veteran from Concord and Lexington in 1775 to those who fought and died on the sands of Afghanistan—Can you identify an American by their physical appearance?—What is the best representation for what it takes to qualify as being an American?—Why, even though they faced discrimination at home, did so many of the victims of persecution and discrimination choose to fight for America?—Quoting the wisdom of Dr. Martin Luther King—How the "Greatest Generation" used free enterprise capitalism, guts, and determination to save America from the totalitarianism of WWII—The Cold War battle against Communism and Marxism—The Biden-Harris administration's 2021 withdrawal from Afghanistan, one of the worst foreign policy disasters in American History!

How many voting citizens cling to the political party of their parents and grandparents without the knowledge of what the party stands for, in modern America?—How to choose a political party affiliation that is most representative of who you are politically—Votes, once cast, have consequences!—How to determine if your candidate of choice is who they proclaim to be—Making the choice between capitalism and socialism a real-time, real-life experience—Examples of lies, lack of unalienable rights of citizens, events, and horrific disregard for the sanctity of human life by Communist regimes—Capitalism raises living standards while Marxism makes citizens destitute.

How our open southern border places American citizens in harm's way and denies our sovereignty as a nation!—Failure of the Biden-Harris administration to uphold their sworn duty to defend the Constitution of the United States—Violation of immigration laws—Key points about the preamble and the Constitution—Using illegal immigration to permanently change the demographics of America's largest Electoral College States to Liberal blue—Deficit federal spending worsened by absorbing millions of illegal aliens—States' health care and school systems are being overburdened.

Remote learning, as a result of COVID- 19, has revealed curriculum that many parents find objectionable. Loudoun County Virginia parents up in arms in opposition to the teaching of critical race theory and transgender issues—Educational achievement is paramount to the success of democracy!—The good, bad, and ugly of education today as compared to education in our past—The alarming comparison of American students' achievement with the countries of the world—Ultra liberals invaded our public schools and higher education decades ago—The wasting of precious instructional minutes in our public schools—Does the federal government's control of public education improve or hinder student achievement?—The left's revisionist history will destroy America!

The Declaration of Independence, the Constitution of the United States, and the Bill of Rights shield Americans from autocratic rule!—Why brave men put everything on the line when they wrote and signed the Declaration of Independence—The left's attack on the Declaration of Independence—The preamble to the United States Constitution explained—How the left's platform of attack shows utter disregard for the preamble and the entire U.S. Constitution—Rule of law versus autocratic rule.

The 1832 democracy in America by Alexis de Tocqueville evaluates the American republic—Congressional bribery of the public with the public's money—Socialists' plans of guaranteed income defies all common sense and natural laws of human existence—The American form of Marxism—The implications of the national debt that is spiraling out of control.

Understanding the language of the "Left"—Debunking Project 1619—George Orwell's book, 1984—Orwellian—Dystopia—Saul Alinsky's 1971 rules for radicals' gradual seizure of power for socialism—Alinsky's disciples in American government—The Neo-Marxists—Attacking the filibuster—Adding two more blue states—Packing the Supreme Court—Patriots must employ the rule of law to fight the Neo-Marxists—The "Left's" attack on law and order—The big steal—Violations of the federal and state constitutions in the battleground states in the November 3, 2020 election—Russian collusion an unproven hoax—Putting America first was a good policy for the future of America—Biden and the Green Bad Deal for America—Compare the stats of American capitalism with the stats of the failed economies of the Soviet Union, Cuba, North Korea, and, yes, China too—Where are the Neo-Marxists taking our America?

Prologue

Today is Saturday, August 21, 2021. I am putting the finishing touches on my book during this weekend. Obviously, I wrote this prologue many months ago! However, I have found it necessary to add two points to this prologue before you read the original one.

My first point is one that jumped out at me as I was in the finishing stages of editing my manuscript. During the editing process, I noticed that there were passages and chapters that took a soft approach as I presented my positions about what has and is happening in America as well as my predictions of what will happen if there are not immediate mitigating actions taken. A mostly soft approach was my intent as I wanted to engage you in this thought process and study of the great America story much the same way that I taught U.S. history. I never wanted to influence students to agree with my way of thinking. It was my goal to provide an opportunity for my students and my readers to be introduced to issues and factual information with questions that facilitate learning. The hope was that with such analysis of facts, conclusions and positions could be reached and supported with sound factual evidence. I did that in the classroom, and for the most part, I feel I have done that in this book. But I noticed that there were times when I deviated from that soft approach!

As you read, it will occur to you that there are times when my points and positions are more stern and more direct. I call out people and groups when I believe they must be held responsible, and I do not like to be lied to. I especially do not like revisionist history that lies to children! Since I began this book on December 26, 2020, there have been times that I have witnessed events that have evoked great emotions and, yes, at times anger. The words on these pages are an expression of what I truly believe in my heart! That is how this book evolved. Unfortunately, there is a second point I want to present to you because it supports the very reason I have written this book.

The second point that I am adding deals with the horrific catastrophe that is developing, as I write this addition to my prologue, in real time. I am writing in present tense! Chaos in Afghanistan, during the withdrawal of August 2021, represents a debacle that clearly illustrates incompetence and a lack of experienced leadership on the part of the Biden-Harris administration. Not only does it illustrate a lack of common sense, it is an example of people who do not recall history and are guilty of repeating history that was detrimental to the United States and all citizens. While the fall of Saigon in April of 1975 was bad, this 2021 debacle is far worse. This catastrophe is the botched withdrawal from Afghanistan that began to unfold with the fall of Kabul, Afghanistan, in mid-August 2021. You are watching this international crisis at the same time I am writing this addition to my prologue. When you cast a vote for the leader of the free world, it is the most important decision you make as a responsible citizen of our democracy! This debacle in the Middle East is an example of just how quickly things can become very nasty. You can read my detailed presentation about this debacle at the end of Chapter 7, "All Gave Some; Some Gave all!"

This book is the culmination of a lifetime of leisure reading about, intense study of, and teaching the subject of American History. United States history is the subject I have loved ever since I began reading the American story during my fifth-grade year, 1962, at the one-room school I attended in the Allegheny Mountain region of southeastern West Virginia.

While the life story of America, like any other life story, has its dark moments and skeletons that we all must acknowledge, even though we would like to forget, it is still a beautiful story of freedom, hope, achievement, and perseverance. The real history of America, not the revisionist history that is designed to divide us and gather membership of the dissatisfied, must be told with accuracy. The revisionist history, being taught in order to propel a misguided movement, must be brought out of the darkness into the light of day to be castigated for the lies being told. The true history of America, warts and all, has to be taught to all Americans, young and old alike. How else can we learn of tragic mistakes, glorious triumphs, prevent past mistakes from recurring, replicate our success, and strive to live up to our high and lofty ideals?

Everyone knows some American History. Some know a lot. I have always wanted to connect the events of American History into a thematic story that shows both our failings and triumphs. Together, our failings and triumphs tell the story of struggle by a nation of imperfect people who have been trying to do something that has never been done before. While trying to climb this mountain of ideals, we have stumbled and fell short of the top many times. Yet we get back on our feet and resume climbing that mountain of high and lofty ideals expressed in our founding documents. That is the American way!

Many of us have learned history piecemeal. Many have learned some history but do not understand how the cause-and-effect relationship of events are woven together into such a spectacular story, *the great American story.* To fully understand America and what it means, we must go back into the history of Europe in the *times of castles and knights.*

During the course of the past few decades, I have become irritated, alarmed, fearful, and now angry at the false narratives being put forth by activists. Who are these activists that seek to tear down the nation that gives us all sustenance? It seems to me that they are a coalition of liberals who are left of center on the political spectrum, power-hungry seekers of wealth and control, and radical leftists who embrace socialism and ultimately the necessity of autocratic rule in order to maintain power and socialism. So I may use the terms *liberal, power seekers, radical leftists, progressives,* or *socialists* singularly or combine them into the term *leftists.* That is okay, because they are all joined at the hip of political propaganda in a common effort to fundamentally change America into something unrecognizable. And I believe they are all influenced and funded by powerful forces from within and from outside the United States. These politicians and activists are persons who seek personal gain and/or are being used by foreign nationalists seeking advantages for nations that are our adversaries. I am sure you are aware that there are nations who have much to gain if radical changes in America weaken us to the point that we become an inconsequential nation on the world stage.

My goal, with this book, is to take the dark-stained brushes from the activists' hands and replace them with brushes that paint the complete and colorful picture of America. Those activist painters only dip their brushes into the stains of our past and then attempt to paint a broad-brushed dark story of how terrible this nation has been and continues to be even today. There is more to the American story than just our failings. There is and always has been much good that we must also paint into the picture and put on display for all to see. Hopefully, this book will rightfully paint a brighter picture of America so that readers will be motivated to fight for the preservation of this great nation. Hang the real artwork of the American story in the gallery of world history and it will shine forth as a "masterpiece," despite the stains. I hope to paint you a real picture of America that is based upon facts and true history. This book's presentation of the real facts of American History will be the weapon I will use to expose the fallacy of the rhetoric that radical forces are using to divide and destroy America. I hope you join me in this study!

Stan Duncan
December 26, 2020

1

"A Fire Bell in the Night!" (Quote written by Thomas Jefferson to Holmes April 22, 1820, regarding the Missouri Compromise debate)

Was November 3, 2020, the USA's rush to repeat the darkest failures in world history? Did you hear "a fire bell in the night" on November 3, 2020?

The greatest country in human history is at risk!

We must, save this treasure of freedom for our children and the hope of the world!

You may or may not agree with the fact that I am about to sound an alarm about our nation's current situation and the path that our country is now traveling. There are always improvements and changes that need to be made as gadgets, processes, and systems are analyzed. I do not see the proposed changes, by the radical left, in our country as being minor tweaks that will preserve and improve the integrity of our system of governance that has served us well. I shudder as I look ahead at the destinations and fearful impacts along the way of the path we are now set upon. At the same time that I look ahead with great fear, I am looking over my shoulder to evaluate the history of our past and the fruit that our past has yielded. When I look ahead, down the path we are now traveling, I see a dark and stark contrast with the many good things of our past that have sustained us for over two hundred years. The left is set upon an agenda that will make this nation unrecognizable. What we are about to face is not small tweaks; rather, they are like volcanic eruptions that will forevermore change the "landscape of American life." To me, these changes being pushed by the left are like replacing the automobile with a horse and buggy, and the horse has terminal cancer! Perhaps you will see what I see as we evaluate history and current events in the following pages.

During the weeks following the presidential election of Tuesday November 3, 2020, an unbelievably large number of people in the United States were drunken with elation and joy that the Biden-Harris presidential ticket was proclaimed a winner by left-wing media sources and finally by the electoral college. Their counterparts were openly sickened, saddened, and fearful for the future of the country. Trump and some seventy-five million voters claimed that the 2020 election was fraudulent due to numerous violations of the U.S. Constitution and the state constitutions of the battleground states. Trump and his supporters were scorned by the announced winners of the election.

Was the 2020 election a major pivotal point for the U.S. in the twenty-first century? How radical might the changes to the nation be after January 20, 2021? Would such radicalism destroy the very foundations of this country? Are there destructive forces being unleashed that may well deny us the capability to continue to provide the hope of a good life for our children and grandchildren?

The aftermath of the 2020 election has left the nation even more divided. To me, it seems more important than ever that we Americans become more aware of the inestimable value of our nation as well as what it takes to create and sustain such a *one-of-a-kind nation*. We Americans must remove the blinders and assess what must be done to preserve this nation. We must understand what is happening and why it is happening.

America and our "rule of law" is a great umbrella of protection for human rights and free enterprise possibilities. To fully appreciate this umbrella of protection, you need to contrast our life with the persecutions we discover during a study of the great trials and sufferings of Europeans and Americans over the past five hundred years. These shared experiences and knowledge of the centuries of trials and sufferings of humanity were in the DNA of the *seeds of freedom and hope* planted on the Atlantic shores of America in the early years of the seventeenth century. To fully appreciate why we do not want to lose what we have, you must study historical events in order to fully understand *why* the seeds germinated and grew into what became the United States of America. Those seeds were deliberately and desperately planted on our wilderness shores. And we must learn and teach our children why this nation has subsequently become a destination coveted by millions desiring citizenship in the land of the free, where upon their own efforts they might turn opportunity into a better life.

It is my belief that far too many Americans do not realize how good life in this country is because they do not know how awful life can quickly become. They have little or no knowledge of the history that clearly explains why a great nation, based upon so many freedoms and opportunities, took root in a wilderness and became the envy of the world and equally hated by many powerful forces the world over. I have some simple questions for all Americans.

Do you know the vital history, both recent and in the distant past, that is necessary prerequisite knowledge for you to make a sound voting decision? Before you cast your vote to decide who will lead our country and the free world, you must be well informed? Do you bother to read the facts of the planks of the party platforms to which the candidates subscribe? Do you vote for the party that your parents and grandparents supported? If so, why? If not, why not? Is the exercise of your right of suffrage a vote cast to satisfy your immediate wants and self-gratification? Or is your decision the product of a thoughtful deliberation upon facts and knowledge of how we can best provide for the greater good and the preservation of the nation?

How much do you know about the cause/effect events of world history and American History? I am talking about the ones that resulted in the human struggles and persecutions that formed visions of freedom in the minds of the oppressed. Those horrific experiences would forge, in steel, the courage to create the USA and ultimately thrust us onto the world stage. What have been the contributions of this country to the world? The survival of democracy is dependent upon voters who realize the seriousness of the act of casting votes. Voters must be well informed with facts coupled with a knowledge of history rather than just absorbing propaganda fed to them by any source of media!

Too many people in the USA often do not appreciate the blessings of liberty and freedoms they enjoy. Many never recognize when that freedom is threatened. Truly, many of these people do not even realize they are free nor recognize their gradual loss of freedoms because they have never suffered without unalienable rights. As you lose freedoms, you begin the downhill slide toward autocratic rule, and your life will become a horrible and unbearable experience. Many Americans do not understand that freedom is not free and certainly do not know how high the cost that was paid to secure their blessings of liberty.

And I can assure you that there have been countless billions of people, throughout world history, who never tasted the sweetness of real freedom and liberty that permitted them to live their lives as they saw fit. Those people clearly understood that they were not free to worship God in their own way, assemble and speak their political thoughts and beliefs, or enjoy freedom of enterprise to better their lives. They also understood the religious, political, and economic persecution they suffered under the rule of tyranny. Some of these victims developed an unquenchable thirst for life, liberty, and the pursuit of happiness. Our American forebears were willing to pay the price to secure the blessings of liberty for themselves and for their children.

"Listen, my children, and you shall hear of the midnight ride of Paul Revere." This is the opening line of the famous poem written by Henry Wadsworth Longfellow. Why and when did this great poet write this national treasure? Why was this 1775 midnight ride of Paul Revere, and others in eighteenth-century America, so important to the birth of our nation? And what benefits did these midnight rides provide for your life, even though you live in the twenty-first century?

I wish to discuss the story behind this great poem and countless other events of world and American History in order to illustrate that the American journey outlines one of the most amazing success stories in all of human history; the birth, survival, development, and evolution of the United States of America! You will discover events in history, both good and bad, that have contributed to the great American story, the story of the United States of America. Though the birth of this nation is officially July 4, 1776, one must look at events in world history long before 1776 to fully appreciate why millions of people bore great hardships just to reach our shores. You will read about the mix of great tragedies, wrongs, and the many triumphs found in the pages of both world and American History that have impacted the American experience. Then, and only then, will you be able to balance all of these concepts and events with the whole story about this nation in which we live. From that vantage point, you will be able to judge the history and accomplishments of the USA from both the long term and broad view required for anyone to fairly judge the value of the birth, struggles, development, and preservation of our nation.

Countless millions have paid a great price with their blood, treasure, and lives just to build and keep this country the "Land of the Free." The United States of America, both in our current daily life and throughout our brief history as a nation, has been an imperfect nation and is still far from being a perfect nation. And how could the USA not be an imperfect nation? How could we have been perfect throughout our past, perfect today, or perfect in the future? Nations, whether they are ruled by dictators or operate as a democracy, are led by imperfect beings. Instead of focusing on past failures, to the detriment of the present, we should study and seek to learn from those failures, not erase them. We should focus on the possibilities we can achieve because of the ideals our country is based upon. We acknowledge our failures; after all, is failure and seeking to improve on the past not the essence of the responsibility we must embrace as citizens and as caring members of the human race?

Yet through all of history, I dare you to try to favorably compare any nation, that has ever been assembled on planet Earth, to our great nation, the United States of America. No nation, in the history of the world, can come close to the ideals, protections, and accomplishments of the USA for the citizens of this country and, yes, for the world. The knowledge of the many sufferings of mankind throughout history, as well as the personal and shared sufferings of our founding fathers, is evidenced by the wisdom displayed in our foundational documents by those founders.

Before you begin to turn the pages of this story, ask yourself, what is so special about this nation in which we live? I believe you will find numerous events that will answer your question many times over as you read this great story.

Since I have authored this story, I must tell you that I am left with one great question. The answer to my question is yet to be answered. What does the future hold for our nation, the United States of America? The answer to our fate rests in the hands of informed American citizens, who love their country. There are dark and ominous clouds hanging over our nation and the world at the start of 2021!

Does November 3, 2020, mark the Unites States of America's step back into history's darkest failures? Do you believe the greatest country in human history is at risk? If you do, then you should recognize that there is a mandate for patriotic Americans to employ the principles of the democratic process, immediately, in preparation for the 2022 election! We must save this treasure of freedom for our children and the hope of the world!

The futures of our children and grandchildren hang in the balance. We must first understand both our history and world history in order to value this nation. Such understanding is necessary so that we realize why we must fight to keep the values, traditions, and institutions of our country for the posterity of not only our country but for the world as well. Preservation of the United States is the last great hope for the world! American patriots must do this in order to preserve "life, liberty, and the pursuit of happiness" for our posterity to enjoy.

Consider, if you will, these overarching questions. Why have so many people sacrificed and fought to come to this country throughout our history? Why are people not fighting to leave this country? The answers to these questions should be proof that what we have built and fought for is really a pretty good thing. In fact, nothing on the world stage of history can come close to our way of life and our accomplishments.

If you dare to study this story, you will begin to value, like gold, this nation that was conceived, grew, and flourished because of the desperate state of countless millions around the world. As you read this story of history, you will find just how bad life can become! I pray to God we can avert those tragedies of past history. Life can become very nasty, very quickly! Since you have read this far, I believe you have accepted the dare to study with me. I can tell you this is a daunting challenge for me!

Now, read this story, both young and old alike, and you shall hear of the many stories and events that motivated the founding and preservation of this great nation, the United States of America. Read and discover the reasons we are and must continue to be a shining example for the world. Fighting for the preservation of this nation, as it was conceived, is the only way our children will have a chance to enjoy life, liberty, and the pursuit of happiness! The cost of freedom has always been great, and it will continue to be so! President Ronald Reagan proclaimed on July 6, 1987, "Freedom is never more than one generation away from extinction. It has to be fought for and defended by each generation." Have you heard the *fire bell in the night*?

I suspect you have looked ahead at the title of the next chapter. You may be thinking, why do I want to read about Martin Luther and the Protestant Reformation in chapter 2? Or, for that matter, Henry the VIII in chapter 3. You may be thinking, *I will skip ahead.* You can, because you are the reader! I encourage you to not skip ahead as chapter 2 and chapter 3 are so foundational for both your appreciation and understanding of what the *great American experience* is all about. Chapter 2 is only 2,631 words! So please get aboard history's time machine with me as we travel to medieval Europe for a close look at the bloody religious and political turmoil of that era. We are going to study the impactful effects that religious and political turmoil events, in medieval Europe, had upon the early settlement of North American in the areas that would become the United States of America.

2

Martin Luther—The Protestant Reformation

About this chapter!

The very nature of humanity illustrates the fact that there are numerous stimuli that fuel deep emotional responses and sometimes violent reactions. Numerous pages of world history provide evidence of how religious dissension between the world's various religions has spawned much persecution, violence, and, yes, even wars. Armies have marched in the name of religion! Effective teachers of history often employ the concept of cause and effect as an effective tool that enables students to tie a string of events together for not only an understanding of the past but perhaps, more importantly, a prediction of the future. As you read the following chapters on this subject, search for the important causes of events and the effects they produced as you employ the concept of cause/effect in the study of European history. From that perspective, you will begin to recognize how the events in European history produced effects that, in turn, caused the founding of our nation. You will discover how the effects of this religious and political turmoil affected those Europeans and caused them to understand the importance and necessity for governance by "rule of law." They came to believe that governance by "rule of law" would provide for and protect the freedoms of the unalienable rights, which fosters the realization and respect for the worth of the individual.

*****

Whether you are an individual who has deep religious convictions or one with little or no religious convictions, you cannot deny the immutable fact that religious convictions often produce deep devotional and emotional responses. This knowledge of how the depth of religious conviction and devotion yields great emotional responses has not escaped the observation of both religious and political leaders. Unfortunately, unscrupulous religious and political leaders, throughout the ages, have sought to harness those emotions as a tool for their quest to gain and maintain both wealth and power.

It is a fact that devout Christians, whether they were Catholic or Protestant, were often used as pawns in a chess match by religious and political leaders in a serious game to acquire territory, wealth, and power. Many of the so-called nobility and religious leaders, whether they were Protestant or Catholic, often caused the slaying of millions just because the slaughtered were perceived to be religious and/or political adversaries. Numerous such examples have been manifested throughout history. Clearly, there has been much conflict among various religions between a particular religion and the nonreligious, as well as civil authority persecutions of religious groups. Often these conflicts resulted when there was an established goal of violent persecution and attempted destruction of a religion. So strong are the emotions that arise due to religious conviction that individuals and groups have been forced to seek refuge and protections for their religious practices.

Religion is so important to the devout that they will suffer great hardships, endure persecution, and willingly make any sacrifice in order to serve the deep *convictions of their heart* for their Maker! That was true in sixteenth-century Europe, and it is still true in America today, though secularism is growing in our country. There has been much carnage as a result of the religious strife that has occurred throughout the ages. Clearly, a solution was needed to bring an end to the persecution and bloodshed of religious conflict in Europe. The answer to this problem has seemed very simple to we Americans for a very long time. The obvious answer was religious freedom based upon tolerance of diverse religious practices. Europeans just could not seem to come up with that simple solution because they felt that religious tolerance might well doom their souls to hell. And when you add the quest for power by various religious and political leaders who manipulated the minds of the devoutly religious, well, then you had the perfect storm. As a result of these travesties, there would have to be a long and violent period in the history of Europe of religious strife and bloodshed! Due to this political and religious persecution, over centuries of time, is it not apparent why by 1620 and into the 1630s thousands of Europeans were willing to risk everything in a voyage across the Atlantic into a harsh and unknown wilderness seeking their personal religious freedom?

To understand religious turmoil in Europe or Western civilization, we shall look at religious dissention created during the Protestant Reformation and the Catholic inquisition from about 1517 and after. Please note this is not, in any way, intended as a debate of any religious doctrine's superiority or rightness as opposed to any other religion. I believe those debates are best left to the heartfelt convictions of others, as I feel that is where they belong. Nor am I taking an anti-religious position. My goal is to allow readers to be reminded of the threats that may arise, at any time, to the personal practice of their religion, their right to not practice or pay homage to any particular religion, or of the right to not be required to support a religion that someone else may want to choose for them.

We have been protected from religious persecution since the passage of the First Amendment in 1791! Does this not, clearly, point out to all open-minded readers of the great American story of the blessings bestowed upon our nation by the wisdom of the founding fathers when they wrote the first ten amendments to our constitution, the Bill of Rights. In America, since 1791, our system has provided that we should be able to go to bed and arise in the morning under the umbrella of protection provided by the "constitution and the rule of law." We Americans should not awaken to find that a tyrant has taken it upon himself to decree that we must live differently in order to serve his personal pursuits. If you do not believe this, read on and see why the protections of our constitution are immeasurable. See just how miserable life has been in the past and can become again, in your present and future. You shall recognize the trials of religious persecution endured by millions for centuries.

Before you hasten to point out the obvious black marks that our nation wears, please remember, we must look at the big picture over time when we fairly evaluate any organization, religion, or nation. Every organization, religion, and nation has suffered, at times, under the despotic rule of unscrupulous leaders.

I open this discussion with the religious dissension that began to manifest itself quite vividly in Wittenberg, Germany in 1517. Martin Luther, an Augustinian Catholic monk, dared to commit heresy when he began to question the practices of the Catholic Church and the pope in Rome. I must, however, point out that there were earlier voices of questioners and those seeking reform of the Catholic Church prior to Martin Luther. Luther's *Ninety-Five Theses*, that he may or may not have posted on the door of the Wittenberg Castle Church of Germany in 1517, included an outline of his beliefs regarding how he interpreted the Bible. These interpretations immediately put him at odds with the Catholic Church. Luther's protestations opened an even bigger can of worms in Western civilization when he challenged the status quo with what he apparently hoped would be internal reform of the Catholic religion to which he belonged. Soon, there would be splinter groups with still other dissenting points of view. Many dissenters contributed to much chaos and death as the battle for religious dominance and for social changes, inspired by the reformation, began to spread throughout Europe.

It is important to note that sixteenth-century European life was dominated by the Catholic Church of Rome and had been for quite some time.[1] Challenges to the authority of the Catholic Church was risky business just as challenges to Protestant denominations of that era would also become a great risk. The question that beg for

---

[1]   http://www.protestantism.co.uk/timeline.html.

answers is, what were the effects Luther's challenge to the authority of the Roman Catholic pope had upon Europe and ultimately North America?

To be very brief and to consider just a couple of Luther's reform suggestions, study of the era will reveal that Luther objected to the practice of selling indulgences by some Catholic priests of the church he served. According to an article found on Catholic Bridge.com (Building Bridges—Healing Divisions[2]), the official position of the Catholic Church is that it has never been and that it is not the doctrine of the Catholic Church that spiritual things can be sold. Specifically, the article points out that "Catholic doctrine has always taught that it is a sin to sell spiritual things, including indulgences, despite some wrong actions by priests 500 years ago." Even today we hear of the difference of opinion between Protestants and Catholics regarding indulgences. Taking a position on the right or wrong of "selling of indulgences" or for that matter to what extent they existed or were sanctioned is not a point to debate within this writing. However, I am sure it has not escaped your awareness that a culmination of such disputes in the 1500s resulted in millions of religious deaths.

Additionally, Luther's presentation of what he called the "Doctrine of Priesthood of all Believers" was recognized as a threat to the authority of the pope of the Catholic Church. Central to the "Doctrine of Priesthood of all Believers" was the position that it was not necessary to have the intercession of a priest to represent "Believers" before God.

As a multitude of different views on many religious points of contention were put forth by Luther and other religious thinkers, anger and opposition rose among numerous parties. I would be remiss if I did not point out that in addition to controversary over doctrine, nobles, kings, Protestant, and Catholic leaders alike had a thirst for power and territory. Unfortunately, many leaders seek their personal advancement by using the devout emotions of the multitudes as tools to create, build, and sustain a movement.

---

[2] https://www.catholicbridge.com/catholic/indulgences.php.

By contrast, life in the USA, where Catholics and Protestants may still debate religious doctrine, such debate is quite peaceful when it takes place. Our system of government, so often attacked by the left, has allowed our citizens to live in relative religious peace under the umbrella of the "rule of law" and the protections of our First Amendment rights! Surely, the previous pages and pages still to be read have convinced or will convince you that our system is a blessing. Nobody wants to repeat the history of Europe and the Protestant Reformation! We study history to avoid repeating the mistakes of the past that caused such human misery. To offer more proof, there is a necessity, I believe, for a brief research of facts that illustrate a very small portion of the carnage and suffering from war with examples of persecution that would follow.

While European history has volumes of books written about this subject, I feel that it is only necessary for me to provide just a few historical examples of the religious carnage and persecution that took place in sixteenth-, seventeenth-, and eighteenth-century Europe. A limited number of such examples will illuminate, for you, some of the tragedy of religious conflict in Europe during this era.

(Five of the Most Violent Moments of the Reformation is an article written by Katy Gibbons, Senior Lecturer in History, University of Portsmouth. You may access this article at https://theconversation.com/five-of-the-most-violent-moments-of-the-reformation-71535).

The massacre on Saint Bartholomew's Day of August 24, 1572, in Paris, France, bears witness to an extremely bloody day of the Reformation. Some two thousand French Protestants were murdered on the streets. Curiously enough, this massacre took place during a celebration of the marriage of a Catholic princess and a Protestant king according to an article written by Katy Gibbons, Senior Lecturer in history, University of Portsmouth on January 20, 2017, 8.24 a.m. EST.

The August 21, 2018 article of History.com Editors at https://www.history.com/topics/reformation/thirty-years-war provides valuable insight into the Thirty Years' War. The carnage of the Thirty Years' War from 1618 to 1648 was perpetrated by many of the major powers of Europe. This war would be one of the longest in human history and extremely brutal. An estimated eight million died from a combination of battle, famine, and disease. Some historians contend that this war witnessed some, if not the first, witch hunts in history. The cause of the war was a religious conflict among the Catholic and Protestant states or countries of the European region of the Holy Roman Empire. One of the major effects of this war, according to many historians, would be geopolitical change in the map of Europe helping form and outline the boundaries of the nation-states of Europe with a treaty, Peace of Westphalia. One lasting effect of this war, that continues to this day, seems to be a reduction in power and influence over the new nation-states of Europe by the Catholic Church and other religions.

"How Medieval Churches Used Witch Hunts to Gain More Followers" is an article written by Becky Little on 1/10/2018, updated 9/1/2018.[3]

Visit any mall in America in October of each year and you can buy a witch costume for you or your child. It is all in fun! Yet during the reformation in Europe from about 1560 to 1630, some eighty thousand people were accused of being witches, and some forty thousand apparently were executed in what has become known as the "Great Hunt." Burning at the stake was a method of execution! Sounds like cruel and unusual punishment to say the least. Not something to celebrate and it happened all during the year in those days, not just on Halloween night. Seems to me that under the USA constitution, our rule of law forbids cruel and unusual punishment. My unsuperstitious mind does not believe that even one of the accused forty thousand executed for practicing witchcraft was guilty. I am going to go on record and say I like the "rule of law" we enjoy in our country. How about you? You may be asking yourself why witchcraft and burning at the stake of witches came about during the reformation.

---

[3] https://www.history.com/news/how-medieval-churches-used-witch-hunts-to-gain-more-followers.

"How Medieval Churches Used Witch Hunts to Gain More Followers" is an article found on History.com and written by Becky Little on 1/10/2018, updated 9/1/2018. It is interesting reading because Little references an article written by two economists, Peter Leeson and Jacob Russ, published in *The Economic Journal.* These two economists have developed a new theory to explain the horrific witch trials in Europe after 1517. They point out that from nine hundred to one thousand four hundred, the Catholic Church did not prosecute cases for witchcraft. You may be thinking, why the change in position? The theory is that both the Protestants and the Catholics competed with each other, via executions of those charged with practicing witchcraft. This search for and resulting punishment of witches was each church's advertisement of evidence of how divinely and determined of a battle against the devil they were willing to wage. Each religion hoped their burning at the stake of those accused of practicing witchcraft and doing the devil's bidding would, in fact, convince the population to join and follow them because they were demonstrating a willingness to protect all from the devil. Hard to imagine some forty thousand innocent and terrified people being killed and burned at the stake because religious and political leaders played upon the fears and superstitions of the populace in the name of religion and the eradication of devil worshipping. Yet it did happen!

I hope you found those 2,732 words of chapter 2 informative. Can you, for just one minute, put yourself in the shoes of those millions of suffering people forced to endure such religious and political persecutions? Imagine how many times those people yearned for someplace to breathe free and live in a way that they aspired to live. I really believe the words of this chapter are foundational for the understanding of all chapters to follow. Chapter 3 will prepare you for Chapter 4, "Escape to a Wilderness." Chapter 3 is only 3,291 words, and they take us closer to the settling of the thirteen English colonies of America.

3

English King Henry VIII

This is the story of English King Henry VIII's break with the Holy Roman Catholic Church during the 1530s. We will discuss Henry's establishment of the Anglican Church of England, the resulting political power struggle, and the religious wars. Look for the direct correlation between the events of this chapter and the early settlement in America by the English. This is another story about real oppression![4]

English King Henry VIII was born June 28, 1491, and died on January 28, 1547, at the age of fifty-five. His reign as king of England lasted thirty-six years. During his reign, England would become embroiled in the Protestant Reformation. Henry was a Catholic, and his writings attacking Martin Luther's proposed reforms of the Catholic Church prompted Pope Leo X on October 11, 1521, to proclaim Henry as the "Defender of the Faith." King Henry VIII's religious posturing during his reign would prove to be most self-serving as his Catholic piety would soon come into question.

We Americans have looked upon autocratic rule with both disdain and fear since we took action to defy tyranny in 1775. Actually, we did not like tyranny even before 1775. The absolute power of a King Henry VIII allows such tyrants to completely change the life of the citizenry because of a personal whim. That is why we call

---

[4] http://www.protestantism.co.uk/timeline.html.

them despots. Benevolent autocrats who work for the greater good of the society at large are rare in history. Citizens who yearn for freedom demand protection from such absolute and all-powerful rulers. Consider the facts of Henry's actions regarding religion in England and you can formulate your judgment.

Shortly after ascension to the throne of England, upon his brother Arthur's death, Henry married his brother's widow, Catherine of Aragon. This union would produce six children, three males and three females, all of whom died in infancy except Mary. Mary would eventually take the throne and earn her place in history as Mary the First or "Bloody Mary." Having only one surviving child, a female, put Henry in an unhappy state of mind. He did not have a male heir to his throne. Additionally, Henry was prone to discard wives and remarry not only in search of a male heir but also to form alliances that were advantageous to him, and as a side note, he searched for marital bliss. The lack of a male heir for Henry, in Henry's small mind, had to have been Catherine's fault, and the way to remedy this problem was to marry Anne Boleyn. Apparently, in Henry's mind at least, the solution was out with the old and in with the new. The obvious solution was a marriage with Anne Boleyn whom Henry had become quite infatuated.

Yet there was a problem with the solution. Henry was a Catholic, and the English king who had been dubbed "Defender of the Faith" already had a wife, Catherine of Aragon. But surely, a king, especially one known as the "Defender of the Faith," would have no problem in getting a divorce from Catherine. How could Pope Clement VII refuse such a request of the king of England? Well, the pope did just that! Henry's dilemma becomes more desperate.

Apparently, Catholic Church doctrine and a papal ruling that was contrary to the desires of an English Catholic king was no problem. The "Defender of the Faith" would take the matter in his own hands. Catherine be damned and the pope…well, I guess we have to judge Henry's actions to conclude what the king may have said when he learned of Pope Clement VII's refusal to grant the divorce. If Henry VIII could not control the pope in Rome, then, why not create his own church?

So on November 3, 1534, Henry did just that and declared himself the "Supreme Head of the Church of England." Parliament and local clergy supported these actions. Now King Henry VIII could require citizens of the realm to not only pay tribute, tithes or taxes, to this new church, the Anglican Church, but he could also seize Catholic properties, such as monasteries, and further add to his wealth. He seized Catholic Church holdings that members had tithed to in order to build those properties. Unfortunately for devout Catholics, they still wanted to pay support to their Catholic church. Supporting two churches was a financial burden on all, not just in England but Ireland and elsewhere in the British lands. And what about those devout Catholics living and worshipping in England, Ireland, and Scotland? That was simple; force would be used against Catholics to make them accept the king's usurpation of the power of their pope. They would also have to accept some other changes in church doctrine as time passed. It was a life-and-death decision for many. As with all tyrants, Henry wanted what he wanted, and concern for others was way down his list.

And how does Henry justify defiance of the pope and essentially become part of the Protestant Reformation? The answer is simple: just bring forth a new theory known as "rule by divine right." God chose the monarchs to rule over their subjects. Henry's proclamations would serve to further the establishment of the fact that a monarch's power and authority were unquestionable and absolute. The royal rulers claimed they had their blessing from God, and it does not get much better than that.

Yet later in history we will discover there would be those who would refuse to live under any such oppression. These people had backbone and began to put forth claims that individuals were endowed by their creator with certain inalienable rights, something they would demand and fight to gain. Today, there are people who question if those in power may be ignoring those inalienable rights. Yet for the time being, that proclamation along with Henry's actions would further cause growth of a very distinct relationship between political rule and religious rule. We call that "no separation between church and state." To quote Lord Acton, a nineteenth-century British politician, "Absolute power corrupts absolutely."

Wait a minute, isn't there something called "separation of church and state"? No, not in sixteenth-century England. Not until our founding fathers recalled the tyranny of past history and established protections in our "rule of law," the Constitution of the United States and our Bill of Rights in eighteenth-century America. If you do not think the wisdom of our "old guys" is not important and necessary in order to counter tyranny, then you should study history and gain a perspective of Catholics and later Protestant Puritans who had real issues with the Anglican Church of England. If that historical study is not convincing enough, fast-forward to the witch trials perpetrated by the Protestant Puritans of Salem in seventeenth-century Massachusetts Bay Colony. That should convince you!

The formula for combining religious fervor with absolute political power produces a drug effect that has made many tyrants drunk with the desire to use that power to persecute and kill. And in the case of Henry VIII, he would also be free to discard and conquer new wives at a rate that would allow for six marriages in his lifetime of fifty-five years. Why not? As king, he ruled by "divine right," and it did not matter that he was excommunicated from the Catholic Church; he was head of his own church! Since he was the head of his own church, it was within his power to have as many divorces as he darn well pleased. And he did!

Catherine was divorced, Anne Boleyn was charged with high treason and adultery for which she was beheaded, Jane Seymour died from complications of child birth after giving Henry a son who would survive, King Edward VI. Finally, Henry had his male heir, but he would marry three more times. He would divorce his fourth wife, Anne of Cleves, and then become close friends with her. Catherine Howard became the fifth wife and supposedly engaged in extramarital activities, a crime for which she would be executed. The heads of her suspected two lovers were placed on London Bridge. It was of little consequence to Henry that he could not even spell fidelity because his hypocrisy knew no limits. His final wife was Catherine Parr, and she would survive Henry. For the most part, one would have to say it was dangerous to be married to Henry VIII. The biological irony of Henry's lifelong quest for a wife that pleased him or for one that would bear him a male heir is the fact that the male parent determines the sex of his offspring, not Henry's unlucky wives.[5]

The question you are asking now is what persecutions took place in England, Ireland, and Scotland after Henry's rebuke of the pope and his elevation to supreme leader of his own church, the Anglican Church of England? While Henry's early Anglican Church would retain much of the doctrine of the Catholic Church, minus the pope in Rome, his persecutions would not be limited to just his wives.

Do you know what document(s) would be created and instituted, later in history, to curb the persecutions of such tyrants drunken with power? Henry's early Anglican Church would retain much of the doctrine of the Catholic Church, minus the pope in Rome.

Sir Thomas More was an attorney who, in reality, desired to live his life as a devout Catholic. He would become the lord chancellor of the English Parliament on October 26, 1529. Later, Sir Thomas More would not take an oath that was a denial of the supreme power of the pope of Rome. For this and other false charges, he was imprisoned in the Tower of London. On July 1, 1535, he was tried as a traitor. Richard Rich apparently perjured himself when he testified that he had heard More say that Henry was not the supreme head of the Church of England. There would not be enough rope in all of America if you could be sentenced to hang for such disparaging utterances today. Could such convictions take place again? Sir Thomas More was sentenced to death as a traitor to be drawn, hanged, and quartered.[6]

Such an execution is a special act of torture designed to strike fear in the subjects of the realm. I, thankfully, have never witnessed such an execution of punishment for being found guilty of high trea-

---

[5] https://www.historyhit.com/the-6-wives-of-henry-viii-in-order.
[6] https://www.britannica.com/biography/Thomas-More-English-humanist-and-statesman/Years-as-chancellor-of-England#ref5009.

son. To view a demonstration of being drawn, hanged, and quartered, watch the 1995 movie *Braveheart* that depicts the execution of the Scot, William Wallace, by the king of England. The drawn part of the execution may have been the dragging of the condemned by horse on a board or disembowelment by cutting out the intestines and sex organs of the victim. The organs were to be burned or trampled upon. Secondly, you were to hang, until almost dead. Finally, after having been cut open and being hung just short of death, you would be laid out on an execution block and beheaded, your body severed into four parts, and then the head plus the four quartered parts of your body were put on display for all potential traitors to see. Some sources claim the quartering was accomplished by tying the four limbs by four different ropes, one rope tied to one of four farm horses that would pull your body into parts.[7] Either method was a gross example of cruel and unusual punishment, something that our "rule of law" does not allow.

While the horror of the execution was most impactful, justification of More's execution was not widely accepted. Pope Pius XI would canonize More in 1935 as St. Thomas More. There were many more things that happened under the rule of Henry, but there was more to come from some of his heirs and others who would sit on the English throne.[8]

Henry did, finally, get a male heir, Edward VI, and he would take the throne upon his father's death. It is not King Edward VI that I want to discuss with you. It is the two half-sisters, Mary I who became known as "Bloody Mary" and Queen Elizabeth I who would persecute the religious citizenry of England. Each would change the religious status of England as they began their rule. They abused both Catholicism and Protestantism in England. Can you see what you get when you do not have separation of powers with a written rule book? To whom do you appeal injustices when you live under autocratic rule? There was no supreme court to protect the rights of the oppressed in "unmerry old England!"

---

[7] https://simple.wikipedia.org/wiki/Hanged,_drawn_and_quartered.
[8] https://www.history.com/topics/british-history/henry-viii.

"Bloody Mary I" was born in 1516. She was the only child that survived from the union of Henry and Catherine of Aragon. She took the throne upon the death of her half-brother, Edward VI. She would wage ruthless persecution upon Protestants as she reengaged England with Catholicism from 1553 to 1558.

According to the writing of Eric Norman Simons, author of *The Queen and the Rebel: Mary Tudor and Wyatt the Younger* and others, we find that Mary I apparently did not put much stock in advisors as she took the throne refusing the sound advice that might have avoided the violence associated with her rule and the label of "Bloody Mary I." She told the Protestants that she would marry Phillip II of Spain, a Catholic, and that her personal life was her own. Within England there were many who had profited by the confiscation of Catholic properties under the rule of Henry VIII, her father. If the English queen were to marry Catholic Phillip II of Spain coupled with the knowledge of Mary's intent to reestablish Catholicism as the state religion, then Mary would immediately be at odds with the Protestants of England.

Sir Thomas Wyatt, a Protestant, would lead an insurrection against Mary. Mary rallied thousands to fight, and Sir Thomas Wyatt was defeated and promptly executed. When Mary I reinstated Catholicism as the state religion along with a restoration of heresy laws, the religious turmoil and violence escalated. According to Simmons, for three years rebels hanged from gibbets, and some three hundred were burned at the stake. After years of religious persecution and unrest, perpetrated by the English rulers who claimed rule by "divine right," the persecuted hoped that with the end of the rule by Mary I, someone might be seated on the throne that could lead England into an era of a better life for all. That was not to be the case for Catholics as it was once again their turn for being persecuted.[9]

---

[9] https://www.britannica.com/biography/Mary-I.

Elizabeth I

I wish to cite the article "Elizabeth I Queen of England," written by John S. Morrill, assistant master and professor of history, Selwyn 790 College, University of Cambridge, as well as the consultant editor for the *Oxford Dictionary of National Biography*. May I suggest you read this article as a source for greater factual details? The article provided this author with valuable facts and insight into the subject. You can access this article at https://www.britannica.com/biography/Elizabeth-I.

May I also recommend the article by Volubrjotr titled "England's Greatest Coverup—England's Catholic Genocide: Roman Catholic Guy Fawkes—The Rustle For America Begins!"

This article can be accessed at https://politicalvelcraft. org/2012/02/16/anonymous-resistance-to-englands-catholic-genocide-roman-catholic-guy-fawkes/. The article provided this author with valuable facts and insight.

Queen Elizabeth I, the virgin queen, was born September 7, 1533, to Anne Boleyn and King Henry VIII. She would be coronated Queen Elizabeth I upon the death of her older half sister, Mary I, in 1558 and retain the throne until her death in 1603. Prior to coming to the throne, Elizabeth's allegiance to Queen Mary's Catholicism came under suspicion in that it appeared she favored Protestantism. For that, Elizabeth's older half sister, Queen Mary I, threw Elizabeth into the Tower of London. Elizabeth was released when there was not enough proof presented to substantiate the charges or suspicions. As I have stated, she would take the throne in 1558.

While many rejoiced and Elizabeth did gain a great following, her rein brought much dismay to the Catholics of the British empire. Elizabeth would restore England to Protestantism. In 1559 Parliament would pass the Act of Supremacy, and Elizabeth I would become supreme governor of the Church of England. Catholics were not happy, and curiously enough, Protestants were also not happy because they were not satisfied that Elizabeth had gone far enough. The Protestants wanted revenge upon the Catholics, and Catholics wanted to get even while they scurried to protect themselves and often hide their worshipping. I sometimes find it hard to realize the reality was that both groups worshipped the same Christ and Heavenly Father! While religious differences played a major role, do not forget that political goals of power and wealth went hand in hand.

However, Elizabeth had done enough to earn the wrath of Pope Pius V when in 1570, she was excommunicated from the Catholic Church for being a heretic. The religious turmoil that had existed for so long in England would continue. The "teeter-totter seesaw" of Catholics on one end and Protestants on the other end of the "up and down board of political and religious power struggles" in England would continue. The path toward "Separation of Church and State" was a difficult passage, and it would be decades before anyone had the wisdom and guts to separate the two.

Is it any wonder that our founding fathers formed a governmental structure subject to checks and balances within a written constitution of separation of powers among our three branches of government—executive, legislative, and judicial? We enjoy the protections of a written law and not the law as proclaimed by the self-serving interests of a monarch or dictator.

Unwittingly, Elizabeth I would rule over one of the great turning points in world history, the 1588 defeat of the Spanish Armada in the English Channel. Catholic King Phillip II of Spain assembled a might fleet, the Spanish Armada and an army. The goal was to conquer Protestant England. A combination of bad luck and bad weather along with the cunning of English forces would destroy the Spanish fleet and save Elizabeth's Protestant rule. Phillip's goal of conquering England for the glory of Spain and the Catholic pope would never be realized.

Prior to this defeat, Spain had become the most powerful nation on earth with great riches plundered from the Incas of South America and the Aztecs of Mexico. Spain dominated the seas of the new world, and none could challenge Spain's wealth and power in Europe or in the Americas. With the defeat of the Armada and the rise of Britain's mastery of the seas, it would soon be proclaimed that "The sun never sets on the British empire." The power of Spain would begin a long decline. Now, there was no nation that could prevent Elizabeth's England from exploration and colonizing of the new world. This colonization would begin in 1607 at Jamestown, Virginia. The London Company sent settlers to Jamestown, Virginia, seeking gold and silver. The Spanish had been successful finding great wealth after Columbus got credit for the discovery of America for King Ferdinand and Queen Isabella of Spain. The English intended to get rich too. They did not find precious metals in Virginia, but they did find starvation and death in the swampy areas of the James River.

Thus far we have studied and learned of events in Europe that paint a picture of a place and time that do not seem at all alluring to me. But I have lived in a country that has evolved into a land of freedom. It is hard to imagine that people had to try to survive in a world such as I have just described. Trust me, my study of history has proven that history can and does repeat itself. It may be happening again, and in all places, the United States of America. I have jumped ahead of myself, haven't I? We have only, just now, completed our visit of sixteenth-century Europe and are now ready to take a peek at the events of the seventeenth century.

We are ready to pass over into seventeenth-century Europe where English men, women, and children are ready to make an "Escape for a Wilderness," the title of the next chapter. I believe we have painted an excellent picture of the political and religious landscape of Europe in the sixteenth century. While it is true that the first English settlers to establish a permanent settlement in Virginia, Jamestown, came in the search of gold in 1607, the chaos and persecution in England led others, in 1620, to settle in Plymouth of New England, seeking opportunity and freedom to practice their "separatist" religion. Much of this early settlement, in the area of North America, was the result of the chaos in England. The struggle and suffering in this wilderness would be a terror. Only the strong would survive. These survivors would begin to build the foundations of a mighty nation! Keep reading. Our journey is far from over. In fact, the American journey is just now about to begin!

4

Escape to a Wilderness

We Americans of the twenty-first century live in isolated rural areas, small towns, and cities of various sizes. We live in a time of cell phones, internet, and space travel. We are so used to the benefits of so many luxuries and machines of complex technological development that satisfy our every want and desire that we are unable to imagine a time before the existence of so many inventions that supposedly make us modern. Such technology, at our fingertips, has created a way of life that makes it almost impossible for the average American to relate to the reality of struggle with the raw forces of nature that our ancestors dealt with on a daily basis. We have become soft! We have lost touch with the reality of struggle for life and the natural laws that govern sustaining life. Life has never been a picnic. The bounty of life has to be earned; it is not free as some would lead the naïve to believe! We had better relearn that reality and employ that philosophy in our modern life, or we risk being castigated into a life of want and arduous struggle.

Too many people believe that government and others who work owe them a living. Imagine a life in which you struggle daily to acquire food, shelter, and clothing. Most of us who work do that every day. We do not do it in the same manner as the first settlers in America did. Most of us do not have to remove a rifle from the mantle and go out to hunt our breakfast or dinner! We do not plow the land with a team of horses in order to grow the grain for our daily bread. Our ancestors fought nature daily, armed with just a bare minimum of the most crude and manual tools.

Stop for a moment, if you will, and try to imagine how your life would change without any technology, electricity, clothing stores, apartment houses, and the grocery store. Better still, imagine that you are about to be dropped off deep into the wilderness of Yellowstone National Park with nothing but a few hand tools and a black powder gun. Let me embellish this scenario further. Relax, put your mind into a mode to imagine life in the early 1600s, as you read the following passage I wrote many years ago. You can imagine yourself as one of the original gold-seeking settlers of Jamestown, Virginia, in 1607 or a passenger of the Mayflower in 1620!

*****

The evening sun was but a crescent that left behind only a fiery glow on the waters of the Atlantic. Since first lighting the earth, this life-giving furnace had risen in the east and proceeded ever westward with a daily precision that seemingly could never end. A lone star on the horizon was soon to be all that would light the way for the tiny vessel of wood and sails of canvas that edged toward the southwest upon the Atlantic waters. When you consider the power of the oceans and the winds, such tiny wooden vessels with canvas sails were almost as insignificant as a tiny acorn drifting down a raging river.

All oceanic travelers of the seventeenth century were mercilessly dependent upon the prevailing winds for both their survival and trip's progression. Many a voyager prayed for divine providence to accompany them on such a perilous journey in the seventeenth century. No one would have objected to a little luck.

While on deck, one might be lucky enough to feel a rare sense of peace and serenity. Experienced oceanic travelers, of the era, knew that the sense of peace and serenity would be short-lived and was a false sense at best. Waves might lap lazily at the ship's sides in rhythm while a cool soothing breeze dried the deck and propelled the ship toward its destiny. All aboard knew that waves and gentle breezes could be quick to anger and might smash this tiny vessel with little effort and with no residual remorse. Since the dawn of travel on the high seas, even the most dullard of voyagers were keenly aware of human weakness and insignificance when pitted against the fury of the earth's oceans and seas. Yet to struggle against the odds and survive those awesome forces of nature was an exhilaration experienced by all successful pioneers who sought escape, a better life, fame, fortune, or religious freedom in the wilderness of North America.

The new and alluring wilderness of North America afforded many people, of the Old World, a chance to enjoy those conventions or traditions they cherished and to escape the persecutions and destitution they could no longer endure. With great effort, daring, and a willingness to engage in a daily life and death struggle, one might create a better life, find fortune, parlay acquired skills into wealth or daily sustenance, or acquire freedom from autocratic rule and religious persecution. Was it risky to venture forth from Europe into the New World? You bet it was! America was so distant, wild, and undeveloped that your past could well lose its hold upon you as you became lost in a wilderness far from king and country. And those adventurers and pilgrims could die a horrible death in an instant or suffer a slow death of starvation and exposure to the elements. For sure, if you survived the perilous ocean voyage and stepped off the boat onto land, you would be engaged in a most fierce battle for your life!

Imagine that you have just climbed down the side of the ship, boarded a small boat, and are rowing ashore. You step into the water and set foot upon the beach of the looming wilderness. Just past the sandy beach you look into a dark and dense forest with a canopy so high and thick that sunlight struggles to penetrate. You are stepping out of the light, of the world you have known, into the darkness of the unknown wilderness. There are no man-made structures, of any type, visible to you because there are no Europeans there who could have built them. There are no wells for water, no gardens for gathering food, and no shelters from the elements. There is nothing but the forces of mother nature, and you suddenly realize that nothing has been created and prepared for your arrival. You will have to create, from the natural resources available, those things necessary to sustain life for you and your family. Those in your company will not be able to look to government for a handout. There is nothing but you and the reality of the natural world's laws of survival.

You have heard there are natives who will seek to kill you, and they may well do that. These natives see you as an uninvited, strange, and fearful trespasser in their territory competing for the limited resources necessary for sustaining life. You sense the possibility for much bloodshed. And you are not wrong! Two very different cultures will fight for control of the land.

You look over your shoulder at the vast ocean you have just spent some two and a half months crossing. You realize you cannot go back, even if you wanted to. You are committed because there are no other options for you. You may drop to your knees and say a prayer of thanks for the divine providence that has brought you thus far. Pray to God and rely upon faith because you are going to need much faith in order to overcome the struggles and challenges you are about to face. Look to your left and to your right. If you survive, the persons you see may well be dead in six months.

These adventurers and pilgrims were not stupid people. They knew before they left what they would face. They made the journey anyway. Would you have embarked upon that journey? Perhaps you would have been made of the "right stuff" to have made the journey. Perhaps you would have begun the fight for survival, and maybe you would have lived, beget heirs who would then demand the inalienable rights due to all humanity, and stood with the dignity that comes from the feeling of self-worth and "rugged individualism." Our ancestors did just that, and they gave us a wonderful gift, the United States of America! Read on, and we will discover just what these European settlers created for "We the people!"

When I titled this chapter "Escape to a Wilderness," I did so because I felt the title was most appropriate, given the story of English settlement of a wilderness. The wilderness would ultimately be transformed into the thirteen English colonies of North America. Granted, the concept implied by the word *escape* does not seem like one you would attach to the words *to a wilderness*! However, there was obviously something very wrong in the lives of many English citizens, who were so desperate, that they would consider moving to the hostile and uninviting wilderness of the Atlantic coast of North America. Those actions, and even the consideration of such a move, did not speak well about life in England for many people who yearned to breathe free or for those who sought opportunity that was not readily available to them in England. Political and religious oppression, as you have read, was extensive in "unmerry old England." Many in England were so destitute that they were little more than economic beggars for their daily sustenance. There were people who had been displaced from estates where they had worked for landlords and eked out a sparse survival. Eventually, multitudes would sell themselves into indentured servitude for a period of seven years just for the transport to America. That action, at least, gave them hope of procuring land in the wilderness, once they completed their voluntary servitude to a master.

I hope you enjoy this chapter! I will attempt to tell the story of struggle, defeat, and triumph that took place as the hopeful battled the wilderness of North America. As a result of this fierce struggle to survive and build a civilization for Europeans on the Atlantic shores of North America, a sense of rugged individualism and independence would grow. The oppressed, who had experienced religious, political, and economic chaos in England and Europe, would plant seeds of thoughts and ideas, in the wilderness, that would sprout and grow into a very unique set of freedoms for religious, political, and economic practices. They would demand these freedoms, and more importantly, they would die fighting for them!

I wish to cite the July 31, 2019, History.com article, "What's the Difference Between Puritans and Pilgrims" by Dave Roos (an excellent source for my discussion regarding the Puritans and Pilgrims.)[10]

Drive through any town, in our country, and count the many different churches that open their doors each Sunday morning. What you will find is many different churches preaching slightly or significantly different doctrines. Just in the small town of two thou-

---

[10] https://www.history.com/news/pilgrims-puritans-differences.

sand five hundred residents in which I reside, you can attend services for Catholics, Baptists, Methodists, Episcopalian, Church of Christ, Lutheran, and Church of God. This variance illustrates that when it comes to convictions of the heart, for religious worship, there exists many different religious views on just how one can best reach the goal of everlasting life in heaven. In America, you have the freedom to choose! Convictions of the heart produce strong emotional responses, especially when they involve one's mortal soul. Obviously, this was also true in Great Britain. With such diversity of religious organization, thinking, and practices, does it not seem the height of naivety to think a government can impose a single religious doctrine as a one-size-fits-all in your country? Religious freedom has existed for so long in our country that theocracy seems absurd. And absolutism of autocratic rule is revulsive to the thinking of citizens who have enjoyed the harmony that the real freedom of democracy allows.

Just as the Protestant Reformation in Europe gave rise to Lutheranism, Calvinism, and the Anglican Church of England, so too did the Church of England experience splinter groups with different religious thought and practices. Just as the Roman Catholic Church of Rome would see millions choose membership in other churches, the Anglican Church would experience the same circumstance of events. It is ironic that the Church of England and the English monarchs would resist and chastise groups that sought reforms of or total separation from the Anglican Church doctrine in a fashion similar to how the Catholic Church and its popes fought against the threat of the Protestant Reformation. In all cases, from both sides, we saw far too much persecution. Again, all of these many groups worshipped the same God but found it necessary to do so in different ways. These dissidents in Europe, regardless of their religion, never knew real freedom!

Earlier we spoke about Protestants in England who were dissatisfied that Elizabeth I was not more aggressive with Catholics. Northern England would foster a movement of thinking that wished to reform the Church of England. These dissidents felt that the Anglican Church needed to be cleansed further of Catholic rituals. In short, their church was still too much like the Catholic Church.

This dissident thinking of this new religious group branded them as Puritans, which the Anglicans derisively called them. The expressed desire of these Puritans was to further "purify" the Church of England of Catholic rituals.

Also, there would arise another group of dissidents who became known as "Separatists." They felt there was no hope of purification of the Anglican Church, and their solution was to leave England in 1608 and seek refuge in Leyden, Holland. Once there, it became obvious to these "Separatists" that their children were losing their English customs and identity, something parents did not want to give up. Faced with the desire to be separated from the Anglican Church and the added fear of the loss of English cultural identity for their children, their solution was to go to the New World where they would be free to practice religion in their own way as Englishmen and women. They secured permission for building a new colony in Virginia. They would take a great risk in a leap of faith and set out for an American wilderness. Is this not proof that deep religious convictions of the heart cause deep emotions that motivate people to take a stand for what they deem vitally important?

These dissident separatists would become our "1620 Mayflower Pilgrims!" When a social or religious group takes such extreme steps, and at great risk, beware when you try to contain them or limit their freedoms. Read the history of the "Mayflower Pilgrims" and you will learn of the great sacrifices and efforts made to just set sail from Europe. The voyage of over two months was cramped and anything but healthy for the 102 passengers. In addition to stormy seas, a structural problem of the ship caused fear they would all perish on the Atlantic. They landed in Cape Cod Bay of Massachusetts, far north of the intended area of Virginia that they were supposed to settle.

Their settlement would become known as Plymouth Plantation. After surviving the voyage, their plight remained a most daunting challenge due to the fact that they landed in the dead of winter. Imagine what it meant to land in a wilderness such as 1620 New England during winter. There was no Motel 6 and not a single grocery store. Talk about adversity! These pilgrims came face-to-face with the life-and-death reality of what it takes to survive some of nature's most challenging elements. Landing on the shores of a wilderness, in the dead of winter, they would have to provide for themselves the basic needs of life—food, shelter, clothing, and water—while protecting themselves from the native inhabitants who did not look favorably upon strangers camping in their backyard. As you can see, the Pilgrims risked everything when they took on the hardships and daily struggle for survival as they sought something that was a novel idea, something not realized before: religious freedom.

I think it is appropriate, at this time, to contrast the sacrifices and struggles in life's real-world laws of nature that the Pilgrims contended with to that of the fairy-tale modus operandi of today's America. The Pilgrims' experience was one based upon the reality of a struggle to survive. You cannot change this immutable natural law of existence, experienced by the pilgrims, with cradle-to-grave handouts from government, lest you create a society that is bankrupt and too weak to survive the inevitable challenges of life posed by the many adversarial countries on this planet. When our government can no longer print funny money or borrow to provide a lifestyle for citizens that they cannot afford or are unwilling to work for—the shock and despair will be unparalleled in our country! It seems to me that everyone, today, avoids the most important question.

Everyone one in the stadium would ask, "What is that elephant doing in the back of the endzone?" Yet nobody seems to ask the obvious question about where is our country going based upon the path we have been traveling for decades? Also, we do not ask how Americans will be equipped to cope when our nation reaches what promises to be an economic and social disaster. There is an economic, political, and social disaster on the horizon that threatens the destruction of this nation. Have the citizens of this country become so fat and sloppy, through decades of being spoiled and kept by the government, that we are too soft, or worse still, unwilling to fight for freedoms.

The Pilgrims went toe-to-toe with natural law just to survive in a wilderness. They were willing to do battle with and accept the challenges of nature to be self-sufficient and independent of others. Far too many people in our country truly believe that someone owes them something! Nobody owes you anything other than the right to struggle to survive just as the Pilgrims did. Only the hardy can survive such challenges as the Pilgrims faced, and that we will surely face in the twenty-first century if we continue to ignore the realities of nature's law of survival as well as fiscal responsibility.

Before the end of their first year, half of these adventurous Europeans were dead! When we look back at Plymouth and Jamestown, we can see the birth of the "Great American Spirit." Many of these settlers were from good stock. They, and others who followed, possessed the grit and determination that would be needed to settle the continent from the Atlantic to Pacific shores. Those were the ingredients it took to accept the challenge of surviving and building the most successful and powerful country in all of human history. No handouts! Self-esteem was earned, not conferred, upon Americans who built this nation. There was no expectation of cradle-to-grave sustenance from a government that would divide earnings of the population, at large, in order to take care of all, especially those who want more and more but who are unwilling to work and struggle for their wants. It was Captain John Smith in Jamestown who said, "He that will not work shall not eat!" Too bad the truth behind that statement does not shine through today.

Do we have a society today that resembles, in any way, the "Greatest Generation"? You know, the generation that volunteered for the military by the hundreds of thousands after the Japanese attacked Pearl Harbor kept military factories running twenty-four hours a day, or who stormed the beaches of Normandy and countless others in the Pacific! Do our young people have any idea what was at stake if those heroes did not storm the beaches or if they had failed? We had better teach them!

At each of our births begins the difficult daily struggle to live. Life's struggle lasts until death because that is, and always has been, the reality of life.

Decade after decade, as our country expanded from the Atlantic to the Pacific shores, people would ask, "What is it about these American pioneers that makes them struggle and bear great hardships to attain success against great odds?" They flocked to our shores as if a great wind was at their backs, ever pushing them toward America. The wind was a wind of desire for freedoms denied them in the lands from whence they came. They thirsted for just a chance to pursue work and free enterprise to better their economic lives. America and all that it has become was the dream they pursued! I believe the answer to the question was the fact that these pioneers had a "spirit of rugged individualism," a spirit that grew from a self-reliance that prompted them to work to achieve self-sufficiency. Their pride, along with these characteristics and accomplishments of self-sufficiency, led them to a spirit of independence and freedom. For this, they held their heads high, and they appreciated America because for the first time in their lives, they gained self-respect and the knowledge that they were as good as any man or women. Those people had a deep sense of pride, and they wanted to stand on their own two feet and hold their heads up with a knowledge they were equal to anyone and they did not need to bow before none, except their "Maker!" They were Americans, and the world would be forced to deal with that spirit time and time again when they tried to subjugate the Americans!

If you expect to find an easy path to achieve success, likely as not, you will be disappointed. Work, sacrifice, and perseverance seem to be a better bet. That is something the Pilgrims already knew or learned very quickly.

To be sure, the Separatists on the Mayflower were not the only people who joined this dangerous voyage. Not all aboard were Separatists from the Anglican Church. Some were "strangers," or those onboard who were not seeking religious refuge. These "strangers," as the Separatists called them, were people seeking the opportunity that the New World might provide. Both the Separatists and the strangers surely knew they were far from any civil authority and protection and that they must make preparations for some measure of control for their society in the wilderness. Yet only one group aboard this ship would have power going forward.

The "Mayflower Compact" is one of the foundational documents of America that we all have read in U.S. history class. It is unique in that it is a written document that helped along the concept of self-government in the New World. It was not a constitution nor was it a structure of government. It is worthy to note that self-governance, as it may be needed from time to time, would be propelled by what was truly a theocracy. While there were fifty men on board, only forty-one were religious Separatists or Pilgrims, and only they voted for and signed the Mayflower Compact.[11]

The compact, a pledge of agreement, would be on the condition that only male members of the church could vote in what would be an example of theocratic direct democracy. That compact of 1620 was quite different from the separation of church and state and representative democracy put forth by the signers of the U.S. Constitution on September 17, 1787, and the 1791 signing of the "Bill of Rights," the first ten amendments to the 1787 constitution. Read the Mayflower Compact and discover, for yourself, what is so surprising about this primary source document.[12]

> In the name of God, Amen. We, whose names are underwritten, the Loyal Subjects of our dread Sovereign Lord King James, by the Grace of God, of Great Britain, France, and Ireland, King, defender of the Faith, etc.:
>
> Having undertaken, for the Glory of God, and advancements of the Christian faith, and the honor of our King and Country, a voyage to plant the first colony in the Northern parts of Virginia; do by these presents, solemnly and mutually, in the presence of God, and one another; covenant and combine ourselves together into a civil body politic; for our better ordering, and preservation

---

[11] https://www.mayflower400uk.org/education/who-were-the-pilgrims/2019/november/the-mayflower-compact-the-first-governing-document-of-plymouth-colony/.

[12] https://www.britannica.com/topic/Mayflower-Compact.

and furtherance of the ends aforesaid; and by virtue hereof to enact, constitute, and frame, such just and equal laws, ordinances, acts, constitutions, and offices, from time to time, as shall be thought most meet and convenient for the general good of the colony; unto which we promise all due submission and obedience.

In witness whereof we have hereunto subscribed our names at Cape Cod the 11th of November, in the year of the reign of our Sovereign Lord King James, of England, France, and Ireland, the eighteenth, and of Scotland the fifty-fourth, 1620.[13]

Should we be surprised, or not surprised, that these Pilgrims who were separated from James I, King of England by sixty-six days of sea travel, chose a one-man one-vote of equal power for decision-making equal to that of each male member of their church? The struggle and success of this Plymouth Plantation Colony did not go unnoticed, and there was plenty of room for more restless English men and women in the wilderness of what would become known as New England.

Previously I mentioned a second group of dissenters within the Church of England, the Puritans. They too would make the harrowing journey to the New World. Massachusetts Bay Colony of Puritans was comprised of three early settlements in the area of Salem, Boston, and Cambridge. The settlement of these three areas became known as the Great Migration. This migration began in 1630. John Winthrop initially led some one thousand Puritans, well provisioned and possessing many different skills, to settle in the Massachusetts Bay area in 1630 after they had secured a charter from King Charles I. By 1640, the colony would grow to some twenty

---

[13] History.com Editors, https://www.history.com/topics/colonial-america/mayflower-compact.

thousand. Massachusetts Bay Colony flourished, but it seems the more things change, the more they stay the same.

The old country saying that you can take the boy out of the country but you cannot take the country out of the boy seems to be an analogy for lots of things. The Puritans could flee England's religious persecution, but they could not leave behind their superstitions, theocracy, and habits for persecutions of those they feared or those who disagreed with them. You have only to read about the 1692 Salem witch trials to be reminded of one of the most horrendous events of the Protestant Reformation. Some fifty-nine people were tried for witchcraft, thirty-one convicted, and nineteen hanged in Salem, Massachusetts, in the New World. Neither the Separatists nor the Puritans came to Massachusetts to nurture religious freedom for all. They came to be free to practice their religion. The Massachusetts Bay Colony was governed by the Puritan Church. Massachusetts Bay Colony was designated a theocracy. This theocracy did not tolerate any disagreement with the church's beliefs or practices. A fact that would soon serve to bring a change to colonial America.

Roger Williams became a victim of Puritan intolerance when he had the audacity to put forth the position that Indians should not have their lands seized without just compensation. Unfortunately, fair treatment of American Indians never caught on during our American "manifest destiny." Roger Williams, a minister from Salem, had another ridiculous idea: The government should not be involved in religion.

In 1635 Puritan New England, such challenges to the church and state authority of the Puritan Church theocracy would not be tolerated. Williams would be exiled. Though he was not burned at the stake and was only banished into the wilderness of what would become Rhode Island, I would ask you, does this remind you of behavior in "unmerry old England?" This was an example of persecution of Williams because he voiced a challenge of the church and state authority in Massachusetts Bay Colony. He was suggesting—yes, you guessed it—separation of church and state and the freedom of speech to suggest such heresy! His courage to voice such protestations would bring about change in America, and eventually his voice would be heard around the New World. Real freedom had been born in America, but only for some only in some ways. There was an evolvement of freedoms and thought taking place in the wilderness. It would continue to grow!

Roger Williams and his followers would move to what is now known as Rhode Island where they founded Providence. In 1644, they were chartered by parliament as the colony of Rhode Island. And what did Williams and the government of the new colony do? Everybody became free to practice religion based upon their personal convictions. Just as important, the activities of church and state would now be separated. Theocracy was out! With these two liberating concepts, the seeds were sown that would ultimately guarantee enormous freedoms and prevent the level of persecution that had been the tool of the powerful, when church and state had been joined at the hip. Talk about radical change for the good.

Contrast the impact of these liberating actions of the new government led by Williams with the events of religious and political autocratic rule that killed millions in Europe in the years that followed 1517. This was real progress, and more people could now breathe free! Many more settlers were now attracted to Rhode Island. I believe there is much historical evidence to prove the great benefit provided for humanity by the courageous actions of Roger Williams. Good news and good ideas can spread as quickly as a tidal wave. Question, how would you like a life in America without such freedoms? There are those who would think nothing of taking them.

Maryland became a proprietary colony under the ownership of George Calvert, the first Lord Baltimore, in 1634. His purpose was twofold in that he hoped to make a profit as well as to provide a safe haven for English Catholics. Curious, is it not, that both Lord Baltimore and the Puritans of New England both had issues with the Church of England and the king. Both sought and found a solution in America. The second Lord Baltimore would be most active in making Maryland a successful venture. The Maryland Toleration Act of 1649 provided religious freedom for all Christians. Just as with any historical event, there are different points of view as to the motivation to pass such a law. And for sure there would be periods of time in which this freedom would not be protected between 1649 and the passage of the First Amendment.

The Maryland colony grew, and success also attracted new settlers who were Protestants. Some historians claim that the Catholics were afraid they might become a minority and once again suffer persecutions. Therefore, the decision was made to protect themselves by guaranteeing religious freedom to all Christians even though they worshipped Christ via different doctrines and rituals. The act forbade making disparaging remarks about different Christian churches. Whatever the motivation, the mere fact it was passed served to impact the passage of the First Amendment. Soon others hurried to America to enjoy what was not available in Europe.

William Penn
(English Quaker leader and colonist)

William Penn became sole proprietor of the colony of Pennsylvania which he considered his "holy experiment." Religious tolerance was a cornerstone of his "holy experiment." He established Philadelphia, the "City of Brotherly Love." The colony would become a safe haven for the Society of Friends or Quakers. Pennsylvania would provide religious freedom for many different religious groups including Jewish colonists. Quakers, who were pacifists and practiced faith without clergy and formal churches, were originally assembled by George Fox. Just as so many religious groups before, the Quakers experienced much persecution in England from both Anglicans and Catholics. Penn was outspoken, and he was attacked for his exercising of free speech and freedom of the press when he authored numerous books about faith.

According to Frederick B. Tolles' article, "William Penn, English Quaker leader and colonist," Tolles writes the following statement about William Penn: "In his first publication, the pamphlet *Truth Exalted* (1668), he upheld Quaker doctrines while attacking in turn those of the Roman Catholics, the Anglicans, and the Dissenting churches." For this and other such speech and writing, Penn would end up in the Tower of London.[14] As you can see, Pennsylvania was Penn's creation of a special place where he sought to correct the persecutions he suffered and witnessed in England. Only in America could he find a place far enough from king and country to protect his Quakers and others for whom he secured religious freedom and free speech! Gaining such freedoms and escaping so much persecution, surely, led many to value a place called Pennsylvania in America. Europeans journeyed bravely to America in pursuit of their dream. And their pursuit created the "great American dream" for the millions who followed. We can all pursue that same dream, but we must protect the dream!

My second year of teaching in public schools in Virginia found me in an 8:00 a.m. U.S. history class of some thirty eleventh-grade students. The year was 1974. One of the students in that class was a young lady, whose face I can still see. That day, it was her goal to put this young teacher, age twenty-one, on the spot. She achieved her goal most emphatically, though I am not sure how many students were awake to appreciate my lack of knowledge on the subject as well as my utter embarrassment. Her chance came during a discussion about the rights found in the First Amendment. She asked me how John Peter Zenger's trial, in 1735, impacted the amendment. I confess, with almost as much embarrassment today as I experienced in that early morning class forty-seven years ago, that I did not know! How is that possible? I do not know! I can still hear the glee in her voice when she said, "You mean you don't know who John Peter Zenger was?" I can tell you this: By the end of that day, I had studied everything I could find about Mr. Zenger!

I am proud to say that by 2008, I had improved my knowledge and teaching of U.S. history enough to be named Gilder Lehrman Institute of American History Teacher of the Year 2008 for my home state of WV. I competed for National Teacher of the Year 2008, and I considered that an honor even though I did not win! And I assure you there are many questions about U.S. history that I cannot answer

---

[14] https://www.britannica.com/biography/William-Penn-English-Quaker-leader-and-colonist.

even today. If you have not had the pleasure of meeting Mr. Zenger, I intend to remedy that situation today. And I can tell you that I have not forgotten the lesson that young lady taught me. Nor have I forgotten John Peter Zenger. This *escape into the American wilderness* by thousands of Europeans was not only a result of religious persecution, freedom to speak your mind was also oppressed in England and elsewhere.

British officials and especially the monarchs of England had no tolerance for criticisms or attacks, either verbally or in print. It did not matter whether your statement was true or false; it was considered libelous if the officials did not like what you said or printed. You had to be very careful when you uttered or printed any criticisms as you could be jailed for libel and sedition. In short, freedom of speech and press did not exist. Censorship is a valuable tool of autocratic rulers who refuse to tolerate criticism of their policies or activities. Until recently, in America, we could neither understand such a curb on free speech or press, and moreover, we would not tolerate such censorship!

Seems to me that chastisement for not speaking in terms of political correctness was the beginning of censorship of freedom of speech and press in recent years in the USA. Today, those charged with not being politically correct suffer much blowback from the media and public officials. It is not pleasant to be labeled a racist, bigot, or a white supremacist, especially when you are not guilty. What you have to understand is that such accusations are a ploy to silence you, as you are their opposition. Being intimidated into being silent is tantamount to surrender, something most Americans cannot stomach. When you do not challenge, do not question, and fail to criticize obvious abuses of power and counterproductive policies, you fuel the "bully" in the powerful. Without fail, the abuse or curtailment of freedoms will continue and increase in severity if there is no resistance put up by the oppressed.

Democracy cannot survive such timid behavior, but tyranny thrives when timidity is the rule of the day, and under those circumstances, tyranny becomes even more abusive. A free and objective press is the natural extension of freedom of speech and is necessary in order to generate debate. Debate is the essence of workings of a democracy. People who love America are of high moral character, work within the framework of the constitution, and who can put forth good arguments in debate are in a position to help government achieve the most positive for the "greater good" of society. That is the theory, but watch some of the major news outlets and you will see anything but an objective press.

The press will present a narrative that stymies much good that could be accomplished economically and politically. Case in point, President Trump operated under the slogan, "Put America First." He insisted on trade deals with China that did not put our economy at a disadvantage and one that was more supportive of American workers. His lowering of the corporate tax rate was designed to bring back, to our shores, corporations that would not only bring home trillions of dollars but would employ American workers as well. Sounds good, does it not?

The problem was too many corporations, rich and powerful entities, and powerful persons had great stakes of investment in China. These groups were able to influence the far-left press to attack President Trump and his policies, both foreign and domestic. When he moved to shut down travel between the U.S. and China when the COVID pandemic emerged, they called him a racist and xeno-phobic. The left-wing press, today, is no longer a watchdog for the protection of America. They have economic and political agendas, and that is why they push propaganda and half-truths. They actually hide behind the label of a free press and use that label for protection in order to put forth political and economic agendas for the far left. These statements about free speech are representative of the perspective of many Americans.

The concept of freedom of speech and of the press was quite different in the formative years of America, both before and after the passage of the First Amendment. Our foundation for freedom of the press and for free speech first took root in colonial America far away from the powerful and absolute rule of king and country. Has editorializing for a cause always taken place? Yes, but to the detriment of America to the point that seems treasonous—I don't think so. Has the press been trusted too much throughout our history? I think so. That is why we should never believe everything that is presented in the press. My opinion, we must be more discerning today than ever before.

The seeds of freedom were planted and received nourishment from those with the courage to stand up to royal governors in the colonies and ultimately to be defiant of King George III. Without question, the greatest of all defiant moments was the presentation of the document known as "The July 4, 1776 Declaration of Independence." Now, that was an example of sedition and the ultimate exercise of freedom of speech and press in the eighteenth century. Enough digressing. What is there that you should know about the trial of my old friend John Peter Zenger?

You may read more on this subject from an article at the website for National Park Service where you will learn about Federal Hall Park in New York, a national memorial, from where George Washington's oath of office was administered.

John Peter Zenger was a German who emigrated to New York where he began to print the *New York Weekly Journal.* The royal governor of New York at the time was William S. Cosby. Apparently, Cosby was corrupt enough to be harshly attacked for rigging elections and other nefarious activities. Though Zenger did not write any critical articles, he did, in fact, print articles that harshly criticized Cosby. For this act of seditious libel, Zenger was thrown in jail where he would stay for a year.

On April 16, 1735, two attorneys, James Alexander and William Smith, were set to defend Zenger. Unfortunately for Zenger, the court disbarred both attorneys and appointed John Chambers, an attorney of little experience and who had conveniently praised Governor Cosby. Not to be outdone so easily, Alexander and Smith secured the services of a most able attorney, Andrew Hamilton, born in Scotland and living in Philadelphia, Pennsylvania.

According to the referenced article from NPS, Hamilton addressed the court as follows: "When Andrew Hamilton spoke, he was made famous for arguing that 'the truth is a defense against libel.' The jury returned with a not guilty verdict." John Peter Zenger, with the able representation of Andrew Hamilton, went free and carried the banner for "freedom of press and speech" into American History books.

What do you think about Hamilton's powerful defense statement on behalf of Zenger? What a novel idea. It is not libelous sedition if you speak or print the truth. And you should not be punished for proclaiming the truth! Talk about standing up to the corruption and sentencing abuse of powerful autocrats! So on April 16, 1735, a defense was put forth that planted yet another seed in America's fertile ground for the birth of real freedom. This historical court case helped lay the groundwork for freedom of speech and press in our bill of rights.

So based upon Hamilton's defense of Zenger, you cannot be libel if you speak or print the truth. That is the hallowed basis for freedom of the press that we have revered for so long. This reverence for freedom of the press and the expectation that the press would not risk libel by printing a lie has given us all a false sense of security.

I grew up thinking that if you read the front page or listened to the nightly news broadcast, then you could accept that report without question. It was true—it had to be! That kind of naivete qualified me as a lamb being led to slaughter. Foolishly, we have thought of the press as a guardian and watchdog for the corruption that exists in government ran by crooked politicians. A free and uncensored press existed to protect us from exploitation. That is a basic cornerstone of our system, and we have cherished it since the days of John Peter Zenger and the ratification of the First Amendment. But what happens if the press is not honest or uses the shield of free press to perpetuate an agenda?

There are many examples of a compromised press throughout our history, but it seems to me that today's press has sold out to those who wish to hide behind the shield of a supposed free press in order to manipulate our society and elections. Fact-check the press and you will find lies that go unchallenged and cause people to be misled. Those who take the bait march off to make stupid statements and engage in dangerous activities. Does real and honest journalism still exist today? I mean the honest journalism that was expected to be our watchdog and that we have held in such high esteem because of our values and traditions! We have revered the First Amendment rights of America. The most important responsibility of a free press is to tell the truth and not spread propaganda. Perhaps we should ask more questions and say we will believe it when we can verify the story. Maybe it is time for me to present another example, actually my second example, of what seems to illustrate that Americans are being betrayed by the press!

The headlines on the front pages of major newspapers and the day-after-day emphatic charges of guilt for corrupt behavior by Donald Trump by the cable news organizations dominated the news for months. "Trump is a Russian asset. Trump colluded with the Russians and Putin to defeat Hillary Clinton in the 2016 Presidential Election. Trump must now repay his debt to his friend Putin. We have the Steele Dossier! We have the smoking gun to impeach and remove Donald Trump from the presidency!" The press beat these drums daily for years. Why? The press said these things over and over because they knew it would raise doubts and erode support for President Trump. If you repeat a lie often enough, the naïve, who do not question validity and sources, will come to accept the statements as truth. After all, it is in the news. It has to be true!

Wrong! Unfortunately, you must verify before you can trust the news provided by multiple news organizations today. Just because you read the news of the paper or hear a news broadcast you cannot and better not accept the story as gospel. First and foremost, you must question, and you must fact-check! I was aghast when I heard the charges put forth by the press against President Trump. You decide if the press intentionally lied. If they did not lie, then they are grossly incompetent and should be fired. Regardless, they could not pass a Journalism 101 course! You may be questioning with a very simple interrogative. Why would you say that about the press, Stan?

Not one of the assertions or charges I outlined above that were made by the press against Donald Trump was true. Not one! Because not one was true, I feel confident in saying that there was a conspiracy of collusion within the left-wing press and between that press and powerful ultra-left forces. President Trump was not guilty of collusion with the Russians. It was the majority of the press that conspired to lie in order to weaken Donald Trump. In short, President Trump was too successful! Had he been guilty, the Muller investigation would have presented evidence of Russian collusion, and President Trump would have been impeached for those charges. They did not and could not present any evidence after almost two years and millions of dollars spent in the "witch hunt" designed to weaken a presidency. There was no such evidence! Has anyone heard even one retraction by any news organization or one apology for the baseless slander and libel against President Trump and his family? I have not, and I bet you have not either. We do, now know, that the Steele dossier was fake, and we know who paid for it, don't we?

Could we offer more historical events? Yes, but the knowledge you have gained, after reading these early chapters, will enable you to reflect on what the First Amendment to the United States Constitution means to people who love freedom and America. You also know the history behind the First Amendment and understand that the First Amendment's intentions can be a wonderful protection of individuals' rights. However, you have also learned that we must question sources, motives, and do fact-checks on the press. Additionally, you now know why these freedoms were so valued by those early Americans who fought to not only gain freedom but to sustain freedom as well. I doubt that you want to experience life without the freedoms guaranteed by our written "rule of law." Can you possibly imagine a life in the United States if freedom of speech and press did not exist?

The great escape to the American wilderness was accomplished. The struggles of these escapees and pioneers were daunting and quite challenging. Many died, but more survived, and they grew the fruit of freedom in the American wilderness for all of us to enjoy.

Though we discussed the First Amendment at length, this chapter was about more than just freedom of the press and speech. In the next chapter, we will take a close look at all parts of the First Amendment. Please, read on. I am enjoying the telling of the story of the "greatest nation on earth," ever!

5

Our First Amendment

Congress shall make no law respecting an establishment of religion, or prohibiting the free exercise thereof; or abridging the freedom of speech, or of the press; or the right of the people peaceably to assemble, and to petition the Government for a redress of grievances.[15]

Brief History of Our First Amendment

During the constitutional convention debate that took place from May 25, 1787 to September 17, 1787, at what is now known as Independence Hall in Philadelphia, Pennsylvania, there arose a serious difference of opinion between federalists and anti-federalists. Federalists, who favored a strong central government, were opposed by those who were more in favor of states' rights because they feared the power of a strong central government such as Parliament and King George III had represented. The opposition, known as the anti-federalists, feared their successful efforts to rid the colonies of King George III might be negated if they accepted this proposed constitution that would become the "supreme law of the land" for the United States of America.

---

[15] https://www.history.com/topics/united-states-constitution/first-amendment.

Basically, after having defeated the British, the anti-federalists wanted assurances of more protection for specific unalienable human rights. The constitution was ratified with the understanding that a bill of rights would be added to protect the natural rights of those fortunate enough to be Americans.

I began this writing because I feel too many people, both young and old alike, do not appreciate our American blessings. Far too many Americans do not know history, either because they have forgotten or more likely were never taught. And far too many have never been taught how to think because it is easier to allow others to tell you what you should believe and accept rather than do the hard work of research and analysis. I would never present an ideology lest I offered a plethora of facts. You should never accept, blindly, any proposition for which you do not have the necessary facts from which you can make informed decisions on your own. Too much brainwashing takes place in the media twenty-four seven. Additionally, too much of this baseless propaganda takes place in classrooms at many levels of education.

Parents, one of the greatest contributions you can make toward your children's education is to put them in a position in which they must analyze factual data and draw conclusions for which they can offer supporting evidence in order to solve problems and defend a position taken. None of this is possible if your child is weak in the skills of English language arts. You must closely monitor your children's achievement in reading, comprehension, and writing! Democracy is doomed when the electorate cannot read, think, evaluate, and make good decisions. Do you think there are forces in our country and the global world that benefit because large numbers of our voters are illiterate? Voting is a decision, is it not? Votes, once cast, always have consequences.

Do not allow me, in this book, or anyone else to tell you what to think! Remember, evaluate facts and history with careful analysis. The goal of the first three chapters was to provide you with a baseline of knowledge about historical events that would stimulate your thinking about how horrible life has been and can become again. I hope I have painted an accurate picture of history with ample facts and historical events. If I have not done so, I encourage you to do more study, research more facts, and please recognize rhetoric that seeks to add you as a blind follower with herd mentality. Your greatest protection is one simple question: Why? Follow this with a simple statement: Show me the facts—just the facts!

So how did colonial Americans begin to solve the dark failures of society that many had suffered? Was one of their solutions self-governance? What value is there in the utilization of rule of law in a written constitution accompanied by a bill of rights? Does our rule of law provide a "protections of individual rights umbrella"? Does our constitution and the bill of rights prevent the tyranny and persecutions suffered in Europe before the Pilgrims came to America? You decide how you answer these questions, but I think I know your answer! The constitution and the bill of rights have done a good job for a very long time, but both are under attack today. The first three chapters of this book provided numerous accounts of persecution for centuries. In America we rejected autocratic rulers who used absolute power for vindictive and self-serving purposes because they always strip citizens of their God-given, unalienable (natural) rights. Our founding fathers chose the protections of rule of written law when they ratified our constitution that provided for separation of powers into three branches of government with checks and balances to prevent tyranny and persecution. The constitution was followed with our first ten amendments, the bill of rights! These unalienable rights found in our bill of rights were sacred to many of these early Americans, as they are to millions of Americans today!

What does it mean to you when you read "Congress shall make no law respecting an establishment of religion, or prohibiting the free exercise thereof"?

Based upon your recent reading of history, in the first three chapters, I hope you recognize the wisdom of our founding fathers' vision to separate church and state. I believe your study, thus far, has armed you with the knowledge that allows you to stand up to those who would belittle these rights and enlighten those who are ignorant of the great blessings we Americans enjoy. Protections and blessings for which our ancestors fought and died to gain for themselves, and even more wonderful is the fact they secured these blessings for their posterity. Can we allow their sacrifices to be devalued because we do not remember their sufferings, do not recognize how valuable our freedoms really are, or are unwilling to make the necessary efforts to preserve these unalienable rights for our children and grandchildren to come? We have been given much in this land we call America. Religious freedom can only be enjoyed when the government cannot encourage or restrict the free practice of any specific religion nor the pursuit of individual religious convictions of the heart! What dark events in history can you now cite that motivated the founding fathers to structure our government as they did? Your rights are protected by this written rule of law: "Congress shall make no law respecting an establishment of religion, or prohibiting the free exercise thereof." Tax money or other governmental acts cannot favor or support any religious group. Nor can government take action or use the public's money to attack a religion. Do you remember the Obama-Biden administration's proclamation that infuriated the Catholic bishops in America in 2012?

Google https://www.cnsnews.com/news/article/100-catholic-bishops-oppose-obama-s-contraceptive-mandate to read the article titled "100% of Catholic Bishops Oppose Obama's Contraceptive Mandate" written by Michael W. Chapman on February 17, 2012. The following is a quote taken from Chapman's article:

> All 181 Catholic bishops in the United States oppose and have publicly denounced a regulation issued by the Obama administration that would require every health insurer to offer contraceptives, including those that induce abortion, free of charge. The bishops oppose the mandate because, they argue, it is a violation of religious liberty under the First Amendment—in this case, the federal government forcing individual Catholics to subsidize products and services that are contrary to their religious beliefs.

A violation of the FIRST Amendment? You decide.

The different branches of government must do their constitutional duty to protect freedoms. Do you remember King Henry VIII's requirement that his church was to be supported by all? Such a limitation on governmental power, as our separation of church and state, is the only way to assure religious freedom for all! Additionally, government cannot impose restrictions on any religion unless that religion begins to deny life liberty or pursuit of happiness to others. One axiom I always emphasized to my students was that your rights end where the rights of others begin. Our founding fathers put forth great effort in designing a system that protected "We the people" from suffering through a repeat of history's dark persecutions.

Unfortunately, there seems to be a concerted movement in this country that ignores the constitution. The facts are clear; thousands upon thousands of Americans died in 2020 and 2021 from COVID-19. Did the government restriction of religious services during the pandemic violate the free exercise of religion and, for that matter, free speech? Does the constitution empower Americans to make decisions regarding their personal health considerations and where and when they will assemble to practice their religious rituals? Does the government have a duty to curb the rights of some when it appears the exercising of such individual rights as peaceful assembly might injure or deny the rights of others? These are serious questions during dangerous times! It would be false to claim that such curbs on individual freedoms have not happened in our country during different national emergencies.

One extremely controversial curb and denial of rights happened in this country immediately following the December 7, 1941, surprise attack by the Empire of Japan on the U.S. naval base at Pearl Harbor. It is noteworthy that there were peace talk envoys from Japan in Washington, DC, discussing the disagreements between our country and Japan close to the time of this sneak attack. About 2,403 Americans died that morning, eighteen ships were damaged, two battleships—the USS *Arizona* and the USS *Utah*—were sunk, and one hundred eighty aircraft were destroyed. As you can imagine, the anger in this country was unimaginable. Thousands upon thousands of Americans rushed to voluntarily enlist in the military to defend this country. The great fear was that the Japanese would invade the west coast of the U.S. They did in fact invade and occupy part of the Aleutian Islands off of the coast of Alaska. Unfortunately, overwhelming numbers of Japanese American citizens, loyal to the United States, would suffer a loss of civil liberties as a result of the horrific event of Pearl Harbor (https://www.nps.gov/perl/learn/historyculture/japanese-american-units-of-world-war-ii.htm).

During the COVID-19 lockdown, pastors were arrested for holding services in violation of "stay at home orders" issued by the government. Do you have an answer for these questions that you can defend with factual evidence? I hope I have stimulated your thought process. Let us dig a little deeper into this umbrella of protection, the First Amendment.

The First Amendment phrase, "or abridging the freedom of speech, or of the press," is equally important as the first phrase of the amendment. In fact, this clause, "or abridging the freedom of speech, or of the press;" works hand in hand as a necessary protection for "Congress shall make no law respecting an establishment of religion, or prohibiting the free exercise thereof." You may remember the John Peter Zenger trial, and now you know that the founding fathers were aware of the lesson learned from that trial and other horrible denials of unalienable rights. "Truth is a defense for libel!" Challenging corruption and infringement of basic rights with both the written and spoken word is a duty of all citizens of a democracy. That is how we protect the "greater good of society" with the democratic process.

The news media in eighteenth-century America was a printing press that printed broadsides and newspapers that were passed from reader to reader, posted on public buildings, and in the town square. Twenty-first-century American press outlets, by contrast, are obviously light-years more advanced and numerous. Today we have everything from newspapers, radio, cable networks, social media, internet, and the list goes on. The free press envisioned by our founders was one that was a watchdog that sniffed out abuses of power and corruption. Obviously, that was not always the case, and you would be foolish to ever think that. To be fair, the press has always editorialized different points of view as well as the different ideologies of the time. And that is fine. A free press is fundamental to a successful democratic society because getting out the different points of view is essential to having a choice and for making decisions. There must also be objective reporting of facts so citizens can decide. Remember, just because you read it on social media, in the newspaper, watch it on TV, or see it in this book does not mean it is true or free of bias. You must read critically and demand or search for the facts. Analyze and think for yourself. Research if you must, but always ask "why" and demand the proof. Recognize propaganda because the goal of propagandists is to draw you into their herd of mindless thought. There is, and always has been, various interpretations of news facts via an editorial point of view which is also acceptable.

Many suggest that we do not have an honest and free press today! Are they right? You should get the facts and then decide for yourself. I will give you a homework assignment similar to one I gave my students. Use your recording device to make a recording of a popular evening news broadcast of at least one that is considered to be liberal and also one for what you would consider to be a conservative source. Then do a recording of both a perceived liberal and conservative cable network news talk show from prime time. You can then put your analytical skills to work in order to see not only the big picture but to find the propaganda that leaves out important facts or distorts events.

I enjoyed assigning this homework activity. I routinely switch the channels from network to network to see the different presentation or the omission of any presentation on hot topics that are important to the country. You can too! Contrast the news leads on a subject that the different networks provide at the start of the story. Search for key words that point to an immediate effort to force their bias upon you in order to influence your thinking. Analyze their presentation in order to see if they present any real facts and if they present the whole story rather than just the convenient short phrase of the total story that conveniently hides and distorts the total context of the story. This distortion is a gross misrepresentation of the whole story, and it serves to advance their false narrative. When you see such instances of bias and "yellow journalism," the red flags should start to fly. Watch out, because if you are not a critical thinker, you will be led down the primrose path of propaganda that is designed to use smoke and mirrors to convert you to an ideology that is void of facts and reality. This is how blind followers are secured in order to bolster nefarious movements that should really be suspect because they have ulterior motives that can do great harm to the country.

A dishonest press that exists in a country, that supposedly has a free press, can be a dangerous weapon that is used to gain power that will suppress the greater good and destroy any faith in honest reporting. Such activities can lead voters to make wrong choices that serve to hurt the country and the efficiency of democracy. In fact, groups and governments have captured control of the media in order to hide facts, mislead the public, and to create a groundswell of support for a movement based on false and misleading presentations or the withholding of information that the public needs to see in order to make informed voting decisions. More than seventy-four million American voters are convinced that is precisely what happened in the days leading up to the 2020 presidential election.

I call your attention to the story that broke in the *New York Post* just prior to the November 3, 2020, presidential election. The story documented evidence that was taken from the computer of Hunter Biden, son of democratic candidate for president, Joe Biden. Along with the testimony of Tony Bobulinski, there appeared to be much damning evidence that Hunter Biden and the Biden family, at large, received large sums of money from China and other countries. Accusations were made that money was paid to Hunter Biden while Joe Biden was vice president of the U.S. as well as after he left that office. The inference was that Joe Biden's office of the vice president of the United States was used for influence pedaling, for pay, by certain members of the Biden family. That access to Biden, for pay, was alleged to have occurred not only with China but Russia and elsewhere.

Such a revelation, just prior to an election, could prove to be a game changer on the outcome of an election. The *New York Post* investigation revealed there had been an ongoing investigation of

Hunter Biden, and there was evidence taken from his computer that was most alarming. Perhaps even more powerful was the Tucker Carlson interview of Tony Bobulinski, former business partner of Hunter Biden. Bobulinski made many serious allegations about Hunter and Joe Biden. Don't take my word for this because a Google search, provided it has not been censored and purged, will show you the *New York Post* articles of accusations along with their supporting facts. Tucker Carlson's interview is certainly preserved for your viewing. You are probably asking yourself how this enters into our discussion of freedom of speech and of the press.

The success of big tech in the form of Twitter and Facebook is nothing short of phenomenal. Worldwide millions upon millions of people use these social media giants daily for hours at a time. Users surf there in order to visit friends and family while sharing photographs, stories, and a plate of food to show what they are eating for dinner. Glad I do not visit those sites, because if I did, I would not have time to write. Most importantly, millions use these media giants as their daily news sources. Curiously enough the *New York Post* used their account with these social media giants to post their article and findings on Hunter Biden. So what was the problem, you ask? Big tech shut down the *New York Post*'s account and would not allow the posting of the story to stay up, thus preventing millions of Americans from seeing the report on Biden before the election. Couple this with the fact that the mainstream media would not air accounts of the story and you had a thunderous news story that did not get out to millions of American voters. Is this censorship and a violation of free press by the tech giants? You decide, but it is curious to note, is it not, big tech took down such a potentially damning article on the Bidens but left articles posted about President Trump up for millions of potential voters to see.

According to a November 24, 2020, article written by Jordan Davidson, and posted at federalist.com, Davidson cites a report from the Media Research Center that indicates suppression of the Hunter Biden story by both the regular media and big tech may have cost President Trump the election. I would contend that while the suppression by the media of this scandal was a major cause, there were many other nefarious activities taking place in battleground states that contributed to the defeat of President Trump. The data on a poll presented in this article put forth that 17 percent of Biden voters would not have voted for Biden had they known about the suppressed Hunter Biden story. If that is true, those kinds of numbers would have created a swing in votes that could have delivered an electoral college landslide for Donald Trump. So what is the real point I wish to make about this story and the suppression?

The point is that big tech allows the *New York Post* to use their sites as well as allowing millions of other users to post on their sites. Everyone is free to read various postings and have been for a very long time. In fact, these social media sites are the go-to-sites for news and entertainment of millions of American voters. In other words, it has become a common everyday acceptance by the public that you can post and write on these sites, subject to various guidelines. So if you are free to speak on these social media sites, and that is a common practice, why, all of a sudden, is such a venue no longer available for an article to be made available to an audience of millions that use the sites on a daily basis? Does this seem like political censorship of free speech by a media that is biased for one candidate? You decide! The power of these giant corporations is staggering because they are in a position to bombard their millions upon millions of members with stories and opinions that they wish to push as an agenda and at the same time suppress stories they view as damaging or counter to their agenda. If this does not scare you, then you may be missing the point. These tech giants of social media enjoy the same dangerous monopoly as did the Soviet Union's news agency TASS, the only news agency allowed to print or broadcast the news in the USSR. TASS was controlled by the only party in the Soviet Union, the communist party that ruled the government with an iron fist that suppressed the truth in order to control the citizens. Now, are you scared? Was this action, by big tech, an attack on the freedom of the press in order to control the outcome of an election? Their power is staggering when it comes to influence. What happens if such a powerful entity comes under the control of foreign enemies? Did it? What do you think? Does big tech have financial interests in China? Just asking!

You have but to google censorship of the press and look at the official government news agencies, such as TASS in the old Soviet Union, to see how the public was kept in the dark and controlled by the one-party autocratic system of the USSR. Check out the press in North Korea and China of both the past and today! If that does not make you appreciate the First Amendment, I do not know what will.

Unfortunately, even in America, freedom of the press in the many forms of media has not guaranteed honest reporting. But your freedom to voice your concerns and ask questions has been safeguarded by your First Amendment rights anytime you witness corrupt media sources and corruption from elected officials. Yet the biggest question being asked over and over in living rooms, eateries, and break rooms at work is, "Do you think the political correctness speech chastisements many of us are experiencing is an attack on our free speech that threatens the loss of free speech?" Too often we are charged as racists or bigots when we question or voice a counterargument. If you do not stand up to such ridiculous infringements of your free speech, you will lose that precious right. Such attacks on your speech by the *left* is their way of shutting you up. They attack loudly and viciously to over-shout you into silence so you cannot be heard. They do this to avoid criticism for actions that they cannot defend in a debate! They have no facts to put forth in a debate, so they loudly shout at you in order to gain the upper hand!

The final two phrases of the First Amendment are as follows: "or the right of the people peaceably to assemble, and to petition the Government for a redress of grievances." I wish to discuss these last two phrases in conjunction with my discussion of the Intolerable Acts that were imposed by King George III upon Boston and Massachusetts after the Boston Tea Party.

Most of you are familiar with the historical picture that paints the scene of Boston Harbor when Sam Adams orchestrated the dumping of tea in Boston Harbor as a means of protest. Adams' Sons-of-Liberty, dressed as Indians, threw the British East India Tea Company's chests of tea into the harbor. The British East India Company was actually selling tea at a very low price as a result of the fact that parliament had given them a monopoly on the sale of tea in the colonies when they passed the Tea Act of 1773. Colonial merchants and shipping companies could not compete with the tea prices of the British East India tea even though the colonials smuggled tea into Boston to avoid paying the British taxes.

The British punishment was the Intolerable Acts which punished all of the citizens of Boston! There would be no town meetings allowed no matter how peaceable they might be. Worse still, Boston Harbor was closed for all businessmen until the cost of the destroyed tea was paid. I think this was an example of two wrongs do not add up to one right! Nevertheless, the First Amendment is considered the law of the land, and it is a correct position, don't you think?

The complexity of life and the myriad of today's problems makes everything more challenging. Would it not be interesting to witness the shock and awe of our founders if we were able to resurrect eighteenth-century leaders and let them view our world? Since we cannot do that, what we can do is take a close look at why our founders valued the Second Amendment rights they wrote into the Bill of Rights. I hope you stay with me for the next chapter, "Disarming the Citizens?"

6

Disarming the Citizens? The Right to Keep and Bear Arms?

A well regulated Militia, being necessary to the security of a free State, the right of the people to keep and bear Arms shall not be infringed.[16]

Have you heard anyone say that the Second Amendment should not apply in America today? That the amendment is outdated after a time of over two hundred years and counting? May I politely suggest, the Second Amendment will always be necessary as long as there are criminals who have guns!

After any horrific shooting, whether it is the case of mass murder in a church, school, shopping center, or some social gathering, the drive-by media and the left begin singing the same old refrain. We must have gun control to protect lives. I have yet to hear one of these advocates for taking guns explain to me how they are going to get guns from the motivated criminals and the deranged. So they want to take the guns of all law-abiding citizens, and they say, incorrectly, that confiscation of weapons will stop gun violence. No, it will not! To say that taking the guns will stop such tragedies indicates one of two possibilities on the part of gun control advocates. One, they are really naïve, or two, they have a nefarious purpose for want-

---

[16] https://constitution.congress.gov/constitution/amendment-2/.

ing the guns. It might well be both! Mass murder can and has been committed many times with things other than guns. Whether it was guns, fertilizer with diesel fuel and an igniter, knives, or vehicles, the sick and deranged find ways to kill. Terrorists used box cutters and planes in New York City, did they not? To take guns from law-abiding citizens because a criminal or deranged person uses them to kill innocents would be the same as taking all knives or vehicles from citizens when those tools are used to kill. There are, I believe, two reasons that this discussion is so important. One, Americans are not going to give up their personal property, guns. Two, the attack upon the Second Amendment by the leftists is not about stopping gun violence. The left has used tragic killings to disguise their real reason for wanting guns, and the law-abiding gun owners know that! The militia and the "minutemen" at Lexington and Concord Massachusetts in 1775 refused to turn over their weapons to the autocratic ruler, King George III and his generals. That is why the Second Amendment exists as part of our "rule of law," and the American people know that much history.

There is an Old West adage that says, "God created men, and Sam Colt made them equal!" Long before 1836, when Sam Colt went into business, Americans owned guns. In fact, from the earliest days of settlement of the English colonies, the settlers owned guns. Pioneers hunted for food with guns. Guns were used for protection from predator animals and for protection from attack by other humans. The colonial militia owned guns and used them in battles with both the French and the Native Americans. Guns were considered a tool as necessary as a plow or an ax. Without a gun, in the wilderness of America, your independence and safety was at risk.

The sense of independence of colonists was heightened by the fact that they had weapons. Since King George III did not want his subjects to feel independent or have the ability to question and resist his sovereign will, the decision was to disarm the militia of Massachusetts. That decision did not work well for the king. Since that time, "We the people" have felt that a gun is a deterrent to those autocrats who want to impose their will upon the people. In short, give up your personal property, your gun, and you have made yourself defenseless against those who would become so emboldened as to deny you unalienable rights or attack you and your family in the sanctity of your home. One might say that since those early days of colonial America, Americans in possession of guns have felt more equal to men who might seek to do them harm, criminals or autocrats!

Criminals own guns! Is there any dispute of the correctness of this statement? Is there any factual evidence that criminals will ever not have guns? Are you willing to bet your life and the lives of your family that if you and all law-abiding citizens were to turn in all guns, that all criminals will turn in their weapons as well? Do you believe that future criminals will also be unarmed?

I truly believe that 99.99 percent of our policemen and police-women are honorable and stand ready to protect and serve. How confident are you that the police will always be near enough to your home to assure your protection from the many different types of criminals? Does the fact that criminals can never be sure if there is a weapon in your possession possibly deter crime? Would criminals become emboldened if they knew that law-abiding citizens no longer owned guns? How successful has our government been in their effort to interdict illegal drug sales and stop drug addiction? Do you think there has been great success stopping crime perpetrated by drug cartels, dealers, and the addicted? I do not believe that the left's demand for law-abiding citizens to give up guns is a solution to gun violence in this country. In fact, I believe that their effort to disarm law-abiding citizens is reckless, dangerous, and unconstitutional!

I have a solution! I move we pass a law that says all criminals and drug cartels have thirty days to turn in all of their weapons and to promise not to buy or steal any other weapons. Is there a second to my motion? Even more ridiculous than my motion is the left's position that we can eliminate gun crime if Americans turn in their guns and we abrogate most or all of provisions of the Second Amendment. This subject has created much heated debate. I believe careful analysis of facts along with objective thinking can provide a counter to the argument put forth by gun control groups.

Do you believe law-abiding American gun owners will give up their weapons? I am searching for just one good reason and waiting for somebody to give me one good reason why our Second Amendment rights should be curtailed. Can you offer one? I honestly do not believe anybody can present a defensible reason for eliminating the Second Amendment. What can possibly be gained by denying this right? Truly, the second amendment to the constitution was guaranteed to every American. Our rule of law exists so that no president, congress, or court can just arbitrarily deny the right of self-defense, the right to keep and bear arms, or any other unalienable right! This right is part of our heritage and is fundamental to our right of self-defense. This amendment to the constitution was added because it is a right, and it also guarantees our many other freedoms.

It seems to me that the minutemen of Massachusetts came face-to-face with a very harsh reality when British redcoats came to take their weapons. Did the minutemen take the view that relinquishing their weapons to the British army meant their freedoms and inalienable rights would fall victim to the tyranny of King George III? What do you think? Would you have given the shot, rifles, muskets, and black powder to the redcoats? We all know what their decision was. It was a decision of courage to stand face-to-face with the most powerful military in the world in 1775. They chose liberty, and they risked possible death. They prevailed in the American Revolutionary War and gained their freedom. They ultimately gave us rule of law with the constitution and the bill of rights inclusive of the Second Amendment. They paid the price, and they meant for future generations to enjoy and value the individual rights and power to keep basic freedoms. These patriots fought and risked it all in order to be able to defend, at the risk of their death, the right of freedom and the right to keep and bear arms for their own self-defense. Tell me where I am wrong!

I have never heard someone challenge the gun control proponents with the question that cuts to the chase and gets to the heart of the issue. The basic premise that defines criminal behavior and the one that we must judge all criminals by is that criminals are willing to break laws, even murder, on a regular basis. "Duh," you say. I know, my statement seems really dumb, but apparently it needs to be stated. Here is my question that I would love to hear a reporter or politician ask the people that want the law-abiding citizens' guns. If you were successful in disarming law-abiding American citizens with a law that forced citizens to turn in their weapons, how would you also get the guns from the criminals? The follow-up question would be as follows. After the law-abiding citizens turn over their guns, does it not concern you that the only people who would then have guns would be the criminals who will use them for illegal purposes?

The next follow-up question is, "Would disarming law-abiding citizens, while criminals keep their weapons, cause more gun violence and criminal activity?" Can mass murder be prevented if we pass gun laws that forbid the possession of firearms by law-abiding citizens? I think there is much factual history that supports the fact that there is precedence that suggests that if a criminal wants to commit a crime, they will and always have been able to procure a weapon. But for argument's sake, let's say that nobody would have nor could they get a weapon to commit mass murder. Would we then outlaw delivery trucks, knives, diesel fuel, and fertilizer? All have been used to commit mass murder! Criminals have always found a way to commit crime and mass murder. Especially if they know they have gained the advantage over citizens who do not have weapons. Think about the obvious answers to the questions above and reflect carefully upon my statements.

What are your conclusions about the gun control efforts coming from the left? Why is there this big effort to disarm the law-abiding citizens of the USA? Do the people, who want the guns, not realize that many people feel the need for guns in order to provide for self-defense and see owning weapons as means of protecting themselves and their family?

Consider what has happened to disarmed citizenry throughout history. I would suggest you research Nazi Germany's 1933 disarmament of Jews. The Nazis took their weapons, including all firearms and bladed weapons. March 1933 you would get five years in prison in the Soviet Union if you possessed any firearm other than a smoothbore hunting shotgun, and in 1935, the law would add knives to that ban. Do not forget to research China. Speaking of China, I recall reading about a mass murder in a school by a sick and deranged person who killed eight children and wounded five more. He used a knife! The date was March 23, 2010, at Nanping school. Knives, like guns, are useful tools, and both, unfortunately, can be used to do great harm. Check it out, but be sure to use creditable sources for levels of crime in countries where guns are outlawed.

I suspect there may be other reasons, not stated, for wanting Americans' guns. I know the anti-gun groups use mass shootings, and the drive-by media exploits these horrendous events in order to gain followers for the anti-gun groups. They do this for power in numbers and growing support for the movement. The great emotions of loss, felt when one of those tragedies happens, feeds the frenzy of how do we prevent such gut-wrenching horror from happening again. The consistent answer by the left that leaps to the fore is we need gun control. People should not have weapons, and if they do not have weapons, then these horrible crimes of mass murder cannot happen again. There is no logic or truth in that argument because the statement is not factual. Such a false premise, propelled by grief and the search for prevention of horror and loss, does not meet the obvious reality test.

Criminals, even if some of them did not have weapons, would get weapons via the constant supply of weapons that come from outside our borders. As I write this at 10:22 p.m. on March 30, 2021, thousands of illegal aliens from all over the world are pouring across our southern border unchecked. These illegals include terrorists from the Middle East, MS-13 gang members, and members of drug cartels who are bringing in massive amounts of fentanyl that is killing Americans. Does anyone really believe they do not bring weapons into our country in the dark of the night? Does anybody think that they would not bring in lots of weapons and sell them to criminals?

The arguments between the anti-gun groups and pro-gun rights groups create more divisiveness among the American citizens. The anti-gun groups have been quite successful. Could it be that this is all a smoke screen to hide nefarious goals?

Is it possible there are powerful people or groups of people who are bent upon destroying the country and seizing control and power? Does it stand to reason that if they reached one-party rule and used that power to create autocratic rule, that they would want an unarmed society? How could freedom-loving patriots resist if they had no weapons to defend against the tyranny of a police state? Many suspect this is the real motive for the attack on the Second Amendment. I do not believe they will be successful in that effort. Too many Americans are too suspicious, and they know history. If you cannot get the guns of all of the criminals, why do you want to take the guns of the law-abiding American people?

June of 2021, a story hit the news that San Jose, California, officials passed a law that requires law-abiding, gun-owning citizens to carry insurance to pay for public costs of gun violence perpetrated by criminals. Do not take my word for this! Go to https://reason.com/2021/06/30/san-jose-wants-to-force-gun-owners-to-carry-insurance-and-pay-fees/ and see for yourself! You couldn't make this stuff up even if you tried. Again, as always, you must think and analyze the facts to make your own decisions!

The right to keep and bear arms was a serious issue in 1775 and has become a major topic of debate in the last few decades. A statement was made, and I bet you know what president made this statement: "Americans cling to guns and Bibles." Why would anyone utter such a statement that would disparage or question such fundamental rights held so dear, and for so long, by so many Americans? By the way, Americans have been clinging to guns and Bibles for a very long time. The beauty of America is that you can cling to a Bible, or not! I submit that through the darkest of times in our history, clinging to a Bible has been the one thing that helped many to survive those trying times. And the truth is, Americans own guns for many different reasons and always have.

Owning weapons is something that is ingrained in the American psyche! And there is history to substantiate that fact, and dare I suggest, history suggests necessity as well. To understand why Americans feel the way they do regarding personal weapons and the Second Amendment, we must go back in history to 1775. We have already discussed some of this. There are some who do not know American History or just do not understand the realities of cause and effect. You may, but if you do not, please, continue reading this chapter.

The following poem, "The Midnight Ride of Paul Revere" by Henry Wadsworth Longfellow, tells the story of the patriots at Lexington and Concord in 1775 far better than I could ever hope to do.

The Midnight Ride of Paul Revere
By Henry Wadsworth Longfellow
(https://dltk-kids.com/poems/longfellow/midnight_ride/index.htm)

Listen, my children, and you shall hear
Of the midnight ride of Paul Revere,
On the eighteenth of April, in Seventy-five;
Hardly a man is now alive
Who remembers that famous day and year.

He said to his friend, "If the British march
By land or sea from the town to-night,
Hang a lantern aloft in the belfry arch
Of the North Church tower as a signal light,—
One, if by land, and two, if by sea;
And I on the opposite shore will be,
Ready to ride and spread the alarm
Through every Middlesex village and farm
For the country folk to be up and to arm."

Then he said, "Good night!"
and with muffled oar
Silently rowed to the Charlestown shore,
Just as the moon rose over the bay,
Where swinging wide at her moorings lay
The Somerset, British man-of-war;
A phantom ship, with each mast and spar
Across the moon like a prison bar,
And a huge black hulk, that was magnified
By its own reflection in the tide.

Meanwhile, his friend, through alley and street,
Wanders and watches with eager ears,
Till in the silence around him he hears
The muster of men at the barrack door,
The sound of arms, and the tramp of feet,
And the measured tread of the grenadiers,
Marching down to their boats on the shore.

Then he climbed the tower of
the Old North Church,
By the wooden stairs, with stealthy tread,
To the belfry-chamber overhead,
And startled the pigeons from their perch
On the sombre rafters, that round him made
Masses and moving shapes of shade,—
By the trembling ladder, steep and tall
To the highest window in the wall,
Where he paused to listen and look down
A moment on the roofs of the town,
And the moonlight flowing over all.

Beneath, in the churchyard, lay the dead,
In their night-encampment on the hill,
Wrapped in silence so deep and still
That he could hear, like a sentinel's tread,
The watchful night-wind, as it went
Creeping along from tent to tent
And seeming to whisper, "All is well!"
A moment only he feels the spell
Of the place and the hour, and the secret dread
Of the lonely belfry and the dead;
For suddenly all his thoughts are bent
On a shadowy something far away,
Where the river widens to meet the bay,—
A line of black that bends and floats
On the rising tide, like a bridge of boats.

Meanwhile, impatient to mount and ride,
Booted and spurred, with a heavy stride
On the opposite shore walked Paul Revere.
Now he patted his horse's side,
Now gazed at the landscape far and near,
Then, impetuous, stamped the earth,
And turned and tightened his saddle-girth;
But mostly he watched with eager search
The belfry-tower of the Old North Church,
As it rose above the graves on the hill,
Lonely and spectral and sombre and still.
And lo! as he looks, on the belfry's height
A glimmer, and then a gleam of light!
He springs to the saddle, the bridle he turns,
But lingers and gazes, till full on his sight
A second lamp in the belfry burns!

A hurry of hoofs in a village street,
A shape in the moonlight, a bulk in the dark,
And beneath, from the peb-
bles, in passing, a spark
Struck out by a steed flying fearless and fleet:
That was all! And yet, through
the gloom and the light,
The fate of a nation was riding that night;
And the spark struck out by
that steed, in his flight,
Kindled the land into flame with its heat.
He has left the village and mounted the steep,
And beneath him, tranquil and broad and deep,
Is the Mystic, meeting the ocean tides;
And under the alders, that skirt its edge,
Now soft on the sand, now loud on the ledge,
Is heard the tramp of his steed as he rides.

It was twelve by the village clock
When he crossed the bridge into Medford town.
He heard the crowing of the cock,
And the barking of the farmer's dog,
And felt the damp of the river fog,
That rises after the sun goes down.

It was one by the village clock,
When he galloped into Lexington.
He saw the gilded weathercock
Swim in the moonlight as he passed,
And the meeting-house win-
dows, blank and bare,
Gaze at him with a spectral glare,
As if they already stood aghast
At the bloody work they would look upon.

It was two by the village clock,
When he came to the bridge in Concord town.
He heard the bleating of the flock,
And the twitter of birds among the trees,
And felt the breath of the morning breeze
Blowing over the meadows brown.
And one was safe and asleep in his bed
Who at the bridge would be first to fall,
Who that day would be lying dead,
Pierced by a British musket-ball.

You know the rest. In the books you have read,
How the British Regulars fired and fled,—
How the farmers gave them ball for ball,
From behind each fence and farm-yard wall,
Chasing the red-coats down the lane,
Then crossing the fields to emerge again
Under the trees at the turn of the road,
And only pausing to fire and load.

So through the night rode Paul Revere;
And so through the night went his cry of alarm
To every Middlesex village and farm,—
A cry of defiance and not of fear,
A voice in the darkness, a knock at the door,
And a word that shall echo forevermore!
For, borne on the night-wind of the Past,
Through all our history, to the last,
In the hour of darkness and peril and need,
The people will waken and listen to hear
The hurrying hoof-beats of that steed,
And the midnight message of Paul Revere.

During my school days in the 1960s, we read this poem, and from these words we learned why we should appreciate America. And like patriots before, we would grow to love the nation in which we lived. I do not know if kids read these amazing stories in schools today or not. As for me and my generation, I believe we are better off for having read the stories of heroic events and of sacrifices freely given to secure the "blessings of liberty in the land of the free!"

There were at least two other riders, besides Paul Revere, spreading the alarm throughout the countryside on the night of eighteenth of April 1775. They rode to alarm the minutemen of Massachusetts that British General Thomas Gage was sending his soldiers throughout the area surrounding Boston, for the purpose of seizing powder and arms of the colonial militia. And for sure, the "redcoats" were coming. The king's army of redcoats would find a very unwelcoming group of farmers and militia awaiting in the Massachusetts countryside.

The farmers and militia, who had pledged to be ready at a minute's notice (minutemen), grabbed their muzzle loading black powder flintlocks from the mantle. They slung powder horns and shot bags over their shoulders and ran into the history books. These "minutemen" ran out into the fields to face the most powerful army on the face of the earth. By this point in the book, or from your study of history, I bet you have some ideas about what may have motivated these colonial citizens of the Boston area to stand defiantly as the British approached. What was just one reason these colonial militia and minutemen stood defiant?

King George III and the British Parliament argued the fairness of their claim that even though the thirteen colonies could not send representatives to Parliament, the colonies had virtual representation because they were part of the British Empire. To be sure, the colonists did not want representation in the British Parliament for the simple reason that they would be an outvoted minority. What they wanted was the right to govern themselves in each colony and to set taxation as they saw fit. It was, however, a very emotional and motivation cry of protest to yell, "No taxation without representation was tyranny."

We can also talk about the British economic policy known as mercantilism designed to keep wealth within the British empire while stifling free enterprising business and merchants in the colonies. The expressed goal of mercantilism was to build up gold and silver supplies so as to fund the growing needs of the British army and navy as they patrolled the world protecting their empire. Mercantilism's economic policies regulated what the colonists could produce and what they could not produce. Mercantilism even enumerated products that could only be sold to Britain. The colonies existed to provide the raw materials for British industry. Under mercantilism, the colonies were to be held captive for the purpose of being a market for the manufacturing interests of England. The colonies were told they must buy from British interests even if they could find cheaper products in other countries. Goods bought from other countries and being transported by ship to the colonies were required to stop at a British port to pay the import duties (tax) before being allowed to unload in the colonies. Smuggling became a way of life for many colonial merchants as they sought to avoid taxes and higher costs.

Through long periods of "Salutary Neglect" (period when the British customs was not as active enforcing mercantilism) by the British government, colonial merchants had enjoyed freedom and good profit margins as a result of engaging in free enterprise capitalism and smuggling of goods to avoid the British duties (taxes) on imports. The colonies of America were endowed with great riches of natural resources. Britain's long period of salutary neglect had given the colonies too much freedom from economic control by the crown.

The debt the British empire had accrued, as a result of the French and Indian War in 1763 North America, forced the British to search for more revenue, and they naturally saw the colonies as an untapped source. They felt the colonies were not paying their fair share for their defense, and they set about to rein in the colonies with new legislation and acts to raise new revenue. These actions angered colonists who had taken the "bit of economic freedom" into their mouth long before 1763. Unhappy colonists would have felt naked without their guns. The British did not want colonials to have guns. British soldiers were sent to the colonies to enforce tax laws and to prevent protest and civil disobedience.

Does any of this story sound even remotely familiar to issues we experience today? Somebody, has allowed our medical supplies, steel, aluminum, and so many other products to be made primarily in the land of the Chinese communists. We are being pushed toward electric vehicles, whose batteries are being made largely in China and with Chinese cobalt. The same situation exists for solar panels. Yet the United States of America has plenty of energy to fuel our internal combustion engines. Does this raise any red flags? Did you know that some of the liberal cities are planning to impose a new tax for miles driven? Guess what? Electric vehicular mileage is exempt from that tax!

Generally, there are two sides to every story, and the story of the rift between Great Britain and the thirteen American colonies is no exception. However, I believe that George III was a weak leader who underestimated the resolve of the American patriots, and his arrogance as a monarch led him to make bad decisions. These patriots were rebels, and does that surprise you when you consider that overwhelming numbers of the settlers in America were rebels to begin with? The cry of many colonists was, "No taxation without representation!" Many historians will tell you that, in actuality, the taxes paid by the colonists was not that much when compared to the English in Europe.

I believe there were more reasons for the colonies to be angry than there were reasons for king and parliament to be as punitive as they were. King and parliament in London expected and would not accept anything less than total loyalty and obedience. That was, in my opinion, a great mistake. Clearly the British Parliament and the king did not understand the colonials, and, for that matter, they did not care to. The colonists would be forced to obey. The rugged individualism of colonists fighting for survival on the frontier from 1607 forward created a sense of independence and self-esteem. They hacked out a living in the wilderness, and they began to see their equality with others because they were self-reliant. And they were far removed from the king and the streets of London. Without a doubt, there is a strong argument to be made that the restrictive nature of mercantilism angered businesses and merchants because colonial merchants favored the more profitable and common-sense approach of free enterprise capitalism. They valued free enterprise capitalism as the means to economic prosperity.

Perhaps it was as simple as the question, "Shall an island rule a continent?" It was Thomas Paine's writing in the pamphlet, "Common Sense," in which he wrote,

> Small islands, not capable of protecting themselves, are the proper objects for kingdoms to take under their care; but there is something absurd, in supposing a continent to be perpetually governed by an island.

Paine was an Englishman who rallied to the cause of the thirteen colonies and advocated for colonial independence from Great Britain. What were the specifics that angered those colonial patriots living in the Boston area in 1775?

I want to be brief in my presentation of the events that led to the uprising on the nineteenth of April 1775 in the countryside of Lexington and Concord, Massachusetts. It was there on that day that the British tried to disarm the Massachusetts militia and the minutemen. The British failed in that endeavor! Would you agree that it is most improbable that the United States of America would have been a nation if the minutemen of Massachusetts had given up their weapons to the British? Would the relinquishment of weapons, by the colonists, have ended the autocratic rule of King George III, or would that surrender have resulted in continued tyranny? What happened in the thirteen colonies between 1775 and 1781, as a result of the actions and sacrifices of freedom-loving brave men and women, brought freedom and democracy to millions, not just on our shores but throughout the world. They set an example of defiance and bravery necessary to achieve and maintain freedom from autocratic rule.

The earliest European settlers of what is now the United States of America traveled westward to arrive on our shores. The American expansion was ever westward until about the 1890s when the frontier was said to have been closed. By the end of the French and Indian War in 1763, pioneers had begun pushing westward into the Appalachian Mountains and beyond. With the victory of England and the thirteen colonies over the French and their Indian allies, adventurous pioneers began eyeing the rich Ohio Valley lands. To them the west was now theirs. The French were gone. The soil was rich, and the furs were abundant.

The powers to be in England had decided that the colonies could not settle west of the crest of the Appalachian Mountains and issued the Proclamation of 1763 which forbade such settlement. Worse still, if you had settled west of the Appalachian Mountains, you were supposed to move back east. This would mean the English would not have to defend against the Indians who by now had been pushed westward. The colonies could be controlled by the British government if the colonists did not move further westward. Many historians will tell you that the major motive was the rich fur trade, and the Brits wanted to control the lucrative fur trade and avoid angering the Indians. To frontiersman, this proclamation was an insult to their spirit of independence and self-reliance developed as they struggled to survive in the wilderness. There were new rich lands to farm, and there were furs for free enterprising traders, and besides, these people were not used to being told what to do. The colonials had fought alongside of the redcoats to defeat the French and the

Indians, and they resented being told they could not move in western lands and that they had to move back east of the Appalachians.

I think it is important to recognize that in those days, there were no social safety nets such as welfare, unemployment benefits, stimulus checks, and there were no earned social security payments for retirement. You and you alone had to take care of the family. If you did not, you starved. It was difficult to slow a westward stampede of colonists. Pioneers were not happy being chained east of the Appalachians. This seemed to be an abuse of power by a government three thousand miles away. I might suggest that it was also counterproductive to the economic goals of the British. When you threaten the livelihood of families and citizens, hungry stomachs will lead a revolt.

Do you see any similarities between 1763 and our experiences during the COVID-19 pandemic when restaurants and gyms were forced to close? Today's citizens were not convinced that the science proved that opening the doors of their business was responsible for the spread of the virus. And many were correct, yet they lost their business, and they felt these government restrictions were an abuse of power! Do you remember the chant, "Rules for me, but not for thee!" Many government officials who made the restrictive decrees, under the guise of protecting the citizenry, were caught violating their own mandates.

I remember watching a restaurant owner crying hysterically because she was not allowed to open her business. She stood in the front of her business she was about to lose and gazed across the street where a tent was set up serving food for a Hollywood film production crew. The parallels between 1763 and 2020 are striking. It really does not matter the right or wrong based upon individual perspective. The fact remains, people were angered and felt their freedoms were being denied unnecessarily, and worse still, they were losing their livelihood. That was true in 1763, and it was also true in 2019. Many people do not want a handout, and they protect their independence by demanding fairness and their natural rights. Colonists of 1763 would become even more angry as England ended salutary neglect and became very proactive in gathering import and export indirect taxation to gain revenue. When king and parliament began direct taxation on the colonists, the colonial "anger meter" rose, and the battle cry of "No taxation without representation" was sounded across the colonies.

It is one thing to tax in order to pay debt incurred in the defense of the country as the British claimed. To contrast that era of taxation by the British central government with that of the 2021–22 proposed tax increases by the Biden administration is another thing. The Biden administration will tax to spend even more money, not to pay debt. (In point of fact, my friend Austin has pointed out that if they taxed everything to the max, the Biden administration could not even pay off the pork spending that accounted for 91 percent of the two trillion bill that was passed under the guise of COVID-19 relief aid. My one-room school education in math skills, that I learned during the late '50s and early '60s, tells me that only 9 percent of the money went for actual COVID relief. (I call this bill Joe's 9 percent bill!) Such tax proposals will send more jobs overseas and take more money out of the pockets of the American workers than any received in the so-called stimulus payments.

"The power to tax is the power to destroy!" See Daniel Webster, 1819, when he argued the U.S. Supreme Court Case of *McCulloch vs. Maryland*. Does the study of Economics 101 suggest that raising corporate and individual tax rates in the midst of a crippled economy and a worldwide pandemic is sound fiscal policy? Additionally, Transportation Secretary Pete Buttigieg has suggested either an added federal tax on gasoline or possibly a tax per mile driven. Talk about taxation that would propel the economy into an inflationary spiral and erode your dollar's spending power! Corporate tax increases are passed on to the consumer, and since we transport goods and many services via the fuel of gasoline, those increased transportation costs are passed on to the consumer in the form of higher prices.

I know the title of this chapter is "A Disarmed Citizenry." You may be asking, why is he spending so much time on taxation today? My answer is that taxation was a big part of the hornets' nest of pain and anger that led the minutemen of Massachusetts down the road to Lexington and Concord in 1775. I talk about the taxation today because there are millions of American citizens who are sickened at the giveaway of tax dollars and borrowed money that is being used for illegal aliens and for the implementation of rampant socialism. Just as the colonists of 1775 were angry at the denial of their rights as Englishmen, there are Americans who are sickened because they were told they should not gather as families during Thanksgiving and Christmas and that maybe you might be able to have a backyard barbecue with your family on July 4, 2021! Give me a break! This is America, and Americans of 2021, just as colonists in 1775, resent government being so involved in their personal lives. These are considerations "We the people" should take with us to the polls in 2022 and 2024. The democratic process must be utilized by Americans in order to save our democracy and unalienable rights.

I do not believe that George III and Parliament believed things would get so out of hand as quickly as they did. Angry emotions often do not pause long enough for clear and rational thinking to take place. The point is, the British felt if they seized the weaponry, they would avoid any further trouble out of the rebellious hotheads of Massachusetts. The Brits made a major miscalculation, and they paid a huge price for that error. The colonists were angered about all of the issues that I have outlined thus far in this chapter. The rebels of Massachusetts refused to accept the rulings of the king on these issues. The king was not willing to compromise. It came down to accepting the autocratic rule of George III and servitude or a willingness to defy what they perceived as tyranny by fighting and standing their ground at Lexington and Concord. The strategy of General Gage was to take away the guns and powder from the colonials and thereby prevent any resistance. The colonists of Massachusetts had a strategy as well. They would not render themselves defenseless in the face of tyranny. They would not give up their weapons. The rest is history! This is a lesson that Americans know well.

Am I suggesting a revolt such as the one we read about in the history books? I am not! If that happened, we all lose in this interdependent world in which we live. The horror of such actions is unspeakable. But I must say, I am scared that things will get out of hand. I pray they do not! For these reasons I must reaffirm to you the point of just how important the "rule of law" under our constitution is and how adherence to that document has, in the past, contributed immensely to our survival. If ever there was a time in our history for patriots who love our way of life and our system of governance to get involved in the democratic process, it is *now*; it is *today*! There are very large numbers of the American people who believe in the constitution and in free and independent elections. Yet since November 3, 2020, there are millions who are afraid the "rule of law" and free elections are in danger.

The British wanted the colonist's guns and powder because they believed the natural extension of colonial protests over taxes might lead to armed insurrection. This disarming of the colonists was a preemptive move that was considered necessary because the British had no intention of easing autocratic rule. King George III was not willing to compromise. Refusal to compromise has always been the undoing of diplomatic negotiations. Such a breakdown, all too often, leads to violent conflict. It is necessary to present other events that caused the revolt in Lexington and Concord, Massachusetts, as well as a brief look at those events. Please note cause-and-effect study of history as you link the amendments to previous events.

There is a direct link to the first ten amendments of the constitution, the bill of rights, and the anger of the colonists with the autocratic rule imposed upon them by King George III. Not only did the king's redcoats seek to take the colonists weapons, they also planned to force compliance with all of the king's rulings, with guns pointed at the colonists. Give up your gun and you may well have just the opposite of what Sam Colt accomplished. Colonists without guns were very unequal to the task of resisting regulations that denied them of the rights of Englishmen. It took the guns of the patriotic rebels of 1775 to achieve the freedoms written into the constitution in 1791, the Bill of Rights, known as the first ten amendments!

Amendment III

No soldier shall, in time of peace be quartered in any house, without the consent of the owner, nor in time of war, but in a manner to be prescribed by law.

Have you ever heard of the Quartering Act of 1765? The act required colonists to provide food and living quarters to the hated redcoats. It is one thing to offer meals and a place to sleep to the doughboys going off to France in 1917 or a lonely soldier home on leave from the Pacific in 1944. It is another thing still to have to feed and house redcoats that were in your town to enforce laws that you hated and disagreed with. Obviously, the colonists resented such intrusions, and they demanded that future generations of Americans would not have to suffer through such. As if this was not enough to anger colonials, the British had some more tricks in their bag.

To punish smugglers who were evading import tax duties that were to be paid to the British, the government authorized the use of the hated Writs of Assistance. These writs were open-ended search warrants. To stop smuggling and to locate the smuggled goods, customs agents were empowered to enter the homes, buildings, and ships of all colonists without announcement or any probable cause.

Would you consider it an invasion of your privacy and a violation of the sanctity of your private home if a knock at your door or the forced entry into your home happened when the only excuse offered was, "We are searching for contraband"? It was no different from a search for a meth lab. How would you feel if officials would say, "We are going to search every home in your subdivision to see if we can find a meth lab"? To me, these searches were not reflective of freedom. And property owners were victims of police state actions. Perhaps you can now have a better appreciation of freedom in America. James Otis certainly appreciated this freedom long before you and I. It was James Otis who proclaimed in a Boston court that the hated "writs" violated English common law, "A man's home is his castle."

Amendment IV

> The right of the people to be secure in
> their persons, houses, papers, and effects, against
> unreasonable searches and seizures, shall not be
> violated, and no Warrants shall issue, but upon
> probable cause, supported by oath or affirma-
> tion, and particularly describing the place to be
> searched, and the persons or things to be seized.

Please compare the Fourth Amendment to the Constitution of
the United States to the actions of the British armed with their Writs
of Assistance. The verbiage above speaks for itself, does it not? This
is a freedom that had its first down payment made at the battles
of Lexington and Concord when patriots refused to surrender their
weapons. Do you see why they refused to surrender their weapons?
They refused to live under such conditions, and they knew that they
would have no choice if they were weaponless. They proved they
would fight to secure freedom. All of these patriots "gave some and
some gave all" as they paid for our right to live free under the "rule
of law" and the Fourth Amendment. Further payments were made
with more blood and treasure. We have a multitude of things in this
country that are very special, and this is one of them. Do not take
this freedom lightly. The minutemen and the Continental Army did
not take it lightly. I must say I am proud, and I have no problem
standing up for the Pledge of Allegiance and the national anthem.
We are the envy of generations of citizens throughout the world who
yearned to breathe free!

The colonists were angered that their rights as Englishmen were
denied when those charged with smuggling were tried in Admiralty
(military) courts. They were denied the right to be tried by a jury of
their citizen peers. Advantage went to the British Admiralty courts
for guilty verdicts, and resentment of Admiralty courts, among colonists, heated up and boiled emotions even more.

Amendment VI

> In all criminal prosecutions, the accused shall enjoy the right to a speedy and public trial, by an impartial jury of the State and district wherein the crime shall have been committed, which district shall have been previously ascertained by law, and to be informed of the nature and cause of the accusation; to be confronted with the witnesses against him; to have compulsory process for obtaining witnesses in his favor, and to have the assistance of counsel for his defense.

Again, give up their weapons and these colonists would never be in a position to enjoy the protections of a Sixth Amendment!

You have to love and appreciate James Madison, George Mason, and any others who may have assisted in the writing of the "Bill of Rights" (first ten amendments) to the constitution. The amendments were presented in 1789 and ratified in 1791. Is there one among us that does not feel a little better knowing that there is in existence Amendment VI to our constitution? This amendment, as were the others, is an example of defense against tyranny.

Was the Boston Tea Party of 1773 perpetrated by Sam Adams and the "Sons of Liberty"? Probably. Was it an act of violent civil-disobedience for which a lawful government should punish the guilty and seek restitution for all of the destroyed tea? Yes. The resulting punishment would be labeled as the "Intolerable Acts" by the colonists of Boston, Massachusetts. There was a lot of overreach in the punishment that was rendered by king and Parliament in England. It was like the punishment of an entire class for the sins of an unidentified student who placed a tack in the teacher's chair during recess and threw all of the chalk into the toilet. Nobody would get recess again until the culprit was turned in. Good luck with that kind of disciplinary punishment. Perhaps nobody knew who the guilty party was. The "Intolerable Acts" were indeed unfair and quite punitive because they punished everyone. This was about to become the "point of no return" for compromise and good relations between Bostonians and the Crown.

The "Intolerable Acts" were punitive and were designed with the intention of preventing further protest in Boston and for getting restitution for the tea dumped in Boston Harbor. The actual results were quite different. The first part of the act closed down the Boston Harbor until the tea was paid for. Punishing the innocent in Boston made no sense, and destroying the economy and jobs of a harbor town did not go over well. This action only served to further divide, increase mistrust, and create a feeling of the oppression rained down from a tyrant from afar.

Secondly, the act authorized the quartering of troops in all towns within the colonies.

The third part of the act allowed officials of Britain, who were accused of committing crimes in the colonies, to be tried in England.

Additionally, town meetings for the purpose of self-governance were limited. The natural consequence of the punishment levied on everyone with the passage of the "Intolerable Acts" was that these acts were an abuse of power. Such actions of extreme punishment caused an increase in support for Boston, throughout all of Massachusetts. This support for Boston and Massachusetts as a whole, after Lexington and Concord, began to increase in other colonies as well.

British General Thomas Gage sent troops to seize weapons and supplies at Concord, Massachusetts, and supposedly arrest Sam Adams and John Hancock at Lexington, Massachusetts.

It was Revere, Dawes, and Prescott who rode to warn the militia at Concord that the British were indeed coming. That decision by Gage proved to be a disaster for the "redcoats" on that day and ultimately for Britain by 1781 at Yorktown, Virginia.

Captain John Parker, Massachusetts militia at Lexington Green April 19,1775, around 5:00 a.m., saw seven hundred British marching toward his command of only seventy-seven and said, "Stand your ground. Don't fire unless fired upon, but if they mean to have a war, let it begin here." Talk about courage and pressure of the moment. The time for talk was over, the "die" was cast, and in the words of the poet, this would prove to be a most "fateful day" for all concerned. Some unknown discharged a rifle, and so it began. Here, on this day, all of the protests had ended in violent acts of war responsible for much bloodshed. Farmers with rifles faced off against the redcoats, who were representative of the most powerful military force in the world of 1775. The American Revolutionary War had begun.

The world would never be quite the same because while this was a war that was fought over land, wealth, and power just as most all wars, it was also a war about ideals. Ideals that would produce a country that would be ruled by "We the people" with a system of government constructed under the concept of federalism in 1787. By 1789, the Constitution of the United States of America would be ratified, and in 1791, the "Bill of Rights" would be added as the first ten amendments to the constitution. So the American colonies would become thirteen states, and the people would be the source of power for the representative democracy that would operate under the "rule of law." These American colonists had come a long way since the pilgrims landed on Plymouth Rock. They still had a long way to go in order to cast off the yoke of tyranny and the power of King George III's "rule by divine right."

What would life in colonial America have continued to be had not Captain Parker and his men stood their ground with weapons they refused to surrender? Would life in the colonies have improved? I doubt that he life of weaponless colonials would have improved; in fact, I believe their lives would have worsened. Most Americans, who know the real history of America, think that what was fought for and won is far superior to anything the king of England was selling. They also know, because of this history, that in the face of tyranny, there was and is no choice but to refuse to surrender weapons. Americans are afraid of autocratic rule, and yes, they do cling to their "guns and Bibles!"

April the nineteenth at about 7:00 a.m. in the year of 1775 became a momentous day in all of world history as per the famous words of another poet who proclaimed, "Here once the embattled farmers stood, And fired the shot heard round the world." The fight with the British continued at Concord, Massachusetts. After leaving Lexington, the British found themselves surrounded at Concord where they encountered a hornet's nest of angry minutemen who fired from behind trees, rocks, fences, and buildings at the straight-line marching redcoats who desperately wanted to get back to the safety of Boston as fast as possible. The British would lose some three hundred soldiers as killed, wounded, or missing on the trip to Boston. The British soldiers would write home about the terrible guns of the colonists. They called the minutemen's rifles "widow makers" due to the long-range accuracy of the rifled barrels the pioneers used on the frontier.

Those American rebels of Lexington and Concord did not give up their weapons on the nineteenth of April 1775. It seems to me that the concept of freedom and weapons as a guarantor of freedom was pressed into the American psyche on that day. The Second Amendment may now have a new meaning to you, and you may now have a clear understanding of the price paid to secure "the right to keep and bear arms." Will this change? It has not yet. Americans still have their guns even though the attempt to disarm law-abiding citizens continues still!

So at this point, I feel I should pose a question to you. I realize that I was somewhat aggressive with my thoughts and presentation in this chapter. I do, however, recognize your right to decide your feelings and position. Along with my feelings presented, I have endeavored to present a factual basis for my assertions. That premise is to be kept because it is, I hope, been an axiom of this writing thus far. And the question is, "Do you think the punishments and the oppression of the Bostonians after the Boston Tea Party warranted the stand taken by Captain Parker at Lexington and of all of the minutemen at Concord and beyond on the nineteenth of April 1775?" As always, you decide!

I had to include this poem. It says so much with so few words!

Concord Hymn

Ralph Waldo Emerson 1803–1882

By the rude bridge that arched the flood,
  Their flag to April's breeze unfurled,
Here once the embattled farmers stood,
  And fired the shot heard round the world.

The foe long since in silence slept;
  Alike the conqueror silent sleeps;
And Time the ruined bridge has swept
  Down the dark stream which seaward creeps.

On this green bank, by this soft stream,
  We set to-day a votive stone;
That memory may their deed redeem,
  When, like our sires, our sons are gone.

Spirit, that made those heroes dare
  To die, and leave their children free,
Bid Time and Nature gently spare
  The shaft we raise to them and thee.

"And fired the shot heard round the world." Emerson's use of hyperbole in this poem is representative of one of the most powerful and enduring statements that I ever recall reading. I had a student who did not understand the concept of hyperbole and therefore could not appreciate Emerson's statement, as evidenced by his sincere question, "How could a gun be so loud that you could hear it around the world?" Most days teaching was full of challenges, but this one was fun! I hope you enjoyed these two poems! They tell a great story.

On June 23, 2021, I listened to President Joe Biden make a remark about those Americans who cling to guns. And I quote, "And I might add: The Second Amendment, from the day it was passed, limited the type of people who could own a gun and what type of weapon you could own. You couldn't buy a cannon." End quote! His statement is false, and there is absolutely no history to support this statement. Do your own fact-check. I have. This is a classic example of misleading and false statements used to support a nefarious agenda! Might I add, an unconstitutional agenda!

Next Joe Biden made this statement, and I quote,

> Those who say the blood of lib—"the blood of patriots," you know, and all the stuff about how we're going to have to move against the government. Well, the tree of liberty is not watered with the blood of patriots. What's happened is that there have never been—if you wanted or if you think you need to have weapons to take on the government, you need F-15s and maybe some nuclear weapons.

End quote! First of all, this statement is incoherent! My question, and perhaps yours as well is, "Are American gun owners being threatened by the president of the United States?" F-15s and nuclear weapons—are you kidding me? That is not an example of the campaign promise made by Joe Biden that he was a uniter, not a divider. Mr. President, should you not leave the Second Amendment alone and do your sworn duty, support and defend the constitution of the United States of America? It seems, in light of the hypocrisy we are witnessing and have just discussed, that the left and the president would stop their attack on the Second Amendment! The violent acts of lawlessness during the summer of 2020 when liberal mayors and governors allowed personal property to be burned, stores to be looted, citizens to be murdered, while their cities burned around them makes the case for the necessity for a strong Second Amendment.

Law-abiding citizens and gun owners have real fears of criminal violence and anarchy. Americans sat stunned as the televisions presented the horrible spectacle of anarchy and violence that played over and over for days on end in liberal cities during the summer of 2020. That viewing was enough to make people even more unwilling to give up any guns, and in fact, the sales of guns and ammunition have been soaring for months. The case for the preservation of the Second Amendment becomes very strong when you look at just a few of the incidents that have taken place since lawlessness has run rampant in liberal city streets.

Google https://www.foxnews.com/us/missouri-couple-who-defended-home-have-rifle-seized-during-police-search-report and watch the video of Mark and Patricia McCloskey of St. Louis standing in front of their home holding an AR-15 and a pistol while protestors marched and demonstrated in front of their home. There is a picture of a gate, at the entrance of the neighborhood, that reportedly was destroyed by the protestors. Patricia McCloskey stated that they were threatened by statements made by the protestors. The protestors, according to the McCloskeys, said the house would be burned, that the protestors would return, that protestors would be living in that house, and the family pet would be killed as well. The McCloskeys were charged with a crime! Missouri Republican governor, Mike Parson, pardoned the McCloskeys. There are other incidents that add more resolve to gun owners' refusal to give up their personal property, weapons!

Consider the murder of retired police captain, David Dorn, of St. Louis. Captain Dorn was age seventy-seven and was killed while trying to protect a neighborhood pawn and jewelry shop during riots and looting in St. Louis in June of 2020.

May 31, 2020, in Cleveland, Ohio, Joe Corbo and his two sons stand at the front door of their family bakery, armed, defending their family business against the looting and rioting that was taking place on their street. While the family stood guard, the rioters made a smart decision; they went on to loot other businesses that were not guarded by owners and the Second Amendment.

What a sad state of affairs when there are officials, in numerous cities, telling the police to stand down while others are yelling to defund the police. I have no doubt that the men and women in blue would have done their duty, in all cities. Such cowardice, exhibited by public officials, serves to embolden criminals and puts citizens' lives at risk. One has to wonder, are these officials of the many cities that experienced massive rioting, murder, and looting so cowardly and weak that they cannot do their duty, or do they have an agenda that wishes to add fuel to the flames of rebellion that threatens the destruction of our way of life?

Will American gun owners be disarmed? Will Americans fall victim to autocratic rule? Were the "minutemen" of Massachusetts right to stand their ground and cling to their guns? Why did the authors of the Bill of Rights choose to write the Second Amendment? Why does the left want to take guns and eradicate the Second Amendment? If the left is truly concerned about gun violence, why are they not actively policing Chicago where gangs of criminals are fighting for turf control of the streets of Chicago and killing hundreds of innocents over the past several years? How do citizens prevent tyranny? With so many questions, have you had time to formulate a personal philosophy that allows you to answer the questions?

There is much to think about, in the coming days, before we once again cast votes for members of the House of Representatives and for the U.S. Senate in 2022. Know the candidates and know their announced platform, though we often find that candidates tell us what they think we want to hear. You may need to judge candidates by the past history of the party they represent. You will need to answer the many questions I am posing in this book, and you must know who you are before you make voting decisions. The future of the country rests with "We the people" in 2022 and 2024! Will Americans sit on the sidelines and allow this nation to land on the trash dump of history? Remember what the heroes of America have fought to preserve since April of 1775!

Speaking of heroes, let me say that there have been many Americans who have taken the sacrifices of the American patriots very seriously since 1775. Join me in the next chapter, "All Gave Some; Some Gave All" as we look at the stories of those who dared to protect America.

7

"All Gave Some; Some Gave All!"

The American's Creed
by William Tyler Page

I believe in the United States of America as a government of the people, by the people, for the people; whose just powers are derived from the consent of the governed, a democracy in a republic, a sovereign Nation of many sovereign States; a perfect union, one and inseparable; established upon those principles of freedom, equality, justice, and humanity for which American patriots sacrificed their lives and fortunes. I therefore believe it is my duty to my country to love it, to support its Constitution, to obey its laws, to respect its flag, and to defend it against all enemies. (Written 1917, accepted by the United States House of Representatives on April 3, 1918)

This public-domain content is provided by the Independence Hall Association, a nonprofit organization in Philadelphia, Pennsylvania, founded in 1942. Publishing electronically as ushistory.org.[17]

---

[17] https://www.ushistory.org/DOCUMENTS/creed.htm.

My friend, John, reminded me of this document that he had memorized during his early school days in McDowell County Schools in the southern West Virginia's coalfields.

Short, concise, and to the point, this creed displayed an understanding of some other famous historical documents in American History! Do you recognize them? And why would William Tyler Page be so knowledgeable about American History? William Tyler Page's great-great-grandfather was a member of the House of Burgesses in early colonial Virginia. Page was a descendant of John Tyler, tenth president of the United States. I would say that the time spent memorizing this creed, by my friend John, was well spent. He became a teacher of American History and American government. You can teach a great lesson about America with this creed.

Please, compare this creed to much of the filthy music lyrics our children are exposed to. I bet you have heard some of those lyrics. For those who do not believe our students should memorize such great American documents of history, I ask, is it okay that students memorize the filthy lyrics of music that propagandize our youth with meaningless tripe that does not contribute to the positive values that have contribute to our country's success?

It is this creed, along with many other beliefs, that has propelled millions to put themselves at risk for the sake of America. All of those millions "gave some, and some gave all!" Why? Because millions of Americans, whether they have read William Tyler's creed or not, subscribe to the creed's principles. Contrast the great lessons learned, if we teach America's creed and other classic documents of American History with the "no value" and negative lessons taught and perpetrated upon our young sport's enthusiasts, the kids of America. Our youth are impacted negatively when they see athletes kneel at athletic events during the playing of the national anthem. You decide which lesson you feel would be most worthwhile for your children. Rest assured, they both teach a lesson.

Recently a college basketball team of players and coaches kneeled during the playing of the "Star-Spangled Banner," our *national anthem*. Coaches are supposed to set positive examples because they are charged with the responsibility of mentoring the growth and development of young student athletes. There should be more to the student-athlete concept than just teaching great jump shooting! I will not name the team nor the head coach.

The coaches I have known have been leaders of young men and women. There was no leadership exhibited by this staff. Worse still, this exhibition of disrespect was put on display for hundreds of thousands of impressionable young fans who were about to view a game they love. A game that would be played by their basketball heroes. The university should be embarrassed, but I doubt a word was said. The only evaluation, in this case, will probably be an evaluation of the number of wins and losses for the season. Then there will be a discussion about the amount of revenue the team brought in to the university. Talk about a failed system. Here is an example of a system that ignores important values upon which this nation has always stood. We should stand and face the flag with hand across the heart during the playing of our national anthem. Why? Because it is respectful of the men and women who served in our armed forces and for those millions who were wounded physically and impaired psychologically for life as a result of service in combat situations. Remember, those who gave all in combat, the ones who died defending the very rights the disrespectful avail themselves of as they protest disrespectfully in front of our flag and during the national anthem.

All Americans should stand up for the values that have sustained this nation! The beauty of the American system of governance is that you are allowed to kneel, if you wish. Values for which America stands for and the sacrifices made by millions are symbolized by our flag and anthem. The very least we all can do is show respect for the sacrifices of millions who have fought to create and sustain our system and culture. By the way, it is the same system and culture that allows for a collegiate sports venue and freedom to exist. Heh, the least you can do is shut up, stand up, and cross your heart when the flag is waving and the "Star-Spangled Banner" is playing!

I must tell you I do have some hope, because just a month after the despicable behavior of kneeling, I heard of one college who suspended coaches and players for kneeling in disrespect. I ask you again, which lesson do you want your children and grandchildren to learn, America's creed or the disrespect displayed at a college basketball game as the national anthem was being played?

The Constitution of the United States and the Bill of Rights guarantee you the right to assemble peacefully in protest and to petition the government for redress of grievances. I would defend that right with my life. And you will not go to jail for being so disrespectful. In fact, you have the right to kneel. But why would anyone want to disrespect the very symbols of our nation that are representative of those who sacrificed life, limb, and mental well-being for all citizens of this nation throughout our history? To those who choose to kneel, I ask, "Why kneel disrespectfully before the symbols that are representative of sacrifices that have bought you the right to kneel?" Those sacrifices should not be disrespected because they have brought us all so many freedoms! The last two statements might be head scratchers, but think about it.

Protest with dignity, if you must, but do not sully the symbolism of extreme sacrifice for which we are all indebted! How can protesters be so foolish and obtuse in their thinking that they would sully the minds of impressionable youth by causing them to think that showing disrespect for our nation is the way to bring about meaningful change? Talk about a self-defeating division of society! Do not create a blinding haze of fog that could blind our youth and our nation as a whole to the overwhelming goodness of America. Injustice, yes, there are many examples to be found, but there is a proper way to affect change. If we do not exhibit better behavior, then we are all in trouble and so is the system. Demonstrate bad behavior and poor taste in your actions and you risk a slow destruction of our system, just because there are imperfections. There are millions who are deeply turned off by such a show of disrespect.

Such disrespect will cost protestors support for any of their worthwhile complaints for which they seek redress. I can assure you, paying that price is not worth the cause of change they seek. Destroy this system and we will find the replacement is one nobody likes. At that point, none of us will enjoy our unalienable rights.

This chapter has been written for some time. Today is July 4, 2021, and I decided to add this powerful statement from a Facebook posting. I am quoting as a paraphrase, my wife, Donna. She just shared this statement with me: "If you want another good reason for standing during the national anthem, go to Arlington National Cemetery and see the four hundred thousand grave markers for men and women who have served this country." There are some very interesting scenes for you if you google Arlington National Cemetery. I just came in from my front porch where I saw the American flag in my yard. The spotlight was shining brightly on my flag as my neighbors fired off rockets that burst into "red, white, and blue." It was a great reminder of how many people appreciate living in this great country!

Patriotism in America can be found in all corners of America and everywhere in between. I am especially touched by music and ballads that sing and speak praise for America across the breadth of this land. I hope that those who kneel will sometime be so lucky as to read the words or hear Johnny Cash's performance of the ballad, "Ragged Old Flag." Johnny Cash spoke the following verses:

> I walked through a county courthouse square
> On a park bench, an old man was sitting there
> I said, "Your old court house
> is kind of run down"
> He said, "Naw, it'll do for our little town"
> I said, "Your old flag pole is leaned a little bit"
> And that's a ragged old flag you got hanging on it
>
> He said, "Have a seat," and I sat down
> "Is this the first time you've
> been to our little town?"
> I said, "I think it is"
> He said, "I don't like to brag,
> but we're kind of proud of
> That ragged old flag
>
> You see, we got a little hole in that flag there
> When Washington took it across the Delaware

And It got powder burned the night
Francis Scott Key sat watching it
Writing Say Can You See
It got a rip in New Orleans, with
Packingham and Jackson
Tugging at its seams

And It almost fell at the Alamo
Beside the Texas flag
But she waved on though
She got cut with a sword at Chancellorsville
And she got cut again at Shiloh Hill
There was Robert E. Lee and
Beauregard and Bragg
And the south wind blew hard on
That ragged old flag

On Flanders Field in World War I
She got a big hole from a Bertha Gun
She turned blood red in World War II
She hung limp, and low, a time or two
She was in Korea, Vietnam, She
went where she was sent
By her Uncle Sam

She waved from our ships upon the briny foam
And now they've about quit wav-
ing back here at home
In her own good land here She's been abused
She's been burned, dishonored, denied an' refused

And the government for which she stands
Has been scandalized throughout out the land
And she's getting thread bare,
and she's wearing thin
But she's in good shape, for the shape she's in

Because she's been through the fire before
And I believe she can take a whole lot more

So we raise her up every morning
And we bring her down slow every night
We don't let her touch the ground
And we fold her up right
On second thought
I do like to brag
Because I'm mighty proud of
That ragged old flag

Johnny Cash said it very well! If you go to https://www.you-tube.com/watch?v=XfzJ8UBr-c0, you can hear Johnny Cash's performance. It will warm your heart. Need I say more?

Somehow, I am not as impressed with the ability of the radical left to make things work for the greater sustainable good of America as I am with the proven system created by the eighteenth-century founding fathers of America! Surely, there is enough civic responsibility and intelligence available to allow for appropriate means of protest. Do those who disrespect our flag, anthem, and veterans not realize that such displays of despicable and unpatriotic protest defeat the cause of change they seek? These shameful acts of protest prevent meaningful debate about the issue being protested. It is counterproductive to anger large segments of the population needed to affect meaningful and just change. I am a retired high school coach, and I hope my players were taught and know better. I am, in fact, positive they were. Now, you know I do have some very strong feelings, do I not? I hope that the following stories of heroism and sacrifice will engender strong feelings for all who will continue to read.

Valley Forge

Valley Forge, Pennsylvania, October 1777 into 1778 winter headquarters for General George Washington's Continental Army.[18]

Valley Forge, Pennsylvania, is just over twenty miles away from Philadelphia, Pennsylvania. It was here that Washington retreated for a winter of starving and cold after his army lost Philadelphia to the redcoats.

Few of us know many of the names of those who spent this winter in Valley Forge. And none of those soldiers, or in some cases the families of soldiers residing there in the camp, could ever have imagined the America that we live in today. They were loyal patriots who believed in the "cause" and were willing to pay the ultimate price to gain their freedom from the British. The suffering and challenges for the Continental Army are depicted quite vividly in the article, "Valley Forge," written by the History.com editors in an October 24, 2019, posting.

The facts about Valley Forge are embarrassing and hurtful to me when I think how little I have done for my country as compared to the sacrifice and suffering of all the soldiers and families encamped at Valley Forge, Pennsylvania, during the winter of 1777–1778. Some twelve thousand five hundred soldiers lived in log huts with dirt floors that winter. The doors were often a piece of cloth. I read an account, a very long time ago, that you could follow the trail in the snow to Valley Forge because of blood from soldier's bare feet. Indeed, on December 23, 1777, Washington wrote a letter to Henry Laurens in which he certified 2,898 soldiers unfit for duty because they were without shoes! Also, according to the National Park Service data presented in the article posted by History.com editors on A&E Television Networks and updated June 30, 2020, one-sixth or two thousand soldiers died within six months of the arrival at Valley Forge due to such diseases as influenza, typhus, typhoid, fever, and dysentery. The food rations were woefully inadequate.

---

[18] America: Our Defining Hours by History.com Editors, https://www.history.com/topics/american-revolution/valley-forge.

Though they were starving, freezing, and sick with disease, they clung on to the hope of victory for the "cause." So in 1781, at the victory of Yorktown, Virginia, the band played "The World Turned Upside Down" as the most powerful army on earth was forced to surrender to Washington's American army. The cost of that freedom was high, and those heroes of Lexington and Concord to Yorktown willingly paid the price. Because of their sacrifice, we have enjoyed a life like no others on earth have ever experienced. What was so bad about life that these soldiers would pay such a terrific price to see it end and replace their governance with something new?

I am convinced they made my life better, and I am thankful. The proof of the improvement can be found in the fact that countless millions, ever since, have yearned to get to our shores. "All gave some; some gave all." We owe them a debt we can never repay. Please, stand up for our living heroes and stand for those who have long since gone to eternal sleep.

War of 1812

Thirty-one years after Washington's victory at Yorktown, the British set fires in the capital of the United States of America. It was a great insult and embarrassment to the young nation. Would the "land of the free and the home of the brave" once again be ruled by the British? That question was on the minds of all Americans, and it struck fear in the hearts of American patriots. More importantly, there rose a great furor of indignation and a staunch determination to defend this land and young country. There was no place in the young nation where that determination was more apparent than it was in Baltimore, Maryland.

These proud Americans in Baltimore would defend their city, to the death if need be. It was during the height of the nighttime naval bombardment by the British at Fort McHenry in Baltimore Harbor that Francis Scott Key penned the following poem that has become an enduring symbol of the struggle to preserve the United States against all enemies. Read the words, please!

The Star-Spangled Banner

Oh, say can you see
By the dawn's early light
What so proudly we hailed
At the twilight's last gleaming?
Whose broad stripes and bright stars
Through the perilous fight
O'er the ramparts we watched
Were so gallantly streaming?
And the rockets' red glare
The bombs bursting in air
Gave proof through the night
That our flag was still there
O say, does that star-spangled
Banner yet wave
O'er the land of the free
And the home of the brave?

Most of you know that "By the dawn's early light," Francis Scott Key could see "Old Glory" still flying over Baltimore Harbor's Fort McHenry. The British fleet had to withdraw because the brave citizens of Baltimore stood defiantly and fought with great valor as they successfully defended their city on land and from the aerial bombardment. So the next time you hear the national anthem, please stand up! Stand with the same pride those citizens of Baltimore displayed in 1812! They fought for their freedom. And, by the way, they fought for yours too. All gave some; some gave all!

World War I

American Doughboys served in France June 1917–November 1918! The rallying cry was, "The war to end all wars," and success would also mean that "The world would be made safe for democracy." These two rallying messages were wonderful thoughts that served as a patriotic message for recruitment. This cry appealed to the idealistic nature of Woodrow Wilson and served to motivate many Americans to go "Over There."

While useful recruiting slogans of idealism, these messages ignored the reality of humanity. History has proven, time and time again, that the innate nature of man is to use war to gain wealth and territory for themselves and their country. As we all know, thus far in the history of mankind, no war has prevented the start of another one. But the peace can be kept if you operate from a position of strength with the highest military readiness. That is the only way I can imagine that you are more likely not to have to use your weapons.

"Over There" by George M. Cohan became the most popular song of World War I. If you know the history of WWI, from the American perspective, you will understand the meaning of the lyrics of this song. Google the title and listen to the original song as millions of Americans heard the song in 1917. Read carefully and figure out the meaning of phrases and you will recognize the motivating statements of patriotic war propaganda. Propaganda, yes, but even so, there is ample evidence to support the American involvement in WWI and the call for a declaration of war on Germany by President Woodrow Wilson in 1917.

"Over There"

By George M. Cohan

Johnnie, get your gun,
Get your gun, get your gun,
Take it on the run,
On the run, on the run.
Hear them calling, you and me,

Every son of liberty.
Hurry right away,
No delay, go today,
Make your daddy glad
To have had such a lad.
Tell your sweetheart not to pine,
To be proud her boy's in line.

Over there, over there,
Send the word, send the word over there—
That the Yanks are coming,
The Yanks are coming,
The drums rum-tumming
Everywhere.
So prepare, say a prayer,
Send the word, send the word to beware.
We'll be over, we're coming over,
And we won't come back till it's over
Over there.

Johnnie, get your gun,
Get your gun, get your gun,
Johnnie show the Hun
Who's a son of a gun.
Hoist the flag and let her fly,
Yankee Doodle do or die.
Pack your little kit,
Show your grit, do your bit.
From the towns and the tanks.
Make your mother proud of you,
And the old Red, White and Blue.

Over there, over there,
Send the word, send the word over there—
That the Yanks are coming,
The Yanks are coming,

The drums rum-tumming
Everywhere.
So prepare, say a prayer,
Send the word, send the word to beware.
We'll be over, we're coming over,
And we won't come back till it's over
Over there.

Dig around the roots of most all wars and you will discover that they were fertilized with many of the same evil ingredients. The most common ingredients are a desire to acquire more territory, resources, and a penchant for an unquenchable thirst for power. Sometimes, both sides are guilty of the same nefarious activities. Others are forced into a conflict even when they wish to avoid the waste of resources and human life.

While I cannot go into great detail about this war, it is my hope to outline the causes, some events, and some of the overall impacts on both individuals and the country as a result of the "Great War," World War I. Hopefully, I can illustrate what forced Woodrow Wilson and congress to send the American Expeditionary Force (AEF), under the command of John "Black Jack" Pershing to France late in 1917. You will have to be the judge of whether or not the cost paid was worth the benefits.

The war would cost the lives of 116,708 Doughboys which included 53,513 battlefield deaths and 63,195 deaths from other causes, most of which would be from disease. Additionally, 204,002 were wounded with 71,345 of these wounds coming from gas attacks. The numbers of those who died in later years from complications of gas poisoning raised the death toll to much higher levels. "Shell shock" was the name applied to what we refer to today as PTSD or post-traumatic stress disorder. What are the true numbers of those who suffered through that affliction? How could you know for sure? As it is with all wars, the numbers who face the post-war with hearing loss, loss of limbs, and blindness are staggering. The challenges faced by far too many of war's survivors is so frightening that many survivors, all too often, reflect that the 116,708 who died were the lucky ones. Thankfully, that is not always the case!

So why did the Doughboys go to Europe? Curiously enough, Woodrow Wilson's reelection was aided by the slogan "He kept us out of war!" There was the issue of free trade on the high seas. A point that would be made later in Wilson's fourteen points. The British blockade of Germany posed a difficult issue for American business and the American economy. It was President Wilson's hope that the U.S. could trade with both sides and remain neutral. That was unrealistic and far too idealistic when it came to the state of affairs that existed between the two sides at war. In the final analysis, it was clear that our country could do without German trade more so than doing without trade with the allies. And Great Britain and France were democracies. We could not trade with both.

The German navy of submarines known as U-boats began raiding the shipping lanes of the Atlantic between North America and Europe. The Germans were starving, and strategically they had to stop the resupply of their enemies, France and Great Britain! The United States would become the future allies of France and Great Britain.

The May 7, 1915, sinking of the *RMS Lusitania* by a German submarine resulted in the death of 128 Americans. Wilson, who had been preaching neutrality, hoped that Americans would not have to be sent to Europe. The Germans hoped to win the war before the Americans made the decision to enter the war on the side of Great Britain and France. After promising not to engage in submarine warfare, the Germans announced the resumption of unrestricted submarine warfare. The Germans were desperate to win quickly because they could not sustain the war with the resources at hand.

The Germans also sought some insurance against the U.S. The Zimmerman note, intended for the Mexican government, was intercepted by the British. The note intimated the Germans' desire for an alliance with Mexico. If the U.S. entered the war against Germany, the suggestion was that Mexico would attack the U.S. Once Germany won the war, the Mexicans would be given the states of Texas, New Mexico, and Arizona.

The contribution of the United States to the ultimate defeat of Germany was significant not only from the standpoint of food and war materials but also the AEF Doughboys.

As we all know, the war ended with the armistice that was agreed upon for the eleventh hour of the eleventh day of the eleventh month of 1918. The allied victory brought about the holiday that would be celebrated as Armistice Day. Armistice Day would later become known as Veterans' Day in order to honor all of America's veterans with an annual holiday of respect for veterans on November 11. For sure, that is the day you should seek out vets and thank them.

I never miss an opportunity to thank a vet or a police officer for their service. I hope you adopt that habit. Try it, and you will see appreciation in their eyes that somebody is thankful and will take time to say so. After all, it is the least we can do! Americans have come forth, by the millions, to defend this nation time and time again.

The decision to send the armed forces into harm's way is one of the most dreadful acts that any president will have to make. And I am sure that decision weighed as heavy on the heart of Woodrow Wilson as it did on every president before and since. I know about being sent into harm's way, not because I have experienced harm's way personally, because I have not. I have been told, over and over, by many friends who did have that experience. Time after time they have said to me, "Stan, I am glad you never had to experience harm's way."

What we enjoy and take for granted in this country is a gift given to us all by the sacrifice of men and women who put it all on the line for the United States of America. There is one such veteran that I would like to introduce to you. May I suggest you consider reading Hickman, Kennedy. "Biography of Alvin C. York, Hero of World War I." ThoughtCo, Aug. 27, 2020, thoughtco.com/ sergeant-alvin-c-york-2360159.

Perhaps you have heard of Sergeant Alvin York and his heroic acts while serving in the 328th Infantry Regiment in the Argonne Forrest during the Meuse-Argonne offensive on October 8, 1918. For his actions, Alvin York received the Congressional Medal of Honor from General John Pershing. The French presented him with the Croix de Guerre and the Legion of Honor. He was considered one of the most decorated soldiers of WWI.

York was born in a remote and rural region of Tennessee in 1887 at Pall Mall, Tennessee. Apparently, York was a gambler and heavy drinker prior to WWI but had a religious experience that changed his life, and he became a devout Christian. Born in the late nineteenth century to a way of life that would practically qualify him as a pioneer in the Appalachians, York's life experiences, after being drafted into the military, was quite a contrast to his life growing up in Pall Mall, Tennessee.

After being drafted, York was catapulted into the modern world of twentieth-century America and Europe. Just a minor note, he did not take his black powder mussel loading rifle to France. His life, however, would be changed forever.

He became even more famous when Hollywood legend, Gary Cooper, portrayed York's early life in rural Tennessee and finally his participation in WWI. The movie, *Sergeant York*, would be a box office hit. If you have not seen this movie, you will be touched with some humor and suffer along with York as he struggles with a decision to fight or not fight after being drafted. His newly found religious convictions led him to become a conscientious objector.

When he was drafted, Alvin York was of the opinion that fighting and killing in defense of one's country was not an acceptable option for him. You will learn that he did change his mind when you read the history of his combat experience or watch the details of York's actions in the movie's battlefield scenes. You will be astounded!

When I first watched the movie, I was somewhat disappointed. The movie seemed to be a production that was an example of one of those unbelievable Hollywood stories that was filmed in a way so as to sell more tickets. Some years later I was preparing lesson plans for teaching WWI in my U.S. history class, and I found documentation that showed the movie was very close to many of the documented facts I discovered. I was astounded, once again, to find that Hollywood had been more accurate than I would ever have believed. Rest assured, I have watched the movie many times since then and I have done research.

In addition to that long-ago lost class handout, I am citing ThoughtCo Biography of "Alvin C. York, Hero of World War I" updated July 30, 2019 by Kennedy Hickman. This article's data is not a carbon copy of the movie, yet it closely parallels much of the movie. Many other writings on the subject offer some different facts and varying points of view, but they all clearly point to amazing bravery of York and that he was clearly worthy of the military medals he received. He was responsible for leading a flanking movement that resulted in silencing several machinegun nests of German soldiers and in the capturing of some 132 German soldiers. York never liked to talk about the numbers of Germans he personally killed that day.

I remain in awe of Sergeant Alvin York of Pall Mall, Tennessee. I can only speculate, but I do not believe anyone goes to war and returns as the same person they were prior to combat.

After the war, Alvin York questioned the rightness for America's involvement in the war as well as his own actions. He had the right to do just that because he served and suffered over there! Also, he had the protections of free speech and freedom of religion to stand upon.

Over time and with much deliberation, his thinking changed yet again. He became a believer in the fact that Hitler represented so much evil that the USA had no choice but to fight fascism. In fact, though old and in poor condition, he tried to enlist to fight in WWII! He was turned down. Alvin York knew what he was volunteering to do. He was willing to go again. Alvin York was a hero and patriot! Since you have read this much of this book, I am willing to bet you would enjoy the movie and then do some Google searches about this American hero. You may be asking, why has this author included this story of Alvin York?

Some readers, who want to find fault with our system, will quickly say that drafting a conscientious objector is a violation of religious freedom. Not because they believe that but because it is their way of casting a negative dark cloud on everything American. While some are exempted, Alvin York was not. Was that unfair, and was it proof that America is built on a collection of lies? No, I don't think so. I never said we have a perfect system nor that decision makers in power always make the right decisions. Nothing is perfect.

To those who seek to destroy our system because of the imperfections they loudly proclaim, I would say, if that is the best argument you have, you lose. You do not tear down the whole house because you have a single floor joist that is not perfectly level as you think it should be.

There were many who voluntarily enlisted to fight. I cannot say what went through York's mind when he decided to fight, even though he thought killing was wrong. In fact, he came home after the war with that same belief. That, in itself, speaks volumes to me regarding the mental suffering this man experienced. Perhaps, as the movie depicts, correctly or not, he simply reasoned he should follow the dictates of Matthew 22:21 from the Bible he held in reverence: "Render unto Caesar the things that are Caesar's, and unto God the things that are God's."

Is it possible he decided that there often exists dire circumstances that compel one to fight and kill in order to preserve the right to religious freedom? Could it have been that he thought that the USA was the greatest protection available to allow him and others to continue to have the optimum amount of religious freedom possible? You decide, but the next time someone attacks our imperfect system, you should apologize to them for your failure in not recognizing that they are themselves a perfect being.

I have a question that I would like the attackers of our system to answer. Given the evil nature of regimes in the world today, yesterday, and most assuredly for as long as the world exists, how could our culture and system of government survive without a desperate fight by our citizens to protect the goodness of our imperfect nation? The world is not, and has never been, a fair place nor a safe place for the timid. I would bet that it never will? I am thankful for heroes like Alvin York and many others. I am thankful for all who served, even though they were not proclaimed in the news as a war hero. They are all heroes because "All gave some; some gave all!" Time to move on to the next subject of this chapter.

World War II

Attack on Pearl Harbor

Around 2,403 Americans died on the morning of December 7, 1941, when air and naval forces of the Empire of Japan attacked U.S. naval forces at Pearl Harbor, Hawaii. The physical damage from the attack was eighteen ships were damaged, two battleships—the *USS Arizona* and the *USS Utah*—were sunk, and one hundred eighty aircraft were destroyed.

December 7, 1941, has become, in the words of President Franklin D. Roosevelt's prediction, "a date which will live in infamy." These words were spoken on December 8, 1941, before a joint session of congress at the beginning of President Roosevelt's speech in which he asked congress for a declaration of war upon Japan. His request was granted! Germany, an ally of Japan, promptly declared war on the United States of America. So in less than twenty-four years after WWI, "The war to end all wars," the United States was at war again—it was WWII.

The anger in America was indescribable because there were in Washington, DC, at the time of the attack, peace envoys from Japan. Indeed, the distance from Japan to Pearl Harbor was such that the attack had been planned for quite some time while peace talks were taking place in our nation's capital. Please note, the USA and Japan were at peace with each other. No state of war existed. The sneak attack raised such a sense of furor and patriotism that recruiting stations were overwhelmed with volunteers.

In the aftermath of Pearl Harbor, Americans had many fears. One of the great fears was that the Japanese would invade the west coast of the U.S. They did, in fact, invade and occupy part of the Aleutian Islands off the coast of Alaska. Unfortunately, overwhelming numbers of Japanese American citizens, loyal to the United States, would suffer a loss of civil liberties as a result of the horrific attack of Pearl Harbor by Japan. That suffering by the many loyal Japanese Americans is sad and is representative of a shameful act noted in our history during a time when America was enduring one of the darkest of times in our history.

Unfortunately, the preservation of a nation, at war with those who seek to commit genocide and destroy your way of life, all too often results in what is believed to be a necessary suspension of the basic unalienable rights and guaranteed freedoms upon which your very democracy was founded upon. I cannot condone citizens being forced from their homes, businesses, and being relocated into internment camps. Excuse the actions, I do not think I can. I can only shudder as I try to get into the minds of those charged with the awesome responsibility to protect the nation from invasion. Also, one cannot dismiss the great fear and questioning of the loyalty of Japanese Americans, some of whom might well be spies for Japan. Sadness, anger, and deep emotions were prevalent in the families who lost loved ones at Pearl Harbor and for all of America as well. And the grief and anger of the Japanese Americans for their loss of civil liberties had to a terrible thing to bear. The horrors of war extend far from the battlefield, and often they are as long lasting as a lifetime and can span generations!

For this reason and many other reasons, war should always be the last resort. The intended and unintended effects of war are horrendous and far-reaching. All sides in a war experience great and horrible losses. The Japanese Americans' suffering in America came as a result of the vacating of their civil liberties by the U.S. government. A vacating of civil liberties by a government that felt it had no choice due to the fact of the Empire of Japan's sneak attack upon Pearl Harbor on December 7, 1941.[19]

Nations that long endure must take a firm stand against such acts of aggression, and they must employ overwhelming force of military power and will. That is the only explanation I have, and I believe it is the only one ever given by the government. I said earlier that I would not skirt the dark stories. I will stand fast on the premise that imperfect as we have been throughout our history, we rise far above the standards and records set by the overwhelming majority of other countries

---

[19] https://www.nps.gov/perl/learn/historyculture/japanese-american-units-of-world-war-ii.htm.

throughout all of human history. I have great reason to stand with hand over heart and say the Pledge of Allegiance and to gaze respectfully, and in awe, of what the waving flag represents when the music of the "Star-Spangled Banner" comes across the speakers. Don't you?

Given the anger and fear that was driving the emotions of millions of Americans after the attack on Pearl Harbor, some might argue that internment camps were the only safe place for Japanese Americans to reside. Is that a plausible point? I do not know. I was not there, and it is important to realize that you can read history and the facts, but it is difficult to garner the true and justifiable feelings of those who were experiencing the events at that point in time. What I can tell you is that among the community of Japanese Americans, there were different responses and different perceptions regarding the internment of these Americans![20]

Thousands of Japanese Americans volunteered or were drafted to fight in the American armed forces, and their valor on the battlefields was second to none. These loyal Americans, though their families could rightfully claim denial of their civil liberties, placed great value on the land, culture, and freedoms their country of birth allowed them to enjoy. They marched off to Europe to fight the Germans, who were allied with the Empire of Japan, the country of their parents and ancestors. These American citizens were Japanese Americans known as Nisei. Children born in the USA of Japanese immigrants were identified as the Nisei. The Japanese immigrants were identified as the Issei. The Nisei fought even though their families were placed in internment centers of suffering. I am in awe of the many Japanese American citizens who stood up and fulfilled their civic duty despite the sufferings of their families. They defended their country and contributed mightily to our survival as a sovereign nation. They continued to do this even though events took place at home that were detrimental to the Nisei, their parents.

In 1944, the case of *Korematsu v. U.S.* was argued before the United States Supreme Court. The argument was that the Japanese

---

[20] The Unfinished Nation 8th Edition by Alan Brinkley McGraw-Hill Education 2016.

Americans had been evacuated unlawfully. The decision, by the high court, went against Korematsu. You can research the 1980s for some restitution that was awarded to the Japanese families. Heroics by the Nisei of the United States military in Europe were taking place at the same time of *Korematsu v. U.S.*

The 442nd Regimental Combat Team Legacy Website has a plethora of information that represents a priceless commentary about the valor of these Japanese American soldiers during WWII. The following excerpts, taken from the website (https://www.hhhistory. com/2019/05/the-nisei-americas-442nd-wwii-battalion.html), are direct quotes by people who told this story far better than this writer could ever hope to do.

> All of us can't stay in the [internment] camps until the end of the war. Some of us have to go to the front. Our record on the battlefield will determine when you will return and how you will be treated. I don't know if I'll make it back. (Technical Sergeant Abraham Ohama, Company "F," 442nd RCT; killed in action 10/20/1944)

> They were superb! That word correctly describes it: superb! They took terrific casualties. They showed rare courage and tremendous fighting spirit. Not too much can be said of the performance of those battalions in Europe and everybody wanted them. (General George C. Marshall)

> They demonstrated conclusively the loyalty and valor of our American citizens of Japanese ancestry in combat. (General Mark W. Clark)

> I cannot say, however, that their "Go For Broke" service has ever been adequately honored, but I do know that any objective appraisal of the record of this unit will place it high up in the annals of our military history… Whether in France, Italy or elsewhere, I know of no units in the American Army that fought and perse-

vered more gallantly than did those Nisei companies and battalions. (John J. McCloy, Assistant Secretary of War)

The Nisei troops are among the best in the United States Army and the respect and the appreciation due honorable, loyal, and courageous soldiers should be theirs rather than the scorn and ridicule they have been receiving from some thoughtless and uninformed citizens and veterans. (Major General E.M. Almond)

The members of the Combat Team have made a magnificent record of which they and all Americans should be proud. This record, without a doubt, is the most important single factor in creating in this country a more understanding attitude toward the people of Japanese descent. (Harold L. Ickes, Secretary of the Interior)

The article, "Going For Broke Part Two: The 442nd Regimental Combat Team," that appeared on WWII, the National WWII Museum site on September 24, 2020, contributor Connie Gentry,[21] provides a treasure trove of photographs and text that makes for a very informative presentation about Japanese American soldiers. According to this article, and I quote, "Despite the odds, the 442nd's actions distinguished them as the most decorated unit for its size and length of service in the history of the US military." In addition to this meritorious statement about the dedication of these soldiers and their wiliness to "Give All," the article provides the following statements which says it all. Again, I quote,

The motto of the unit was "Go For Broke," a phrase that meant putting everything on the line in an effort to win big. Just as other minority groups, Japanese Americans faced two wars

---

[21] https://www.nationalww2museum.org/war/articles/442nd-regimental-combat-team.

during World War II—war against the Axis powers and war against racism back home—making
"Go For Broke" an appropriate motto.

For more about their action in Europe, I offer the following
quote from this article:

> In September 1944, the 442nd participated
> in the invasion of Southern France, successfully
> liberating French cities from Nazi occupation.
> The unit went on to fight with the 92nd Infantry
> Division, a segregated African American unit, in
> driving German forces out of northern Italy.

I do not know how you could possibly say it better than the
author of this article has stated the record of these valiant soldiers
in WWII. However, I do want to offer some comments about my
analysis.

My initial statement about these soldiers, both Japanese
American and African American soldiers, comes in the form of a
question. Why, when you consider the socioeconomic hardships and
racism the Nisei and their families were forced to endure back home,
did so many of the young Nisei fight so valiantly in Italy and France?
This question could apply to the African American soldiers as well.
Do not read ahead just yet. I have asked you this type of question
many times thus far in this book. You have skills and knowledge
with which to analyze this material and offer plausible answers to this
question. Will they be right, or will my thoughts be correct? I can't
say for sure, but I believe we will all be very close given the circumstances. So *stop and think before you read on to learn of my thoughts*! To
assure you do not peek, I am going to discuss another thought before
I proceed to deal with the question I posed above. Take a minute and
come up with some sound responses, please.

This section of the book allows me to interject some important
points that I want you to consider about who we are as Americans. I
want you to consider, if there is cause for concern, for the fact that our

American borders are not secure. Do unsecure borders pose a threat to our national security? Read the preamble of the U.S. Constitution:

> We the People of the United States, in Order to form a more perfect Union, establish Justice, insure domestic Tranquility, provide for the common defence, promote the general Welfare, and secure the Blessings of Liberty to ourselves and our Posterity, do ordain and establish this Constitution for the United States of America.

The preamble begins with the phrase, "We the people." What follows "We the people" are reasons why the U.S. needed a constitution and a new government. One reason for the establishment of the constitution was to "provide for the common defense." Is our government living up to that and other premises of the preamble? I do not know about you, but since November 3, 2020, I am not sure our government is assisting in preserving a "more perfect union." Additionally, I want to weave in a discussion about immigration from the perspective of becoming an American citizen and introduce the concept of "state of mind' of being an American. Clearly the Nisei, based upon their actions, knew what the "state of mind" for being an American was. Also, I wanted material of a slightly different but relevant topic to take up space so that you could not peek before answering my question posed in the previous paragraph.

One day my students were greeted with a question on the screen that was very thought-provoking. I had written, "What does an American look like?" That was all I wrote. If you go to Japan, you will quickly recognize the populace as Japanese. The same can be said of many countries such as China, Italy, and of the Middle Eastern region.

This was a bell-ringer activity that I wanted students to write about or reflect upon as I took roll and whatever other admin duties that were required. Does this make you think? Maybe not. But the look on the face of my young students told me that the question was evoking some deep thoughts. I knew this would be interesting. When I was ready to engage the students, I verbalized the written question they had been pondering and followed with some statements. If you go to Japan, you will quickly recognize the populace as Japanese. The same can be said of many countries such as China, Italy, and of the Middle Eastern region.

Then I solicited a response by asking for a show of hands. I did not get a raised hand or an answer. I repeated the question, paused, and then called on a particular student. The response was a blank look with a reply of, "I don't know!" I knew I had work to do at this point. Let me explain further.

Social studies classes provide a great venue for teaching by the Socratic, questioning method. Perhaps you have noticed that I am employing that method with you when I ask thought-provoking questions? This is an ancient method that is coupled with the employment of the inductive method of reasoning. Both methods work hand in hand. It is a way to lead students with questions about what they readily know so that they can reason and conclude an understanding about something new to them. What does an American look like?

Since I did not get an answer, I asked another question, "Why is America called the great 'melting pot'? They may be able to answer that question and maybe not, but if they can, they are on their way toward reasoning to arrive at the answer to "What does an American look like?" "Okay, so where have immigrants to America come from?" "Do they all look alike? If so, why? If not, why not?" Now you have the class engaged, and you are on a roll. You begin to see light bulbs come on, and that is the great fun of teaching. I am not lecturing them to sleep by saying, "Americans do not look alike because we have multiple ethnic origins of immigrants mixed into our society." I am engaging them in the skill of inductive reasoning via Socratic questioning. I am encouraging students to think in order to answer questions, and I am leading them to new discoveries and that is creative teaching that provides a venue for student involvement in learning. They are learning to question and think, which is a skill that will serve them well throughout life. This activity builds skills' abilities, is educational, and we are learning history at the same time. Before I go on to a discussion, about my earlier question that I asked you to ponder upon, I would like to offer some reflection on this activity.

So all Americans do not have certain ethnic features that make them readily recognizable as Americans. "Duh," you say. Then what is an American? Being American obviously has nothing to do with race. Yes, being an American means being a citizen of the country. And may I suggest that in addition to being a citizen, being a real American necessitates a certain "state of mind." Is just being a citizen enough to really make you an American?

I wish to interject the importance that immigrants who come to this country, should come only because they buy into our system of governance and free enterprise. The 9/11 attack upon America and other terrorist attacks should be reason enough for my previous statement. The daily life of our modern-day America is a stark contrast from the time when there was an availability of a vast frontier to settle and farm. That time era that welcomed the unskilled labor of the first three "waves of immigration" has long since ended! Does it not seem necessary that merit-based immigration grants should take precedence when it is decided who can come to our country? Someone, anyone, please tell me how open borders and illegal immigration benefits the "greater good" of this country? It is one thing to come here looking for a job and another thing still when people come here with no skills or assurance that they can be self-sufficient. It is a serious matter when we apprehend terrorists, members of MS-13 gangs, and drug cartel mules coming into this country. I suggest those people will never have the "state of mind" needed to be an American citizen.

Does it take more than just a granting of citizenship in order to be an American? Are there citizens in this country who actually hate this country and have little, if any, real regard for our heritage, values, and system of economics and government? Then what is the "state of mind" that determines that one is truly an American?

The "state of mind" that determines that one is truly an American is, I believe, a recognition of the many great freedoms this country provides and has provided throughout our history. This "state of mind" is one that appreciates our heritage of values, our religious freedoms, equality, and economic opportunities to strive to be all you want to be by subscribing to the concept of "rugged individualism and self-sufficiency." These are, I feel, the prime ingredients necessary for one to possess before you have the opportunity to seek the privilege to become a citizen of the United States of America. We need people who will be proud to be Americans because they recognize that our economic system, political system, and our ideals that support many different freedoms are special in all of world history. Back to the question I asked you to consider several paragraphs ago.

Why, when you consider the socioeconomic hardships and racism the Nisei and their families were forced to endure back home, did so many of the young Nisei fight so valiantly in Italy and France? The answer may have been simple for some and more complex for others. I believe that one thing that was front and center is that they considered it a duty of a citizen to defend their country just like millions of other Americans felt. Could it have been as simple as a "state of mind" about the pride they felt because they were born American? Had they decided to flee to Japan, the Japanese would surely have welcomed them, if for no other reason than a propaganda embarrassment of America. Perhaps they said we are Americans born in this country, and we, like millions before us, will fight to protect our country and the loved ones we have left at home. They may have fought to show all Americans, who despised them and looked upon them with suspicion, that they were wrong. Perhaps they wanted to demonstrate, for all Americans, that race should not be a determining factor for love and loyalty to one's country. Some may have hoped to make life better for their family back home and to make life in America better for them when they returned. I think they were successful in reminding many Americans that you cannot determine what having a real American allegiance looks like by just observing ethnic features.

Please consider the following question and statement: "Given the knowledge we have about all of the sacrifices made by so many Americans, is there not a lot of room and reason for all of us to make some sacrifices for our country? I believe more of us must step up our civic participation to fight the attacks, from within our country, that threaten what others before have fought to gain and preserve!"

Reviewing the record of these Nisei soldiers, it becomes necessary to remark that "All gave some; some gave all!" If that does not qualify one to be an American, then I do not know what is required in order to be recognized as an American. After all, being an American is a "state of mind." Being an American is not determined by belonging to a particular race!

I would be dismissive and disrespectful if I did not at least attempt to acknowledge the sacrifices of at least some of the many different ethnic groups who fought for this nation. Time and space will prevent me from doing justice for all who sacrificed. For that, I apologize in advance, and my omissions should not be construed as a lack of respect for those I do not name.

The first Americans were what we call "Native Americans," or the Indians as they were mistakenly identified by Columbus in 1492 when he believed he had reached India and was greeting the people of India. Talk about a group of people who experienced a total loss of civil liberties! Volumes have been written to detail the sad story of fate that befell the American Indians. I am proud to say that I have Indian ancestors. Just one of countless examples that I could cite is the contribution of the "Windtalkers," mostly Navajo, but there were other American Indians among that group. They communicated military-coded commands and information over the radio in the Pacific, in their native tongue. The Japanese never broke the code because they could not decipher the Navajo language. Their efforts were invaluable to the American war effort. There is a movie that you may want to watch entitled the *Windtalkers*. I would recommend you watch that movie. They fought for their country as did many other groups!

The "Third Wave of Immigration" to the United States occurred during the time period of 1881–1920 at a time of a vast industrial expansion. These immigrants came through the "golden door" of Ellis Island in New York Harbor. They came to escape hardships and abuse in Europe. They huddled in the steerage level of ships desperately holding on to the hope that they would find opportunity in America. The overwhelming majority never returned home. Would you venture a guess as to whether they found opportunity? What were the possible reasons that speak to why they never left? After it was erected, during this period of immigration, many passed by the Statue of Liberty, a gift to the United States from France in 1885.

The New Colossus

By Emma Lazurus

Not like the brazen giant of Greek fame,
With conquering limbs astride
from land to land;
Here at our sea-washed, sunset gates shall stand
A mighty woman with a torch, whose flame
Is the imprisoned lightning, and her name
Mother of Exiles. From her beacon-hand
Glows world-wide welcome;
her mild eyes command
The air-bridged harbor that twin cities frame.
"Keep ancient lands, your
storied pomp!" cries she
With silent lips. "Give me your tired, your poor,
Your huddled masses yearning to breathe free,
The wretched refuse of your teeming shore.
Send these, the homeless, tempest-tost to me,
I lift my lamp beside the golden door!"

These words are written on the pedestal of the Statue of Liberty on Ellis Island. And so, European immigrants came by the millions. They came from many European countries, two of which included Italy and Germany. Certainly, German Americans suffered abuse during both of our World Wars in which we fought Germany. The Italian Americans had similar experiences as well. Both the Germans and the Italians of America had painful decisions to make, and many of these "Third Wave" of immigrants' children fought for their adopted country, even though the circumstances had to have been heartbreaking due to having relatives in their ancestor's native countries. What does that say to you about the value America held for so many?

African Americans, though they could not attend schools with white students, drink from a white-designated water fountain, sit to eat in a restaurant of white people, or vote marched off to war for the

United States during all of our wars. Their hope was that it would earn them respect and gain equality for themselves and their family once they returned home after the wars. Do not ever allow anyone to tell you that African Americans do not love this country. I hear and I see Black Americans' acts of heroism every day when they speak with pride of how this country has grown and provided the opportunity to work and achieve. Truly, some do not, but there are plenty of American citizens, of all colors who do love this country.

I have always been struck by the pioneering example of bravery and determination demonstrated by the pilots of Tuskegee Institute. They became known as the "Red Tails" and first began training at Moton Field in Tuskegee, Alabama. These pilots trained as fighter pilots at the segregated Tuskegee Army Air Field. Segregated because they happened to have dark skin. These brave men would prove that in order to be defined as an American, only one determining factor is required, and that is the "state of mind" of the individual and a sense of duty and personal honor. There should be no test of skin pigment required to be identified an American citizen (https://www.nps.gov/tuai/index.htm)!

Google https://www.nps.gov/tuai/learn/historyculture/index. htm for more in-depth study. I wish to cite the following quote found on this site about the Tuskegee forces. And I quote,

> The Airmen were not just pilots. They were technicians, radio operators, medical personnel, quartermasters, parachute riggers, mechanics, bombardiers, navigators, meteorologists, control tower operators, dispatchers, cooks, and others. Also included were Caucasian officers, Native Americans, Caribbean islanders, Latinos, and people of mixed racial heritage.

Women were included in this effort. But the most important takeaway is that they were all Americans, and they stepped up to fight for America when it counted.

And they did fight! Go to this site (https://www.tuskegee.edu/support-tu/tuskegee-airmen/tuskegee-airmen-facts) for more facts on the "Red Tails." The following facts tell the story of these distinguished fighter pilots of WWII. The following facts were taken from the Tuskegee University site that provides facts about the Tuskegee pilots or "Red Tails." And I quote,

> The Airmen's success in escorting bombers during World War II—having one of the lowest loss records of all the escort fighter groups, and being in constant demand for their services by the allied bomber units—is a record unmatched by any other fighter group.

- The 99th Squadron distinguished itself by being awarded two Presidential Unit Citations (June–July 1943 and May 1944) for outstanding tactical air support and aerial combat in the 12th Air Force in Italy, before joining the 332nd Fighter Group.
- The 332nd Fighter group was awarded the Presidential Unit Citation for its' longest bomber escort mission to Berlin, Germany on March 24, 1945. During this mission, the Tuskegee Airmen (then known as the "Red Tails") destroyed three German ME-262 jet fighters and damaged five additional jet fighters.
- In 1948, President Harry Truman enacted Executive Order No. 9981—directing equality of treatment and opportunity in all of the United States Armed Forces, which in time led to the end of racial segregation in the U.S. military forces.

- (Facts provided by Tuskegee Airmen Inc. and the Tuskegee University Office of Marketing and Communications.)

Sadly, their hopes for equality as American citizens, went unfulfilled for decades to come after WWII. Yet the valor of all of these fighters led President Truman to take a step that eventually led to the end of racial segregation in the U.S. military. President Eisenhower continued the push for desegregation in the U.S. military.

While there are many who look to reinforce the events and incidents that all too often divided our country along the spectrum of our multiracial makeup, may I suggest that we look for the examples of things that unite us as Americans? Building and defending this great nation has been a great effort and the contributions to that end have come from many ethnic groups. May I suggest that all races of Americans could exemplify a more color-blind outlook and join together to fix the problems of this nation? Let us unite and preserve the system that has provided much for us all.

Dr. Martin L. King wished for a time when people were judged by the content of their character and not by the color of their skin. I believe that if he were alive today, he would suggest that his statement was intended as a guiding principle for all races. White, Black, Brown, Red, and Yellow can all be respected equally, and all can respect other races as Americans! He had it right! I have always encouraged my students to judge people by the content of their character and to evaluate people's actions as individuals, not as a member of any particular race! We Americans, of all colors, need to unite and make this country even more great as we uphold the values that have made this the "greatest country" ever!

The Normandy Invasion
June 6, 1944
Led by "the Greatest Generation"

Have you have seen the movie *Saving Private Ryan* in which Tom Hanks had the leading role? If you have not watched this movie, I would encourage you to do so. At least, watch the opening scenes of the allied landings on the beaches of Normandy, France. If you start watching the movie, I doubt you will stop viewing until the end of the movie. Nevertheless, if you watch the opening scenes, you will witness the horror of that invasion. You will be spellbound with thoughts of anguish regarding the fear these brave young men must have experienced during that long day. If you watch their sacrifice, you will surely understand the meaning of "All gave some; some gave all!"

My reading of history and viewing of other movies about the landing on the beaches of Normandy has convinced me that the depiction of the invasion in the movie, *Saving Private Ryan*, is as close to the real event as we can imagine the reality of that day. There are sources available that are original newsreels that recorded this amphibious invasion, the largest in the history of the world. I have never watched anything that was any more important to the allied war effort to defeat Nazi Germany as was the Normandy invasion. The horrific scenes left me so awestruck that I question if I could have mustered such courage. Indeed, those young men belonged to what we have named "The Greatest Generation!" We, as a nation, are eternally indebted to these heroes.

The WWII Allies had already forced the Germans out of North Africa and, for the most part, had liberated most of Southern Europe. Finally, it was time to open the second front that Stalin and the Russian military wanted so badly. The allied command had fooled Hitler into believing that the attack would be made at the French Port of Calais. Instead, "Operation Overlord," as the invasion of Europe was named, took place on the Normandy beaches of France. This landing caught the Germans by surprise, and the allies had done such a great job of fooling Hitler that he remained convinced the main invasion would still come at the Port of Calais. He refused to send the Panzers south to Normandy, where they might have been able to knock the allied invasion force back into the English Channel. Lucky for us, Hitler was too arrogant and stupid to follow the advice of some very good German generals. Why was the defeat of Nazi Germany so necessary?

Without a doubt, the evil of Hitler and the Nazi party, Mussolini in Italy, and the militarists of Japan was so profound that the devil in hell enjoyed one of his greatest triumphs ever with his orchestration of the multitude of ungodly acts committed by the Third Reich, Fascists of Italy, and the warlords of the Empire of Japan. Without a doubt, they were disciples of the devil!

Make no mistake, the Jewish holocaust perpetrated by the Nazis executed over six million Jews, and millions more of innocent people in Europe were likewise executed. Millions were slaughtered for no military reason. Millions were executed because of sick hate.

Google the "Rape of Nanking" at https://www.crimemuseum.org/crime-library/war-crimes/rape-of-nanking/ and you will read of unspeakable Japanese war crimes committed against the Chinese people of Nanking.

Mussolini was guilty of slaughter in North Africa. I suspect, actually I know, that there are far too many people in the USA, who do not know what was at stake for our country as we faced the aggressive onslaught of these three "Axis Powers of evil" in WWII. So what was at stake? Everything!

Germany and Italy were led by absolute totalitarian dictators in Hitler and Mussolini. What is totalitarianism? It means that the authority and power of those dictators was absolute, without limit, and the final word was always theirs. Their orders and desires would be carried out without question. Failure to carry out the orders would result in execution of those the dictators commanded. And they commanded everyone!

Tojo Hideki was the wartime leader of Japan, and according to the source of History.com, he never gained quite the absolute power of the dictators, Hitler and Mussolini. Tojo supposedly answered to Emperor Hirohito. Do not minimize the brutality of Tojo! Because of this knowledge, about the evil of totalitarian dictators, your appreciation for freedom in America is warranted. Here there is an appreciation for the self-worth of individuals and a constitution that protects the rights of individuals. Are you vigilant and watchful for signs that might indicate a threat to the appreciation for and the protection of the rights of individuals as you should be? May I suggest, we should always be on guard, especially if we recognize the examples of autocratic power grabs that fill the pages of history. The members of the "Greatest Generation" were keenly aware of history, and they decided to do something about autocratic behavior.

The June 6, 1944, Normandy invasion was a total commitment to the survival of all the freedoms the peoples of Western civilization had ever enjoyed. This allied invasion was a life-and-death struggle of total war to preserve our way of life against the onslaught of totalitarianism. The United States was an arsenal for democracy, and our industrial output of military supplies and weaponry was the envy and amazement of the world.

The organizational and industrial excellence of the United States' free enterprise capitalism system was already well established, and our success had no equal in the world. Without our industrial output, the British would have fallen, and the invasion would never have taken place. The axis powers of Germany, Italy, and Japan simply could not produce the war materials needed to defeat the allies. (Because of this history, I suggest that aluminum, steel, medical supplies including medicines, and countless other items should once again be mass produced in the United States, not in China!) Our military forces along with all of our allies made the supreme effort and put everything on the line. They faced down every challenge, and they would not be defeated. Our brave men and women went toe to toe with our enemies, and we did not back down.

For the life of me, I cannot understand how so many people in our country do not appreciate what a great gift the United States of America is for "We the People." How could anybody be so blinded by the false rhetoric of the left and their drive-by media puppets that they would want to assist in or allow the destruction of our way of life and governance? How could we have become so delusional as to not recognize that millions upon millions of people generation after generation have valued this way of life so much that they made any sacrifice to preserve this county? The men who stormed the beaches of Normandy and fought across France into Germany knew why they were fighting. Do we not know why they fought so hard? Today and going forward we all can do more in today's fight to protect our country from attack within and from beyond our borders. Will today's fight require as much of us as was required of them? I do not know, but I believe our fight is just as important as theirs was. What is at stake today? Everything! You can find numerous books written on what they did on D-Day. So what did they do?

Hundreds of young men were cut to pieces by German machine guns when the door of their landing craft opened for them to step onto the beaches. Many who survived the first hail of bullets stepped off into water over their head and drowned due to the weight of the equipment they carried. Those soldiers who survived long enough to get onto the beaches then encountered barbed wire impediments and land mines. The first waves were literally cut to pieces, but some were able to get to the base of the bluffs and hold on as more and more reinforcements ran, stumbled, and crawled off of the water's edge. The beaches ran red with the blood of young men who were sent to end the tyranny of Hitler and the Nazis. There was no turning back, and future president Dwight D. Eisenhower, Allied supreme commander, kept pouring in more waves of soldiers and equipment until the Germans, on the bluffs above the beaches, were overran. This was just one of many sacrifices made by the "Greatest Generation" who put it all on the line to preserve the freedoms of the American people. Some might say, "Well, what would have happened had those brave soldiers not fought these battles?"

I can say that life as it was known in 1944 in the U.S., and today, would have all been lost. Study the goals, plans, and philosophy of Hitler and the Nazi thugs; or better still, read about their actions and total lack of respect for life and freedom of ethnic groups and individuals, period! Then, surely, we all will realize how blessed we are to have been preceded by those brave Americans, Canadians, British, and many other countries' soldiers who stormed the beaches of Normandy on June 6, 1944. We live under the protection of an umbrella that these brave Americans fought to sustain for us all. If this does not get people off their knee to stand proudly for "Old Glory," then those folks just do not understand what it was that these soldiers appreciated and fought for. Nor do they realize what a wonderful and successful blessing we all enjoy.

Think about what those brave Americans passed on to us! "All gave some; some gave all" because they knew the dictators of the world meant to destroy our way of life and the "rule of law" provided by our constitution. Our enemies were against everything we Americans stood for. Among our enemies' shortcomings was the fact that they did not know that freedom yields a great resolve within the hearts and minds of the beneficiaries of a free society. There was no quit in those Americans of the 1940s!

Battle of the Bulge
Bastogne!

The Battle of the Bulge symbolizes the fact that there was no quit in the forces of the United States and our allies. The Americans' motivation to fight on and to refuse to surrender, though they were surrounded, was propelled by patriotism and pride that would not allow those soldiers to relinquish the freedoms guaranteed to so many Americans at home. The American "spirit" was as strong and fierce at this battle as it has been at countless other times in our history.

Hitler launched a German counteroffensive against the Allies on December 16, 1944, in the Ardennes Forest under winter conditions. To counter the Allied drive toward Germany that began with the successful Normandy invasion, Hitler hurled almost one thousand tanks and over two hundred thousand soldiers at the Allies in what became known as the "Battle of the Bulge." The Belgians of the town of Bastogne had experienced this circumstance back in 1940 when the Germans forced British and French forces to flee Dunkirk. Hitler's plan was to split the Allied army with a drive through Belgium toward the English coast. The battle would last for a month, and Hitler would fail due to the heroics and the Americans' refusal to surrender.[22]

The stubborn 101st Airborne Division was surrounded at Bastogne, Belgium. Vital to the German advance was the crossroads near St. Vith and Bastogne. It was here that the 101st Airborne Division and American tank forces were surrounded and held on for reinforcements to arrive. What was at stake? The war in Europe!

---

[22] www.army.mil.

Did the acting commander of the 101st at Bastogne realize that if he surrendered, the German counteroffensive could well succeed? I have no doubt that he did. He could have taken the easy way out. His cooks were picking up rifles in this desperate fight. His division was cut off and surrounded, and it was the dead of winter. He was massively outnumbered. Not by any stretch of one's imagination could you predict that the Americans would stop the Germans at this vital crossroads. The Allied war effort in Europe was hanging on by the valor of small cutoff squads who would not yield. The Germans sent the acting commander of the 101st Airborne Division, Anthony Clement McAuliffe, an ultimatum demanding he surrender or the Germans would destroy what remained of his division. McAuliffe's eloquent reply was a refusal of just one word, "Nuts!"

Talk about an "American Spirit of Sacrifice." This commander and his soldiers were willing to pay the ultimate price for freedom as they faced the overwhelming forces of the freedom hating totalitarianism of the Nazis. These determined Americans were not going anywhere. For sure they were not going to surrender freedom to tyranny. Help was on the way!

Help came with the leadership of General George S. Patton and his 3rd Army. Patton pulled his 3rd Army out of a winter campaign, turned them north into the German's flank of attack. His men marched, day and night, to relieve Bastogne. This forced winter march is one of the most stirring segments of the movie, *Patton*. Watch that movie and feel both pride and gratitude that you are an American beneficiary of such an effort. Bastogne was relieved, and the German offensive was stopped. The die was now cast. Hitler and his evil efforts would soon be totally destroyed. The world would soon be, temporarily, safe for democracy.

Do you want to know more about this monumental defense put up by the Americans at the Battle of the Bulge? If so, may I recommend a great source? Colonel Ralph Mitchell's 1986 article, "The 101st Airborne Division's Defense of Bastogne," presented by the Combined Arms Research Library/Command and General Staff College's Combat Studies Institute can be found at https://www. ibiblio.org/hyperwar/USA/CSI/CSI-Bastogne/MITCHELL.asp.

html. This article will provide you with great insight and many factual details.

The desire to fight, in order to guarantee the survival of our "way of life," coupled with the stubborn refusal of commanders such as Anthony McAuliffe to surrender, has been a matter of fact displayed time and again by our military. Are we still unwilling to surrender freedom? I hope so!

I fear that too many Americans have been lulled into a false sense of security and falsely believe that the freedoms of America are untouchable. Nothing is further from the truth. The sacrifices made at the Battle of the Bulge were only an installment paid on the cost of freedom; it was not a cost paid in full forever. New bills for the cost of freedom come on a regular basis, and you must pay a price to keep the "wolves of war" from taking away your freedom. Take a break from the ball game or whatever occupies your time and reflect on the many troubling warnings that point to the fact that our way of life is under attack.

Forces from within are being funded by sources outside and inside our country to push us to the brink of collapse. They present themselves as guardians of democracy when they are really anti-American wolves in sheep's clothing. I hear words such as speaking politically correct, I hear charges of racism, I see borrowed money being spent like monopoly money on a board game, I see American jobs being sold overseas, I watch an open border to our south, I see American energy independence being sacrificed for a "Green Bad Deal," I see foreign totalitarianism becoming emboldened, I see censorship of the press, and I see a press that provides propaganda rather than a reporting of facts. All of these things I see as a concerted effort to destroy life as we have known it. This is not what those brave Americans fought for during the Battle of the Bulge. What do you see? If I am correct, the question becomes, "How many will give some, and will any give all?"

While many Americans have failed to teach or learn our history, others know the history but choose to ignore history, and worse still, they endeavor to cover up history and truth. They do this to present their false narrative. Beware! What I can tell you is that the people who live in and around Bastogne today have not forgotten what the Americans did there in December of 1944. Recently, a best friend of mine attended a Formula 1 race in Belgium. He was amazed at the reverence those people still hold for the Americans who faced down the tyranny of the Nazis in their country. They remember the price the Americans paid for not only American freedom but for their freedom as well. I write this in case we Americans have forgotten or for some to learn for the first time.

The Bataan Death March

General Douglas MacArthur was ordered to leave the Philippines in March 1942. The upper echelons of the U.S. military knew that the U.S. forces in the Philippines were cutoff and that there was no way to get reinforcements to them. MacArthur's generalship was needed for the war that was going to take place in the Pacific. The U.S. would accept nothing but unconditional surrender from the Japanese. The war would be long and desperate, and it was imperative the military must have the best commanders available. Having been ordered to leave, MacArthur said, "I shall return," and he was evacuated from Bataan.

True to his word and prophesy, MacArthur did return to the Philippines when he landed on the island of Leyte on October 20, 1944. Eventually, the Japanese forces would be driven from the Philippines, and they would not return! But between March 1942 and October 20, 1944, there was a lot of war to be fought.

U.S. General Edward King was in command of all ground troops on Bataan. On April 9, 1942, he was forced to surrender to the Japanese. The Japanese then committed one of their many war crimes when they orchestrated the Bataan Death March. The numbers of soldiers, Philippine and Americans, who died of starvation, exposure, and from execution during the forced march of sixty-five miles are almost impossible to determine. The executions, starvation, and inhumane brutality of the Japanese captors was unspeakable. The Japanese commander, Lt. General Homma Masaharu, would be tried for war crimes and executed for his evil treatment of prisoners of war. Knowledge of these and other acts only served to harden the resolve of American sailors, marines, and airmen as they fought their way across the Pacific to free the world of the barbarian totalitarianism that threatened all freedom loving people.[23]

Another story that I wish to share is the story of General Jonathan Mayhew Wainwright IV and his leadership on Corregidor, in the Philippines. After the surrender of General King on April 9, 1942, Wainwright retreated with a command of some three thousand five hundred men and took up a defensive position on Corregidor. Wainwright's men were starving, exhausted, and low on all military supplies. They had absolutely no hope or chance for reinforcements or resupply. Yet on May 5, 1942, they defended their position on Corregidor against overwhelming odds. May 6, 1942, General Wainwright was out of options, and he was forced to surrender his command. I cannot even begin to imagine the mental strain and anguish this man endured as a result of the choice he had to make regarding the surrender of his men to the Japanese. He and those who survived imprisonment and inhumane horror for three years at POW Camp O'Donnell would be nothing but skin and bones when they were finally liberated.

One can only imagine the nightmares these survivors would endure for the rest of their lives as a result of the brutality they experienced and the memories of their comrades who made the ultimate sacrifice in service of their country. These men gave their all! They paid the highest price for precious freedom and unalienable rights that has ever been exacted upon any soldiers. This would not be the last time that the Japanese would see General Jonathan Mayhew Wainwright IV.

For his service, General Wainwright was awarded the Medal of Honor. I wish to cite and present the following statements about this man that were taken from Arlington National Cemetery Website (Webmaster: Michael Robert Patterson, http://www.arlingtoncemetery.net/jwainiv.htm).

---

[23] Elizabeth M. Norman, https://www.britannica.com/event/Bataan-Death-March.

Wainwright, Jonathan M.

Rank and organization: General, Commanding U.S. Army Forces in the Philippines. Place and date: Philippine Islands, 12 March to 7 May 1942. Entered service at: Skaneateles, N.Y. Birth: Walla Walla, Washington. GO. No.: 80, 19 September 1945.

Citation:

Distinguished himself by intrepid and determined leadership against greatly superior enemy forces. At the repeated risk of life above and beyond the call of duty in his position, he frequented the firing line of his troops where his presence provided the example and incentive that helped make the gallant efforts of these men possible. The final stand on beleaguered Corregidor, for which he was in an important measure personally responsible, commanded the admiration of the Nation's allies. It reflected the high morale of American arms in the face of overwhelming odds. His courage and resolution were a vitally needed inspiration to the then sorely pressed freedom-loving peoples of the world.

The actions and bravery of General Wainwright and his men are above any reproach. Their deeds of service and valor leave this writer wanting of any appropriate words. I am not worthy. Please join me when I say, "Thank you," to any survivor and to the families of those Americans!

The Halsey-Doolittle Raid on Tokyo
18 April 1942

The attack upon Pearl Harbor left the military, citizenry, and the government of our country stunned, angry, fearful of a mainland invasion, and vengeful. While the country grieved for the loss of life and for the wounded, the naval forces in the Pacific went into full-scale war preparations to make ready for the defeat of Japan. Even as all of these things were taking place, a plan was developed to strike fear in the Japanese and to do serious damage to their capital, Tokyo.

This plan has most often been referred to as the "Doolittle Raid" by the press, but it is important to note that naval records also call it the Halsey-Doolittle Raid, Task Force 16 (TF-16). The bombing raid on Tokyo and other cities occurred on 18 April 1942. Lieutenant Colonel James H. Doolittle, USAAF, would personally lead sixteen B-25 bombers that would launch from a carrier in Vice Admiral William F. Halsey Jr.'s task force. They would do something that had not been done before. They would launch land-based bombers from the deck of a carrier at sea.[24] And it was a one-way trip! If they were not shot down, they would have to force land in Japanese-controlled China if they had any hope of survival. Please read the above statements again. Let that sink in.

There are numerous sayings that I like to hear. Such sayings as "Luck is when preparation meets opportunity." Admiral William F. Halsey Jr. said, "There are no extraordinary men...just extraordinary circumstances that ordinary men are forced to deal with." I would not ever question Admiral Halsey. Let it suffice to say that there were ordinary men with great courage and a sense of duty that stepped forward to fly Doolittle's planes. Indeed, the circumstances were extraordinary, and their actions were heroic, if ever, there were heroes. I say this without any reservations. The men who flew the sixteen B-25s from the deck of Halsey's task force carrier possessed every fiber of character we attribute to the men and women we call "The Greatest Generation." They would do the unthinkable in April of 1942. They were going to bleed the enemy's homeland. These heroes flew into the heart of the Empire of Japan, and in doing so, they would forevermore live in the hearts of proud and grate-

---

[24] Naval History and Heritage Command, https://www.history.navy.mil/browse-by-topic/wars-conflicts-and-operations/world-war-ii/1942/halsey-doolittle-raid.html.

ful Americans. The audacity of this raid signaled a very clear message to the Japanese. This message did not require the Japanese to read English. The message delivered to the Japanese was simple. The Americans are coming! I wonder if any of the pilots flew into battle with the thought on their mind, *Remember Pearl Harbor.*

Sixteen planes, stripped of everything unnecessary in order to carry more fuel, flew from the carrier. Halsey had hoped to get within four hundred miles of Tokyo before launching, but the task force was discovered by Japanese boats six hundred fifty miles from Tokyo. The question circulating in everyone's mind was, could they deliver their incendiary bombs and have enough fuel to escape to mainland China? What I can tell you is that all sixteen planes flew off the carrier deck and flew into the "hell of war." The bombing raid struck targets in Tokyo, Yokosuka, Yokohama, Kobe, and Nagoya. Incendiary bombs having been dropped, the bombers flew toward Japanese-occupied Chekiang Province in China. These American airmen flew toward China with prayers on their lips, and their planes flew on fumes of exhausted fuel tanks. Fifteen of the planes crashed in China, and only one plane managed to land in the Soviet Union. All gave some; some gave all! Can we Americans not put up a fight in 2021 in order to save what these men fought so valiantly for in 1942?

Time out! I have a sad "news flash!" July 1, 2021, U.S. Air Force fitness training testing is undergoing experimental changes. Airmen will be allowed to walk the 1.5 miles rather than run the 1.5 miles if the airmen choose. There will be modified push-ups allowed. "The new tests, which the service will begin experimenting with in January 2022, will allow Airmen to choose between running 1.5 miles, shuttle running or walking to demonstrate aerobic capacity." Go to https://www.archyde.com/new-us-air-force-physical-fitness-tests-will-allow-walking-instead-of-running/ to find the above quote and other information regarding this story. According to this article, Lt. General Brian Kelly, Air Force deputy chief of staff, says this will allow airmen more flexibility of choice for how they want to be tested. The Air Force claims that there is scientific and physiological testing data that supports their reasoning for trying this new method in 2022. I guess that I may not know enough about this, but I can tell you I have ran a mile for time. I can tell you that at age sixty-eight, I routinely walk a mile. I am sorry, but I am not buying this one!

I bet Lieutenant James H. Doolittle, USAAF, just turned over in his "grave of honor!" When Doolittle and his airmen crash-landed in China, after the raid on Tokyo, they had to run for their lives in an all-out effort to escape the Japanese. I assure you that they did not have an option to choose to run, shuttle-run, or walk away from the Japanese that were searching for them. I am also sure that if they had the flexibility of choice to walk, that the Japanese would not have been good sports and walked as well. Can you imagine the laugh that the Russians, Chinese, and North Koreans must be having since this news has broken? I promise you that these three countries do not train any of their military forces in this manner. Our Navy SEALS, Green Berets, Delta Forces, Rangers, and all of our military forces, retired and active, must be aghast!

While the damage done to Japanese assets was minimal, it was the psychological damage the raid inflicted upon the Japanese that was significant. The real impact of the raid from the American stand-point was the rising spirits of Americans when the news spread of the raid. To Americans, the men of the Jimmy Doolittle Raid were heroes. Now you know what caused the daring raid as well as the effects. What you may not know is that the Japanese would react with an attack upon Midway.

The Battle of Midway
June 3–6, 1942

A History.com article entitled Battle of Midway found at https://www.history.com/topics/world-warii/battle of midway pro-vided the information necessary for the following discussion!

Commander of the Imperial Japanese Navy, Isoroku Yamamoto, hoped to achieve at Midway what the Japanese had failed to do at Pearl Harbor and at the Battle of Coral Sea. Yamamoto hoped to neutralize the United States as a sea-and-air power in the Pacific. He had devised a strategic attack plan for the seizing of the American base at Midway that involved sea, air, and land forces. With the capture of the American base at Midway, the Japanese would not only have a strong base situated halfway between the U.S. and Japan, they might well destroy U.S. naval power. To say the least, this was a vital strategic location for control for the war in the Pacific. Both sides needed the base, and the resulting fight revealed the price both were willing to pay for the control of the Midway Atoll. And the price was indeed very high! This battle illustrated the resolve of both sides! And with that commitment, the fighting and willingness to make the ultimate sacrifice was fierce and heroic. Yamamoto was not the only admiral plotting strategy in the Pacific in 1942.

Admiral Chester W. Nimitz, commander in chief of the U.S. Pacific Fleet, was busy at Pearl Harbor devising plans to protect his fleet and the west coast of the United States. They suspected that Midway would be targeted by the Japanese, and the navy would gamble against the odds and commit whatever forces they had to stop the Japanese. The U.S. Navy had an advantage in this game of strategy due to the fact that U.S. intel had broken the Japanese military communication code. With this advantage, Nimitz decided a great naval battle was about to take place at Midway and made preparations to meet the Imperial Japanese Navy. A great deal was at risk, and even with the naval intel, luck was needed for the desperate and outgunned U.S. Navy to be successful at Midway Island. Heroism was on full display that day, and the Navy made America proud.

Yamamoto had a great plan, but instead of ambushing the Americans, Yamamoto sailed into an ambush of devastation. The American ambush of Yamamoto was orchestrated by American naval intel and the planning of Admiral Chester W. Nimitz and his staff of captains and admirals. No matter how wonderful the plan and the ambush was, it would have been useless without the bravery of the American sailors and the heroic fighting spirit of sacrifice made by the American pilots who literally flew into the "hell" of the Japanese Empire's aggression. Those young American pilots flew to victory and death for the sake of freedom for the American people. Squad after squad of American bombers and torpedo planes went on the attack without the protective umbrella of fighter plane escorts. (The fighter plans were kept back to protect the aircraft carriers.) Time and again that day, most all of these squads were shot down by the anti-aircraft guns and fighter planes of the Japanese. Still the American pilots took to the air time after time. All Americans should be proud of their work done that day! They fought against great odds, and many died, but they fought until they won the day! "All gave some; some gave all!" There is a movie, *Midway*, that you may want to watch. Watch the movie and you will get a feel for what they faced and what they did on that day.

History.com editors' article "Battle of Midway," April 17, 2021, access date from Publisher, A&E Television Networks, found at URL https://www.history.com/topics/world-war-ii/battle-of-midway, provided the following statistical data statement regarding the Battle of Midway. And I quote the following verbatim statement from this History.com editors' article:

> On June 6, Yamamoto ordered his ships to retreat, ending the Battle of Midway. In all, Japan had lost as many as 3,000 men (including more than 200 of their most experienced pilots), nearly 300 aircraft, one heavy cruiser and four aircraft carriers in the battle, while the Americans lost the *Yorktown* and *Hammann*, along with around 145 aircraft and approximately 360 servicemen. [Note: The *Yorktown* was a carrier while the *Hammann* was a destroyer.]

The article referenced above will provide you details of both Yamamoto's battle plan and the Nimitz ambush. There is a wonderful video and narrative that you will find most informative should you desire to study this great naval and air battle in detail.

As you can see, the Battle of Midway was a resounding victory for the United States Navy. The losses of the Japanese were so devasting that the Japanese Imperial Navy would have to fight a defensive battle for the rest of WWII. American spirits soared.

Was it possible that this battle, only six months into the war, was the turning point? There was so much fighting left to do as the

Americans fought the Japanese in battle after battle across the Pacific on their way to Japan's unconditional surrender that would be signed on board the *USS Missouri*. Thousands of Americans would pay the ultimate sacrifice on the beaches and islands of the Pacific. Thousands upon thousands of brave Americans suffered horribly from the physical and mental wounds received in the battles that were to come. Turning point?

Yes, I think so, because the American Navy destroyed four Japanese aircraft carriers, killed almost two hundred of their most experienced pilots, and shot down three hundred aircraft. The Japanese Navy was severely beaten and left Midway much weaker. This victory gave the "Sleeping Giant," the American Industrial Complex, the time needed to convert domestic factories into sites for manufacturing of planes, tanks, ships, and all materials of war. Our free enterprise capitalism economy had created a manufacturing and production system that was finely tuned and second to none in the world. The speed at which domestic manufacturing switched over to production of weapons of war was nothing short of astounding!

While there are numerous examples of outstanding patriotic success stories for American war production, I will only take time to quote one. Go to http://michiganhistory.leadr.msu.edu/wwii-and-ford-motor-company/ and you will be amazed at the contribution made to the war effort by Henry Ford and Ford Motor Company. The article is entitled "WWII and Ford Motor Company" and explains what took place at the Willow Run plant. The following is a direct quote taken from that article found on the Michigan Historical site.

> Ford Motor Company built the giant Willow Run plant to produce B-24 Liberator bombers using an assembly line one mile long. The plant produced its' first bomber in May 1942, and made several hundred aircraft a month from thereon. Willow Run produced at a record rate: one plane per hour (Henry Ford: Helped Lead American World War II Production Efforts)! By the end of the war, Ford had built 86,865 complete aircraft,

57,851 airplane engines, 4,291 military glid-
ers, and thousands of engine superchargers and
generators (Henry Ford: Helped Lead American
World War II Production Efforts)! In addition
to aircraft, Ford plants built 277,896 of the ver-
satile vehicles (tanks, armored cars, and jeeps).
Ford Motor had plants in Great Britain, Canada,
India, South Africa, New Zealand, and even Nazi
Germany. [Please note that the May 1942 Willow
Run production of the first bomber was only five
months after the December 7, 1941, attack on
Pearl Harbor by the Japanese!]

The Germans, Italians, and Japanese had no chance of match-
ing the output of weapons that the United States began rolling out.
Why or how can anyone question the success of the American free
enterprise system? When you hear someone extoll the evils of capitalism and the nonexistent virtues of socialism you might challenge
them to construct an "A" to "B" comparison chart on the creation
of wealth and job production efficiencies between American capitalism and socialism/communism. Then ask them to debate you based
upon the data illustrated on their chart. Also, ask for historical evidence for success for each economic system! I bet you will win that
debate, that is, if you choose Free enterprise capitalism. That is my
choice, for sure! Are you ready to embrace the socialism agenda that
the far left is implementing in our country as I write this book?

Before too many rush to embrace the agenda of the socialists, I
wish to offer a classical example of the failure of socialist communistic systems to provide for the citizenry at large or be able to provide
for the common defense of their nation. When Hitler reneged on
the "German-Soviet Nonaggression Pact," with his sneak attack on
the Soviets, the world witnessed the abject failure of socialism and a
state-run economy. A failure, I might add, that continued for as long
as the Soviet Union existed. The Soviets, with all their population,
land, energy, and minerals, could not feed themselves or produce the
needed war materials to fight the Germans.

It was American free enterprise capitalism's industrial output that filled in the gaps of production for the poorly run economy of the Soviet Union. Just one of many examples is the approximately four thousand six hundred P-39 Airacobras, U.S.-built planes, that were sent to the Soviets as part of the U.S. Lend-Lease program. President Roosevelt (FDR) initiated Lend-Lease in order to get necessary weapons to the Allies fighting the Nazis. To be fair, we also supplied many weapons to the British. The Brits had been fighting the Nazis alone due to the Russians' treaty with the Nazis that saw the Russians sitting out the early part of the war. Nevertheless, the communist economic system could not produce what they needed to successfully fight the Nazis. This inability was due to a lack of technological knowledge as well an inefficient assembling of resources into the products needed.

After WWII, the Soviets spent so much on the military that they could not feed themselves. The Soviets relied on U.S. grain deals to feed their citizens until the time of President Reagan. Ask American farmers if they would have moved to the Soviet Union to be farmers.

To learn more about the incompetent and evil Soviet socialists or communists, fast-forward to the nuclear age in the Soviet Union and you will forget about global warming or climate change. What the environmentalists should be talking about are the ticking time bombs of nuclear radiation that the incompetent and morally decadent communists have dumped into our oceans, seas, and on the land in Europe. The implications of what the Soviets have perpetrated upon the world with their nuclear atrocities makes the bombing of Hiroshima look like a firecracker. Read the story of the Chernobyl disaster in Serhii Plokhy's book entitled *Chernobyl: History of a Tragedy* and in Peter Huchthausen's book entitled *K-19: The Widowmaker*. When you read excerpts from these books or read them in their entirety, you will know about the Soviets' incompetence and dereliction of moral duty to humanity!

The totalitarian, one-party socialist regimes of the world have all been morally decadent. The only thing of importance is the "state!" Individuals be damned! Is our country following a dangerous path toward socialism and one-party rule? Which type of a system do you want to pass on to your children and grandchildren?

Final Thoughts "All Gave Some, Some Gave All!"

WWII ended with the total and unconditional surrender of both Germany and Japan. The United States, along with our many allies, were the victors over a totalitarian dictator in Germany and the militarists of Japan. Both countries lay prostrate at our feet. What happened to these two countries after WWII is a fair question to be asked. The U.S. did not rule those countries, and we did not deny them unalienable rights.

The Soviet Union's response was quite different! And millions suffered until 1991 as a result of autocratic rule by communists under the banner of socialism.

After the war, Germany was divided into four sectors. Eventually that division was reduced to only two, East and West Germany, two separate countries. East Germany was controlled by the "iron red fist" of the Soviet Union. The Soviet Red Army conquered much of eastern Germany before the western allies were able to advance that far. Therefore, the East Germans would suffer from 1945 until the early 1990s under autocratic rule of the communists. That was a fate I would not wish upon my worst enemy. The East Germans were destitute, devoid of many freedoms such as religious freedom, restricted from moving around, and spied upon by the communists. These suffering Germans tried to escape to the West during the Cold War. Early on about one-sixth of the Germans escaped to the West before the "Iron Curtain" was built. After that, most were not able to escape. If a life of socialism under autocratic rule and control is so good, then why would people try to escape over the "iron curtain" to the freedom of western democracies and a reunion with family? For that matter, why should you be so restrained by government that you were compelled to risk your life by escaping the confines of a country in which you are forced to reside?

To my fellow Americans, I say once again, we have a good thing going for us! But we should be on high alert because there are far too many people who seek to seize power and forever change America. When have you ever heard of anyone trying to escape the United States or Great Britain? They do not, and we do not want socialism and one-party radical left rule either.

Life in the Federal Republic of Germany (FRG) or West Germany was a far cry better than the lives of Germans stuck in Soviet-controlled East Germany (GDR). West Germany or the Federal Republic of Germany (FRG) developed a social market economy. A social market economy provided for mostly private production and allowed the market to work in ways that set both prices and wages. To be clear, the government was involved to a certain extent, just as ours is. The FRG enjoyed an economic miracle for success that propelled West Germany to the most prosperous economy in Europe.

Compared to West Germany's economic success, the "socialist centrally planned economy" of East Germany (GDR) produced, at best, only "economic want and stagnation!" West Germany flourished with an economic system that worked amazingly like most any free-market capitalist economies work, and it took root in West Germany. Couple the economic success of West Germany, with the fact that the political system of the FRG was a parliamentary democracy that provided for many rights of freedom, and I suggest that therein lies a formula for success. So I wonder what conclusions you have drawn from this presentation?

An iron curtain divided Germany into two countries with diametrically opposed systems of governance and economic operations. In short, it was democracy and a free enterprise type of economy in West Germany (FRG) versus socialism and communist rule in East Germany (GDR). The FRG enjoyed great success! When the Berlin Wall was torn down and East Germany and West Germany were reunited, the freedom and economic success of West Germany was able to absorb the disaster of socialism and communist rule that had been responsible for so much suffering of the Germans in captivity under the Soviets. This success story came close to not happening.

As quickly as the United States and the Soviet Union were forced, by necessity of Nazi aggression, to become allies in WWII, the USA and the USSR became enemies in a cold war that would last until 1991 when the Soviet Union collapsed. Post–WWII Germany was divided into four sectors with the Soviets, USA, Britain, and France, each controlling their own separate sector. The German capital, Berlin, was located entirely within and surrounded by the Soviet-controlled sector, East Germany. However, the German capital city of Berlin was also divided into four sectors with the Soviets controlling East Berlin, and the British, French, and USA allies each controlled their own individual sectors of West Berlin. It was here that the East met the West, and neither side trusted the other. The Soviets did not want a reunited Germany. The Soviet solution was to try to run the western allies of Britain, France, and the U.S. out of the city of West Berlin.

The Soviets decided to establish a blockade around the allies' sectors of the city of Berlin. They would starve the two million Germans and force the allies to withdraw. With West Berlin cut off from resupply from Western Europe, the situation was desperate. This Soviet Communist blockade that cut off West Berlin from food, fuel, and other supplies that France, Britain, and the U.S. had to deliver to the starving Germans was an example of pure Soviet aggression that showed absolutely no regard for human life. President Truman and the other allies refused to give in to the Soviet aggression of Joseph Stalin.

The Soviet blockade would be defeated by the "Berlin Airlift" conducted by France, Britain, and the U.S for ten months. The allies would land three hundred thousand planes among their three sectors of control in West Berlin over the ten months. At times planes touched down every thirty seconds during the airlift. They delivered almost 2.5 million tons of food, fuel, and other necessities to the desperate Germans of West Berlin. Here is a key point we should all consider. The war with Germany was over, and what did the Allies, led by the U.S., do? We provided humanitarian assistance with the Marshall Plan and the Berlin Airlift. We assisted in the rebuilding of West Germany's infrastructure. What did the communists do? You now know they were aggressors seeking to expand their domination of countries in order to spread their failed system of socialism and autocratic rule.[25]

Freedom-loving democracies that employed free enterprise capitalism stared across the Soviet blockade of West Berlin with great resolve and determination. We helped save millions from the suffering that the Soviets brought down upon East Germany and numerous other countries in Europe. The Soviets' blockade failed. The world is a much better place due to the fact that the Soviet Union also failed! These are the facts that the left hides. It is time to paint the picture of truth about our history. The real history of America depicts what we stand for as a nation and of the millions who have benefited by our willingness to shed our blood and spend our treasure.

There was another major power that was defeated in WWII, and you probably know a great deal about the success of Japan. Japan, after their defeat in WWII, was occupied by the United States. The government of Japan is a constitutional monarchy. The emperor is primarily a figurehead that basically performs ceremonial duties. The economy of Japan is a free market economy of free enterprise. The success of Japan is nothing short of phenomenal when you consider that they are a G7 nation that has the second largest developed economy in the world. How did the Japanese get to this point? The United States helped them, and we provide a defense from the military attack that would surely come from China and North Korea. The Japanese and the South Koreans are surrounded by failures.

Their neighbors are the Russians, North Koreans, and Red China, all of whom have denied basic unalienable rights for citizens. The economy of North Korea and Red China cannot compare to the success of the United States, Japan, and South Korea. It is important to note that the Russians have become more capitalistic than anyone could have ever imagined. Why have the Russians looked to capitalism?

The Russians know that socialism is restrictive and counterproductive to economic success. There are no incentives or rewards that encourage success in a socialist economy. Before you swallow the tripe

---

[25] https://www.history.com/topics/cold-war/berlin-airlift.

fed out by the drive-by media that sings the praises of economic success of the Chinese, I suggest you study that one more closely. Given the evidence that is available for all to see, why are there people in this country openly and secretly pushing socialism? The system has always failed, and it will not work anywhere or anytime. All that system will do is weaken this nation to a point of insignificance, which is exactly what China, Russia, North Korea, and the Iranians want. The actions of the United States and of the communist nations after WWII were starkly different and produced quite different results.

West Germany, Japan, and South Korea would become free and independent nations that produced great freedoms for their people who also enjoyed economic success with high standards of living. By the way, did I mention that the United States led the effort in Korea to prevent the Chinese and North Korean communists from taking over South Korea? We did, and look at the success of the South Koreans! These countries would shun socialism and autocratic rule. Contrast this story with the sufferings of the East Germans (GDR) who were controlled by socialism and the USSR communists. The same abysmal circumstances of a lack of freedom and economic want ran rampant in North Korea and China. Can you see the two diametrically opposed patterns of success and failure by two very different systems of governance and economic productivity?

Numerous times in this chapter you have read the phrase, "All gave some; some gave all!" I can tell you, with 100 percent assurance, that all of those brave Americans did not fight to see this country become a socialist failure stripped of unalienable rights and economic freedom. Those patriots must be rolling over in their grave wondering what land it is that they are buried within. I will end this discussion with a brief statement about the comments of one of our generals when he described what Americans have done.

The article, "Colin Powell—All We Want is Land to Bury our Dead—Truth!" by Rich Buhler and staff posted on March 17, 2015, can be accessed at https://www.truthorfiction.com/powell-empires/.

Colin Powell served the United States as a soldier who would rise to the rank of a four-star general in the army, serve as chairman of the Joint Chiefs of Staff, and he became secretary of state. To learn of the wisdom of this American leader, I encourage you to google quotes made by Colin Powell.

The article that I have referenced points out that during the World Economic Forum in Switzerland, January 2003, the archbishop of Canterbury, George Carey, questioned Colin Powell. According to Rich Buhler and staff, Carey asked Colin Powell the following question:

> He asked Powell whether the U.S. was relying too much on 'hard power' such as military action as opposed to 'soft power' such as appealing to the common values of the major religions and building trust based on those values.

Colin Powell responded with words that I find revealing and uplifting. According to the article presented by Rich Buhler and staff, Colin Powell made the following statement.

> We have gone forth from our shores repeatedly over the last hundred years and we've done this as recently as the last year in Afghanistan and put wonderful young men and women at risk, many of whom have lost their lives, and we have asked for nothing except enough ground to bury them in, and otherwise we have returned home to seek our own, you know, to seek our own lives in peace, to live our own lives in peace. But there comes a time when soft power or talking with evil will not work where, unfortunately, hard power is the only thing that works.

Thank you, General Colin Powell, for your wisdom and your service to your country. There is a big difference between the United States and the other side. I say, let us all continue to climb the "mountain of ideals" this nation has stood for since 1791! We will stumble at times, just as we have in the past, but we will always get back on our feet and continue the climb!

Today is August 19, 2021. I have returned to this chapter to write about a most disturbing and tragic story. The Biden-Harris administration has botched the U.S. withdrawal from Afghanistan. This is one of the most embarrassing and tragic political and military leadership failures in all of American History. The damage done to American foreign policy, intelligence capabilities, and respect for America around the world is catastrophic.

There are estimates that eighty-five billion dollars in U.S. military equipment was left in Afghanistan. Much of the equipment includes highly sophisticated equipment such as planes, helicopters, tanks, drones, night vision equipment, not to mention the small arms and ammunition. The Taliban is now one of the best armed fighting units in the world. It is bad enough that no one was caring or smart enough to bring that equipment home, drop it off in Israel, or at least destroy the equipment and blow-up installations that the Taliban now occupies. The Russians, Chinese, and Iranians can now examine all of this sophisticated weaponry. I am sick to my stomach! But you have not heard the worst of this debacle. There is a far greater tragedy that we must discuss.

Thousands of American citizens and Afghan fighters loyal to the United States war effort over the last twenty years are trapped in Afghanistan. It is unbelievable, for millions of Americans, that the Biden-Harris administration would leave citizens and Afghans loyal to the American military behind in the hands of the Taliban. Yet that is exactly what happened! The American military personnel who fought in the Middle East are beyond angry. These brave men and women do not leave their own behind.

This travesty, caused by fools, will be ranked as one of the great catastrophes in American History. The fallout from this debacle will haunt us for years. Our NATO allies and other allies we used to have cannot trust American leadership, and who can blame them! Our enemies are laughing, and they know that the Biden-Harris administration is so inept and weak that they are free to be aggressors around the world. And they will! The Japanese, Taiwanese, South Koreans, and our NATO allies of western Europe are angry and severely shaken.

The worst thing you can ever do is embolden your enemies by a show of weakness, incompetence, and lack of resolve. The Biden-Harris administration is guilty of emboldening our enemies, and they have done this in the most profound way.

I wrote this chapter several months ago. I knew that I would come back to discuss and give credit to all of our heroes of Vietnam and to those who have also proven themselves on the sands of the Middle East! Without question, our military forces in those theaters of conflict must be acknowledged for their efforts that illustrated that all gave some; some gave all! Our troops did not lose in either of those theaters! When called by their country, they reported for duty, and yes, there were many who volunteered just like other patriotic citizens did in all of our many wars! These Americans did everything and more than their country asked of them. They are all deserving of the highest regard and respect that a nation can bestow upon those who serve to defend our nation. Never pass up an opportunity to thank these veterans.

For days Americans and the world watched the disaster unfolding in Afghanistan. This disaster is the direct result of the botched withdrawal of Americans from Afghanistan. As of September 11, 2021, we do not know how many of our citizens are in harm's way and at the mercy of an enemy that shows no mercy, the Taliban! The Biden-Harris administration has said they are depending upon the Taliban! You cannot make up this kind of insanity. The total lack of common sense, foresight, planning, and professionalism of those in Washington responsible for this debacle is further testimony of the incompetence and amateurism of the Biden-Harris administration. History has just been made, and it is history created by failed leadership. A lack of leadership that will have severe and long-lasting impacts on this nation of "We the people." The overwhelming majority of Americans are sickened by this grossly mishandled withdrawal. By the time you read this, we will know the outcome, maybe! Does history repeat itself?

History does repeat itself, and everyone has heard the cliché that those who do not read history are doomed to repeat history. If you do not remember, or if you would like to refresh your memory, research "The Fall of Saigon," April of 1975. Joe Biden and Kamala Harris and the rest of that administration have apparently forgotten history or never learned the history of Vietnam. Worse still, I see no evidence of common-sense applications that should have been applied to prevent this nightmare. This Biden-Harris debacle is light-years worse, in many ways, than was the fall of Saigon in 1975. A first-year cadet in our military academy could have devised a strategic plan that would have been far better than this mess. The political and military leadership in charge of this withdrawal ignored the intelligence reports and allowed strategic installations to be taken by the Taliban.

The Biden-Harris administration did not demand that the Taliban adhere to a conditions-based withdrawal scenario. And the administration did not provide the Afghan forces with crucial air support. They watched as the Taliban took over Bagram Air Base. The most powerful nation in the world cannot afford such a lack of political and military leadership in Washington!

There is also another story that adds to this debacle in Afghanistan. We left behind many who deserved to be taken out of Afghanistan while removing thousands from Afghanistan who were not properly vetted and who did nothing to support our efforts in Afghanistan. Why? There is no common-sense answer to that question or an explanation for the transfer of thousands of undeserving Afghans into our country. We do not know who most of these people are! Are there terrorists among these people the Biden-Harris administration has dropped off on our military bases? Do these Afghan's survival depends upon Americans who pay taxes? Do these people support the values of America? Do any of these new arrivals support Sharia law? If so, that will conflict with our constitution, will it not?

Leadership and the duties of a commander in chief are paramount, and may I say that when you cast a vote for a commander in chief, who will be the leader of the free world, there are consequences! The Biden-Harris administration has shown that they do not have the leadership capabilities necessary to be recognized as leaders of the free world! The consequences of elections, whether they are fraudulent or not, can be either good or bad. A vote for Joe Biden and Kamala Harris in the 2020 election was a bad choice. There are consequences for voting for people who are not ready and who would never be ready for the awesome responsibility and duty of being president or vice president of the United States. The American veterans and citizens are not laughing; many are crying! Many of us predicted that there would be chaos in the Biden-Harris administration. This tragic incident, along with many others presented in this book, proves our point.

The television interviews of Biden, his handpicked generals in Washington, press secretaries, and cabinet heads have demonstrated gross incompetence, flippant attitude, baseless excuses, and a deer-in-the-headlights look. They have no idea how many Americans they have abandoned in Afghanistan! Obviously, they had no plan before the withdrawal, and there does not seem to be any plan to rescue the Americans in captivity in Taliban-controlled Afghanistan! Nobody, as of August 19, 2021, had seen the VP since this travesty first hit the airwaves. She did appear in a news conference with Biden on Friday, August 20, 2021. She had her mask on! Biden has, during this time, been in and out of the White House as if he can take a vacation during an international crisis that involves American citizens being left behind.

In a television interview, I heard Joe Biden say that really there was no way to predict or prevent the chaos of this situation. Here are the exact words I heard him say: "We're going to go back in hindsight and look, but the idea that somehow, there's a way to have gotten out without chaos ensuing, I don't know how that happens." Heh, Mr. President, how about transporting *all American citizens* out of Afghanistan before you draw down troops, abandon airfields and airports. Also, we would have been most appreciative if you had not armed the Taliban with an estimated eight-five billion dollars of American military equipment! Too bad the soft-touch *left wing agenda supportive press* did not confront the president a little more directly about this travesty.

The America people are beyond angry, as well they should be. The Iranians, Chinese, Russians, North Koreans, and others are laughing hysterically. I cannot even imagine what is going through the minds of our entrapped citizens, our veterans, our active-duty military, and, for that matter, all of our allies which includes the people of Israel. This withdrawal in Afghanistan illustrates, for all of the world, the absolute incompetence and weakness of the Harris-Biden administration or whomever is running Joe and Kamala. This is not an American administration that will prevent the Iranians from developing a nuclear weapon! The left, for the most part, is strangely quiet, and when they do speak, it is from a perspective of deflection of responsibility, ignorance, or outright lies. You have watched this on television. What do you think?

I am sick with fear for American citizens who are hostages of the Taliban. May God protect them all! To our heroes who have fought and served, I say thank you, and I am sorry for how so many of you must be feeling now. I wish to thank all active-duty personnel and those who have retired. I can only imagine how you must feel at this point. My message to all American citizens is, if you know a veteran that is suffering from physical and mental wounds as a result of their service for all of us, please, reach out to them and do anything you can do for them!

Sadly, we could not get out of Afghanistan before a terrorist attack took the lives of thirteen American military personnel. Many other American military personnel were wounded. There is blood on someone's hands because these brave men and women should not have died, and those wounded will suffer for the rest of their lives. So just as countless times before, all gave some; some gave all. Rest assured, there will be more Americans who will perform their duty just as their predecessors have done their duty! Stand up, America! American military personnel stand ready to pay the price for our freedom.

I hope this chapter has been an acknowledgment of the respect that I and so many of you have for our military alive today as well as those who have passed from this earth! I realize this was a long chapter. There was much to tell.

Please, join me in Chapter 8, "Methodology for Determining Political Party Affiliation and Why Socialism Is an Illusion and a Lie." Part of this chapter will place you in an educational project that I used in my classroom for grade 11 U.S. history students. I hope you find it educational, and I hope you enjoy!

8

Methodology for Determining Political Party Affiliation and Why Socialism Is an Illusion and a Lie

What was the methodology you used for choosing the party you joined when you first registered to vote? Did your choice of party have anything to do with the party affiliation of your grandparents and your parents? My grandfather and my father both belonged to the same political party. I can tell you that while there is still in existence a party that goes by the same name as the party that both my grandfather and father supported, about the only thing that is similar is the name. During the sixty-eight years of my lifetime, the party of my grandfather has changed so much in so many ways. When you do a comparison of that party's platform from about the 1930s through perhaps the 1980s with the platform of that same party in 2020, you will find very few similarities. I have met many people who support the political party that their dad, their grandpa, and their great-grandpa supported. They proudly wear that moniker because as they say, "If it was good enough for my grandpa, it is good enough for me!" It does not matter that their grandpa's party, as far as the party platform is concerned, no longer exists. They do not even realize that. That unawareness is a shame, and that puts a democracy in profound jeopardy. Too many people vote for a party name rather than the party planks that make up the party platform. The members all too often do not know what their party stands for, and worse still, if they did, they would have little grasp of the consequences the party platform, if enacted, would have upon the country. Indeed, they have very little idea of what a party platform is or where to find the platform. Ask them what are the issues that have been assigned to the planks of the party platform and you may get a blank stare. I have to share two experiences I had in my classroom.

We were doing a project in my U.S. history class for eleventh graders. Most of my students would be registering to vote during their senior year of high school. The project, which I will present in detail later in this chapter, was designed to help students discover who they were politically based upon their views on major issues. Once the students determined the major issues of the presidential campaign, they would record their viewpoint on each issue. The students would then compare their positions to those of the party planks of each major party. While doing the comparison of their positions taken on major election issues with each of the two major party's platforms, they recorded either a D for democrat or R for republican beside each of their chosen positions. Once the comparisons were complete, the students would tally the number of Ds and Rs recorded. While doing this last step, the silence in one of my classes was abruptly ended.

Suddenly, one of my students screamed, "Oh my god, I cannot be a republican!" The young lady was actually very upset to discover that she did not agree with the party platform of her parents' party, the democrat party. I suspect that her parents might not have been well informed about their party either. I do not know if my student schooled her parents or not!

In another class, working on the same project earlier in the day, one of my students raised her hand and said, "Coach, does President Obama support allowing abortions?"

I replied, "What does it say in his party's platform?"

"It says the party supports abortion," she said rather quietly.

I then asked her another question, "Do you know the definition for a partial birth abortion?"

She did not! Another student explained it to her. I can tell you the student was horrified. She exclaimed, "I could never vote for Obama!" I never told her that I would not either.

Here were two students, and there were others, who claimed they supported a political party only to discover that they did not know what the party of their parents stood for. They were troubled by the party platform planks and realized they did not like what they had thought they would be when they registered to vote. Notice, I did not tell them what they should be; I just put them in a stimulating exercise that made them question, research, and think for themselves.

Should your children or friends read this book or books similar in nature? I think so! The PBL (project-based learning) activity that is presented later in this chapter might just teach people to recognize how important it is to be well informed with facts on issues so that they can make sound voting decisions. Perhaps more students and adults will develop the skills needed to see through the smoke screens of illusion and lure that the liberals, radical left, and power seekers are using to convince people to gravitate toward the assured self-destruction of socialism. Those who participate in the PBL activity will be free to join the party of choice and to vote as they please, but they will be armed with skills of discernment, with which I believe they will be enabled to make wise choices when they join a party and exercise their right of suffrage, voting. Voting decisions should not be made with a goal of immediate gratification that can destroy the long-term ability of a system to sustain itself into perpetuity.

There are real dangers such as a serious move toward socialism in this country, a move that threatens our America. In America, can you believe that? You and your children must not be fooled by the pie in the sky of *free everything*. There are no free lunches. Someone will pay! The problem is, we may not be able to pay our staggering trillions of debt. And our system and way of life may well collapse. I can tell you that the Chinese, Russians, and the Iranians would love that. There would no longer be a strong USA to confront the Russians' goal to control Eastern and Western Europe, the Iranians' goal to restore the caliphate in the Middle East, and the Chinese's goal to control everything else in the rest of the world. They do not want to fight the U.S. and our allies on the battlefield. Our enemies are seeking to take us down from within.

So let us look closely at this thing called socialism. Let us teach our children at home and in our schools on just how you can make good decisions as citizens. We must make better voting choices. We need to teach the skills such as the skills I will present in the PBL later in this chapter.

Do you remember *Aesop's Fables*? The story about "The goose that laid the golden eggs" comes to mind. Greed and immediate gratification killed that goose, and there was no gold for the future, and no offspring would be produced that may have also been able to lay golden eggs for future generations. The analogy is obvious, but I will state it anyway. There are forces that are rushing to destroy the very socioeconomic system that has sustained us quite well for over two hundred years. What we are witnessing today is real, not a fable, and it is being perpetrated by the lefts' greed and grab of power that is destroying our "golden goose."

One particular U.S. history class lesson plan that comes to mind was about comparing and contrasting free enterprise capitalism with socialism or communism. Two of my students remarked that socialism seemed like a good idea to them. I asked, "How so?"

One of the students replied, "Well, I think it would be nice if I did not have to worry about paying for housing. It would be nice for the government to provide that for you."

This is what we teachers call a "teachable moment." I said, "Do you think so?"

Both quickly replied, "Yes!" The two students then gave me a plethora of other pie in the sky reasons. The sad point is, they believed what they said.

These students had heard some propaganda that never presented the whole concept of the reality of life's sufferings that millions had to bear for over seventy years under a socialistic communist regime such as the former Soviet Union.

Please know I did not challenge the students with a frontal assault that implied they were ignorant of the facts. That would have been both rude and counterproductive. In fact, that is not good teaching, and you surely lose students when you practice such foolish engagements and dialogue with students. My job was to be sure they saw the big picture when they chose a philosophy for life. Since it was near the end of class, I knew this "teachable moment" required a special lesson plan that would require a large part of the next class meeting.

An associate of mine, Leon Franklin, had shared an activity he had used in his social studies classes. I thought it was brilliant, and I decided to implement the activity the next day.

The next day I announced we would be doing a special activity. My class had five rows of students. I told the row to my left that they were all "A" students and had been their entire life. I said, "You all make A's because you are smart, are motivated, and you work very hard." It helped that there were several A students in that row. The next row was designated the B students, and I gave them reasons why they achieved at that level. The center row was told they were C students. I explained that some of them could do better but chose to perform at that level, and I said that some students do the best they can do, and that is okay. The next row was designated the D students. I explained that some students just do not care to work, are not motivated, are satisfied with very little, and to be honest, some are just lazy. Some do their best, and that is okay. The last row, you guessed it, they were designated as the row that made an F. Again, I explained that some were very lazy and just did not care to work. Some may really need extra help. I explained that these designations were for illustration purposes and were part of the activity we were now ready to begin.

I introduced this activity by writing the infamous philosophy of Karl Marx on the board. "From each according to his ability, to each according to his need." This is the creed of socialism. So I then tell students that the basis of socialism is to divide resources equally among the people. There are to be no classes of upper, middle, or lower when it comes to wealth. (That is a lie. The reality is that in every socialism/communistic society, there are always the powerful who live much better than the overwhelming majority.) All of the workers share in the total production by receiving equal shares. With these statements, I was ready to engage the class.

I said, "We have a problem here. Does anyone know what it is?" No answer, either because they were shy, unsure, or simply did not know. I said, "We have a problem of inequality within our group." At that time, it was fair to say that only half of my students had cell phones. So I told the students who had phones to please raise their hands. I told them that since I was the head of the government, I already knew who had phones, and I pointed to a couple of students who did not raise their hands. I said, "You will be penalized for hiding that information from the government. Beginning tomorrow, those of you with phones must share them every seven days with those who do not have a phone. There is no other choice. You will do this." I explained that in order to control any violence or argument, as we divided resources equally, it was necessary that the government be the final say-so, and there would be no dissent. Sounds autocratic, does it not? At this point I had the students' attention.

I asked, "What do you think about this?" Several students said they would not do that because the phones belonged to them. "Oh no, they do not belong to you. There is no such thing as private property. The phones belong to the state and are to be shared equally among the people. The police or army will enforce this ruling." Many students were still wondering where this was going.

I then let the students know there was another inequity that we had to handle immediately. But before I could go on, a student said, "With whom do you share your phone?"

I replied, "With nobody. I am a high-ranking member of our single party country, and it is deemed that I need a phone at all times." There was some discussion about that, to be sure.

I pointed to the statement on the board. "From each according to his ability, to each according to his need." I explained to the A students that in order to promote equality and equal distribution of produced resources, they would have to give up their A and B scores. These resources would be given to those students in the F row so they would now have C's. The A row would now get to join the C group. Even though this was a game activity, some of these students were quick to protest that they worked hard, and they asked me what had the F group done to get this reward. I replied, "Absolutely nothing." This was really good because some of this group was already incensed by the concept that "affirmative action" was often a determining factor for acceptance to some colleges. I then told the F row that they were now getting C's. They loved that as some of them did have an F in my class. Needless to say, I had the attention of the class. I then walked over and stood in front of the B row and pointed to the D row. Both rows knew what was coming next. I announced, "B's, you must give up one grade achievement and become C's. D's, you are now equal with everyone as you have a C for a grade. D's and F's, you did not do one thing extra to earn this elevation, but at least everybody is equal in resources." Now it was time for feedback and engaging dialogue as we could now discuss the statement, "From each according to his ability, to each according to his need."

I asked the A row if this would change their behavior in any way. They were quick to point out, as did the B row, that they would not work as hard. They would no longer produce at the same high level as they had. I asked, "Why not?"

The A's said, "I work hard to get an A, and if all I can get is a C, why should I work so hard?" The Bs agreed.

The C's said, "This is not fair!"

I said, "But if resources are distributed equally, does that not mean this it is fair and best for everyone?"

The low-performing Ds and Fs of the class were extremely happy. They said they liked this deal. Makes you wonder about those people in our society who push this "ism," does it not? Now, I was ready to drive the point home and let them judge reality for themselves!

My second step of the activity required that I tell them they had to pretend we were close to the next report card for the second-grade period. I said, "All of you have to step up production because grade resources are now less plentiful." Production is down, and it must be raised.

A student said, "Why should I do that? We all get rewarded the same thing."

I explained, "If you do not all work harder, then everyone will earn a D the next nine weeks. Does anyone know why?" They thought, and I finally had to craft questions to stimulate further thought. Finally, they understood that since the A group and the B's were not working as hard anymore, there were now three grade levels of earnings less in the pot; therefore, there were less resources to divide equally. Now everyone was at the D level of resources.

In other words, economic production was down because less goods and services were being produced. I explained the centrally planned economy that the party set up still took what it needed for military research and development as well as for the military supplies needed around the world for the goal of world conquest. Whatever was left, and it was less each year, would then be divided among the society for food, clothing, housing, and medical needs.

At this point we could now dissect the statement, "From each according to his ability, to each according to his need."

This activity accurately illustrated the lower productivity levels in the Soviet Union that the communistic system yielded as time went on. The socialistic and autocratic communist regime could not compete with the free enterprise capitalism of the United States. They were failures! Too bad people like Bernie Sanders do not understand these simple issues. There are ample historical examples to prove my point. Yet Senator Bernie Sanders embraces the concept and loved communist Russia so much that he went on his honeymoon behind the iron curtain!

It was now much easier to compare and contrast free enterprise capitalism and socialism. You can be the judge of whether you think this activity had merit, but I believe it did. Research, from a creditable source, the real facts about life in a system of socialism. As I stated before, socialism has never worked any place in the world, and it will not work. Socialism has proven time and again to be the most inefficient and unfair economic system ever devised. Autocratic rule comes with this bargain, and if you think that is okay, research the "death camps" in China or the "gulags," prison camps, of the USSR.

How many people are voting members of the Democratic Party and do not know that the "radical socialist left" has taken over their party? I hope they read this chapter and reevaluate their party affiliation!

One more thing. If you want to read a great book, I recommend you read the book *Ablaze* by Piers Paul Read. The story is absolutely amazing and one of the most frightening things you will ever read. The author chronicles the Chernobyl nuclear disaster. You will realize the criminal behavior of the Soviets. The Soviets and the communists were sloppy, inept, short on money, and did not have enough moral will to provide the quality control needed during the construction phase of the nuclear power plant. The nuclear disaster and the lives lost at Chernobyl is indicative of gross negligence by a government that simply did not care about the citizens. The socialism of the Soviets could not produce the resources needed to contain the release of radioactivity that endangered millions outside the borders of the Soviet Union. The nuclear genie was indeed out of the bottle, and the communist autocracy hid the results as long as they could. Are there now and have there been many good and decent people in the countries of the former Soviet Union? I believe the answer to that is a resounding yes! They have been victimized by autocratic rule in the same ways as have countless millions of other people suffering under such rule. Many died as heroes at the Chernobyl disaster. As a young child, I say movies that depicted Soviets dying trying to escape from behind the iron curtain. When is the last time you saw citizens of our country struggle to escape from the U.S.?

Too many kids and adults are buying in to the false narrative and promise of a life where the struggle for shelter, food, and clothing is lessened or negated via redistribution of wealth of successful people. Let the more affluent pay for this they say. "Let the rich pay their fair share!" They do not want to be stressed by those real and necessary struggles of life that have challenged humanity since the dawn of time, and always will!

They think that if you take more from me, I will just work harder and harder and produce more. Wrong! The left spins this fairy tale to gain power as they seek to buy votes while giving away the money of those who have earned their money and by borrowing more and more money that we cannot afford. In short, in their quest for supreme power, they are "killing the goose" that lays the "golden eggs" of our future. Remember, when our economic system and government collapses, we have enemies that are waiting to take us over from within. Makes you wonder if we have been sold out and by whom, does it not? Ask yourself, who stands to gain if our way of life disappears from the world?

So how do you get something for nothing or even entertain such perverse thoughts? Excuse me, but is that not the very definition of stealing? I guess that you look at the big house on the hill and compare it to your smaller house. Why should that person have all of that and I have so little? Should they not share with me? Karl Marx certainly felt that way in 1875 when he popularized the phrase, "From each according to his ability, to each according to his need." Sound familiar? I hear this all the time, but they use different terminology and avenues to achieve this philosophy today.

As a teacher, I never told students what they should believe. That is not the job of the instructor. I wish there were more college and university professors who agreed with me and did not use their bully pulpit to brainwash students. For that matter, I wish that there were not a growing number of public school teachers who are guilty of that same atrocity. Do you think parents are sending their kids to schools where their children are being systematically told what they should believe as the professors paint a horrible and grotesque picture of America? Have you personally experienced or spoken with a friend who was upset by the ideological views their college children professed when they returned home during a break from college? Are our kids in public schools, colleges, and universities being told that we live in a horrible nation? Are they being denied the advantage of hearing multiple viewpoints? Some colleges and universities will not allow speakers who are right of center to address their students in a campus gathering. Are your children being indoctrinated and encouraged to support a reinstatement of historically failed policies that have been proven by history to be social failures? If you are answering truthfully, I bet you had to answer "Yes!" Parents are paying, and students are borrowing huge sums of money (loans that the government wants to forgive at the expense of taxpayers) to send kids to places of learning that all too often have an anti-American agenda.

Additionally, a "Yes" answer to the above questions is indicative of false narratives being presented to students. Students are not told the full story. Students and the public at large are all too often presented with only excerpts of the whole story. When taken out of context, these excerpts are used to cast a negative light on the overall American story of success. That is tantamount to lying for personal gain. And in this case, it is a lie to advance a weak ideology. This is wrong!

Many media platforms do this all of the time as they try to influence public opinion by hiding the facts that tell the whole story. I call this hiding of facts and presenting only the phrases that advance their narrative censorship. Such dishonest reporting is an abuse of the press. If the press is not honest, it can no longer be labeled a free press. The press has been bought and paid for due to very nefarious goals that are anti-American. I want to present an example of how censorship is being used by the democratic party's cronies. You may want to consider this and many other examples of the censorship and misleading stories of the democratic press when you choose the party, with which you wish to be affiliated! Also, question the corporations that are in bed with our foreign adversaries as the corporations and our enemies get involved in politics that are detrimental to America.

Time-out for a newsflash! I must share an example, before I go on, that you can verify. August 16, 2021, saw posts on Twitter made by the Taliban leader after the Taliban retook Afghanistan during that week. Correct me if I am wrong, but was President Donald Trump not banned from making posts on Twitter during January of 2021? An American president is banned and censored from a platform that Americans visit on a daily basis for news, but that same platform provides a venue for the evil monsters, the Taliban! Give me a break…back to the dialogue about the press and our children being ill-equipped to evaluate propaganda and misleading stories to fulfill agendas with nefarious purposes.

If you answered "Yes" to the questions above, I submit, we have not taught our children to think. Such an omission, by parents and public schools, leaves our kids ill-equipped when they walk into a classroom or listen to media sources. These students are at the mercy of being misled by demagogues simply because they do not possess the necessary discerning skills of thought and analysis. Have we taught our kids to respectfully question? We should! Rest assured, if we do not, someone or something will think for our kids. Believe me, this is happening in many liberal school systems around the country. If you do not believe me, I encourage you to do some research! Do some Google research on "Critical Race Theory." Google search the Buffalo school system's curriculum. Read about the 1619 project! Make up your own mind; you are an American, and you have that right!

Too many kids find it easier to listen rather than engage in questioning and critical thinking dialogues. Unfortunately, there are too many teachers who find it easier to lecture kids to sleep, ask students to fill out trite worksheets, memorize the answers, and then take a test on that worksheet. That is not educational, and we are dooming our kids to a lifetime of believing what they hear and accepting it for the gospel.

After all, the media or government is always right and truthful, are they not? If you answered yes to that question, then I am failing in my efforts. Schools and parents have caused this mode of educational deficiency via spoon-feeding of information in a lecture format that does not provide for engaging dialogue. Meaningful life preparedness skills of critical thinking can only happen when classroom teachers force analytical thinking and expression by presenting students with problems or questions that lead to debate over real facts. It is natural to want to trust the adult or the teacher, but I believe it is necessary to encourage thought and effort to verify. Trust but verify is a Russian proverb often quoted by President Ronald Reagan during the time he was dealing with the Soviets during the Cold War. I will also use this Russian proverb and say we must teach our kids to "Trust but verify."

I think you get the message. Do not take my word for any of these statements I have made about the indoctrination of our kids! Think for yourself. You might want to quiz your child when they come home on college break or in the evenings from public school. Socialism is good, and capitalism is greedy and bad, right? We awful Americans are responsible for destroying the planet, and we care nothing about the environment! As proof of the bill of goods that our students are being sold on just these two false charges against our country, I offer the following arguments.

Point to just one country where socialism exists or has existed and prove that socialism works to produce a better life for the people. Socialism, in order to survive, must invoke autocratic rule and all of the dark aspects of communism. Do you need a recent example? If so, please look at Venezuela! The Soviet Union, or USSR as it was also called, no longer exists. And I believe I can tell you why.

The Soviet Union was as autocratic as it gets. The people of the Soviet Union who lived well were the upper echelon of the Communist Party. The vast majority of the people lived a life of want and oppression. If you had gone shopping for food in the Soviet Union, you would have been aghast at the lack of choices, empty shelves, and the meager allotment you were allowed to procure.

Research the grain deals the Soviets bargained for with President Jimmy Carter. What facts of proof, from real events, can be submitted to prove that socialism is an efficient economic system? Or for that matter, a system that provides a good life for happy citizens? I have not seen that proof.

I have heard of numerous cases of people who finally escaped the iron curtain and actually wept when first they entered an American supermarket. I have, in fact, talked personally to a young immigrant who shared with me her utter amazement when first she came to the United States.

Workers and businesses are motivated to work hard and advance when there is an appropriate reward and profit for their labor and effort. That is the basis of free enterprise capitalism. But there was no freedom or private ownership in the Soviet Union. Typically, most people I have met are motivated to get ahead. Socialism does not motivate the production of surplus because you will not enjoy the fruit of your labor. You do not own anything. You get the dole or handout that is your share after it is all divided. The Soviets could not feed themselves. Thus, they sought to buy grain from the successful free enterprising farmers of America. The one-party rule of the communists gobbled up the largest share of resources as they built a military apparatus designed to expand their sick system around the world. With all of their vast and fertile lands, they could not feed themselves!

Research Tiananmen Square (China) and you will realize that there were many Chinese who were not happy with the Chinese Communist government. Many yearned for freedom and democracy. You will also learn what happens to dissenters in communist China. There is very little freedom in China, and the Chinese people do not dare voice a dissenting opinion. It takes very little effort and only a short study of facts and history to find support for my argument. But some will argue success in the case of China because they have a huge economy.

Yes, they do! And that is due, in no small part, to the fact that American companies fled to China because of the high rate for corporate taxes and regulations in the USA. Supposedly, the Biden administration is getting ready to raise corporate tax rates. Big money goes where it can make bigger money, and we will see businesses moving or staying overseas. China has benefitted from the trade policies that favor their economy. These same policies and trade deals have put our companies at a disadvantage. The autocratic rule of the Chinese Communist Party demands much slave labor and enjoys a competitive advantage because they have fewer of the restrictions of operation that American industry often suffers needlessly.

A classic example is the little discussed fact that the Chinese are building coal-fired electric generation plants right and left. I wonder if the exhaust of American factories is cleaner than those in China?[26]

Do you not find it curious that China does not have to abide by the same Paris Climate Agreement edicts as the United States regarding air pollution at this time? And since China does not operate under the same restrictions as the U.S. does today, is there anyone who really believes the Chinese Communists ever will?[27]

China is building 184 coal fired plants as of 2020. And China is sending workers to build coal-fired plants in other countries such as Vietnam, Turkey, Indonesia, Bangladesh, Egypt, and the Philippines.

---

[26] https://www.npr.org/2019/04/29/716347646/why-is-china-placing-a-global-bet-on-coal.

[27] https://greengarageblog.org/20-advantages-and-disadvantages-of-the-paris-agreement.

Sources suggest that all in all, China may now be building, or in the stages of building, approximately three hundred coal-fired plants around the world. Could this move be under the guise of spreading Chinese Communist tentacles around the world's poorer regions and thus gaining more control over countries and forcing them to be more dependent upon the Chinese? Some say China, as the worst polluter in the world, has done some house cleaning of their environment in China. They needed to do just that! Google the smog of China over the past years and you will see why.

So why is China building coal-fired electrical generating plants around the world while the *left* and Biden are touting the "Green New Deal" and have rejoined the Paris Climate Agreement, an agreement that cripples the U.S. economy and puts us at a competitive disadvantage with China? Will the Chinese be into developing and exporting green energy? I believe we have offered some plausible reasons to explain both China's and Biden's actions. Excuse me, but do the prevailing winds of pollution not travel around the planet? As you evaluate my statements that I present as facts, do not take my word. I encourage you to do some research and decide for yourself which viewpoint has validity. Do you want to trade a system that has worked well and is founded in the reality of life's natural law?

Since my job did not include telling students what they should believe or what political party to join, you may be wondering what I believed my job actually was. My job was to put students in a position to question, research for creditable facts, analyze, make decisions, and come to conclusions that they could defend and live with as they defined who they were. I will say, that for those students who learned how to analyze facts and draw logical conclusions, I was often gratified to see them make sound decisions. The decisions belonged to the students. I never asked the young lady what party she joined when she registered to vote her senior year. It was not my business; it was hers. I will say I do not believe the other young lady ever voted for President Obama when he ran for reelection.

Are you still with the same party you joined when you first registered to vote? I am not! I have now had three different registration cards. Can you guess my political affiliations over my lifetime? A hint for the first party would be that I grew up in the deep south of West Virginia near the unionized coal fields. In fact, I was, for a few days, a union coal miner. My father and both of my grandfathers worked in the coal mines of West Virginia. At about the age of thirty-six, I had my own insurance business in North Carolina. Can you guess the party I changed to at that time? When I turned fifty, I found I was once again disillusioned with a party. So when I sold my business and moved home to West Virginia to resume a teaching and coaching career, I registered for a third time. You have enough clues. Perhaps I will give you the answer on the last page of this book.

Earlier in this book, I made a statement that needs to be repeated. Parents, teach your children to question rather than to blindly accept statements that may be designed to mislead them or to get them to join. Teach them how to look for the red flags. Show them how to find facts and how to analyze those facts. Put them in situations where they have a problem they must solve and then let them struggle to reach a decision. Demand they support their decision or conclusion with facts. Teach them to think for themselves. In my opinion, I believe that type of activity is educational, and it is a skill students can rely upon for a lifetime.

Educational fads come and go, and teachers either get sick of them or they embrace the new instructional initiative. Perhaps you have heard of project-based learning, or sometimes it is called problem-based learning (PBL). It is an excellent instructional initiative that forces higher level thinking and develops skills needed for the lifelong learner. I have given you some insight into this type of teaching and learning. What I want to do, at this time, is to invite you to participate in a PBL exercise I used in my U.S. history classes. This particular PBL put my students on a path to determine who they were politically and to reach a decision on which party they might want to join when they registered to vote their senior year. Who knows, you might change your political party affiliation or assist your child in determining theirs, if you dare. Given the dangerous issues and concepts that I have outlined thus far in this chapter, I feel you can now appreciate the importance of teaching the following skills to our students.

Choosing Your Political Party

A Problem-Based Learning Project
2020 Presidential Election
Designed by Stan Duncan
West Virginia's 2008 History Teacher of the Year

Step 1. Write the name of the political party you intend to join or have joined.

Step 2. Write a statement that explains why you chose that party.

Step 3. Assume it is October of 2020. For whom will you vote for president of the United States?

Step 4. List the major issues of the 2020 presidential election!

Issue 1

Prevent illegal immigration with a secure border wall or open the border for all who want to come to the U.S.

State your position on issue 1.

Issue 2

The U.S. should rejoin the Paris Climate Agreement or remain separated from the group.

State your position on issue 2.

Issue 3

The U.S. should allow offshore drilling and fracking or suspend these two methods of energy acquisition.

State your position on issue 3.

Issue 4

Add the District of Columbia and Puerto Rico as the fifty-first and fifty-second states or keep the number of states at fifty.

State your position on issue 4.

Issue 5

The U.S. should increase the number of justices on the Supreme Court of the United States (packing the court) or keep the number at nine justices.

State your position on issue 5.

Issue 6

Remove sanctions on Iran and negotiate nuclear deal or keep sanctions on Iran to prevent them from having a nuclear weapon.

State your position on issue 6.

Issue 7

Bring an end to sanctuary cities or allow cities to declare that they are sanctuary cities.

State your position on issue 7.

Issue 8

Raise corporate and personal income tax rates or keep corporate tax rates and personal income tax rates the same.

State your position on issue 8.

Issue 9

Retain tariffs on Chinese imports while taking a hard-line position on Chinese expansion or remove tariffs on China and improve relations by taking a softer approach on Chinese foreign policies.

State your position on issue 9.

Issue 10

Defend Americans' right to keep and bear arms (Second Amendment rights) or ban all assault weapons and other semiautomatic rifles.

State your position on issue 10.

Issue 11

Pro-life anti-abortion and oppose tax payer-funded abortions or pro-choice belief that it is the woman's right to choose to have an abortion and that it should be government-funded.

State your position on issue 11.

Issue 12

We must restore the full protections of the Voting Rights Act. We will bring our democracy into the twenty-first century by expanding early voting and vote-by-mail, implementing universal automatic voter registration and same-day voter registration, ending partisan and racial gerrymandering, and making Election Day a national holiday. We will restore voting rights for those who have served their sentences. And we will continue to fight against discriminatory voter identification laws, which disproportionately burden young voters, diverse communities, people of color, low-income families, people with disabilities, the elderly, and women. Or voter identification verification for U.S. citizens where they reside on Election Day, stop ballot harvesting, stop mass mailing of ballots, bipartisan viewing of vote counting, and adherence to state election laws as required by the U.S. and state constitutions.

State your position on issue 12.

Issue 13

All Americans should get a tuition-free college education as well as forgiveness of any college debt they have or if you charged your college costs that is your responsibility and you will have to forgo luxuries and pay your own debt rather than go begging hardworking American taxpayers.

State your position on issue 13.

Step 5. Google the following URL to view the 2016 GOP platform details. Note the 2016 platform was used for 2020 as well. Copy and paste the platform onto a document or toggle back and forth (https://ballotpedia.org/The_Republican_Platform_and_ RNC_Platform_Committee,_2016)

Step 6. Google the following URL to view the 2020 Democrat Party platform details. Copy and paste the platform onto a document or toggle back and forth (https://ballotpedia.org/ The_Democratic_Party_Platform%2C_2020).

Step 7. Review the position you took on each of the thirteen issues of step 4. Compare the position you took on each of the thirteen issues with both the Republican (GOP) Party platform (step 5) and the Democratic Party platform (step 5). Once you determine which party platform is representative of your position, mark your selected position in step 4 with an *R* for republican or a *D* for democrat.

Step 8. Tally the number of Rs recorded and write the total down. Tally the number of Ds recorded and write the total down. You may want to prioritize the issues 1–13, with 1 being the top priority for you down through 13 which is of the least importance to you. That will help you decide the most important issues and will help you make a more clear choice of party affiliation.

Step 9. Based upon my analysis and survey of my positions, I wish to register to vote with the _____ party.

Step 10. Write a statement that informs me whether your party selection in step 9 is the same or different from your selection made in step 1 at the beginning of this PBL (project-based learning) activity. Please explain why and offer a statement about what you have learned.

Step 11. Based upon my study and analysis, I wish to vote on November 3, 2020, for _____ to become the president of the United States on January 20, 2021.

Step 12. Write a statement that explains if your selection for president in step 11 is the same as it was when you started this PBL activity in step 3 or if it is different. Please explain why and offer a statement about what you have learned.

Please note that this format can be modified and used for many different important decisions that need to be made. I truly believe this project is educational and helps students learn how important it is to gather reliable facts, do careful analysis, and then make informed decisions that are defensible. Every student in high school should learn these lifetime learner skills in order to be better prepared for life's challenges. Did this project make you think?

I must say that I enjoyed this PBL activity that I developed for my classes. Remember, this activity is very adaptable and can be used in a multitude of learning circumstances or problem-solving scenarios. Perhaps you can use this activity as you read the next chapter.

The next chapter is titled, "Why Must a Nation of Immigrants Close the Borders?" Here is the simple guiding question for you to use in the next chapter. Should the southern border of the United States be closed and regulated as it was under the administration of President Donald J. Trump, or should we have an open border with no regulations as we now have under the Biden-Harris administration? Please continue to read!

9

Why Must a Nation of Immigrants Close the Borders?

Open a discussion about closing any border of the United States and the liberals and their media will immediately scream that to close borders goes against everything that this nation was founded upon. They loudly proclaim, "We are a nation of immigrants!" People who take the position that our borders must be secured are proclaimed to be racists. Even louder are the voices screaming that we must take in these increasing numbers of illegals because they are poor and desperate people. To base any decision upon purely idealistic reasons while not taking into consideration reality is both foolish and a step toward disaster. This is especially true when it comes to the open-border invasion of illegals into this country that the left is pushing.

In fact, Biden has verbally encouraged the illegal wave of immigration that this nation is suffering through in 2021. I predict that this invasion across our southern border will be the worst and the largest in the history of illegal invasions of our southern border! There is data to support the assertion that 2021 will be a record year for illegals entering our country.

During the first Democratic debate, regarding questions about immigration policies of the Obama and Biden administration, Joe Biden said,

What I would do as president is several more things, because things have changed. I would, in fact, make sure that we immediately surge to the border all of those people seeking asylum because that is who we are, we are a nation that says if you want to flee and you are fleeing oppression you should come.

So what did President Biden do to aid this surge on our border by illegals from all over the world that is responsible for the crisis at our southern border?

Biden made sure there was a surge when he ended the "Stay in Mexico Policy" which was an executive decision by President Trump. By the way, it was working! Biden-Harris also terminated much of the deportations by reinstating the insane Obama-Biden catch and release of illegals who promised they would report to a hearing sometime in the future. Please, you cannot make this stuff up, can you? Biden has gone one step further in that his administration is busing these illegals, many of whom are positive for COVID and the Delta variant, into the interior of our country. COVID positive illegals are entering our country by the thousands while the Biden administration is now pushing vaccine mandates. I took the vaccine and will take the booster when I have the opportunity. That was my choice based upon my assessment of relative risk for taking the vaccine versus the relative risk for not taking the vaccine! I must respect the right of those people who do not want to take this vaccine. People are now being fired because they refuse to take the vaccine! Consider all the medical caregivers and first responders who battled COVID-19 before the vaccine was available. These people put their lives on the line, and there were deaths. Does it make sense to you that people who do not accept this vaccine mandate and refuse to be vaccinated are now being fired? Medical caregivers, men and women in our military, first responders, police, and all Americans have rights. We do not have enough medical personnel! He stopped construction of the border wall!

The White House has a fence, and I agree that it should. Should the American citizens living on our border have the protection of a fence as well? A fence that would protect all of America, I think so, but what do you think?

Because of these actions and policies of the Biden-Harris administration, the illegals have poured into the country. The have come to the tune of hundreds of thousands that we know of and hundreds of thousands that have not been detected crossing our borders. All undocumented aliens are illegals, and they are in violation of existing federal immigration laws of the United States. Legal immigrants must go through a formal process in order to gain admission into our country. When immigrants do not go through the established legal process for seeking admission to the United States, they are breaking our laws, and they become illegal aliens.

All sovereign nations must satisfy a "who and why scenario" for the people they allow to come into their country. Failure to regulate immigration prevents the government from being able to provide for the common defense of its citizenry. Read about how immigration into the Roman Empire was one of the causes for the fall of that empire!

Additionally, allowing masses of people to enter our country will overburden our ability to provide services for American citizens. This massive influx of illegals will surely cause an eventual collapse of the system. Is that what the Marxists want? If that is not their plan, would someone tell them they are causing great harm to this nation and the nation's ability to persevere? And ask them why they are willing to cause such great harm to "We the people." We simply cannot take in all of the poor of the world. I have said it before and I will say it again: The best chance for the world is best served by a strong and free United States of America participating on the world stage!

I have always thought that a president's and vice president's oath of office required them to uphold the laws of the United States and to follow the dictates of our constitution. Am I wrong?

The preamble to the United States Constitution sets forth a clear expectation about the purpose of our government. Our constitution dictates how our government is supposed to operate. We the people spoke in the late 1700s. We the people have spoken many times since as we have fought to maintain this organization of government. Please read the preamble once again. It seems clear to me!

> We the People of the United States, in Order to form a more perfect Union, establish Justice, insure domestic Tranquility, provide for the common defense, promote the general Welfare, and secure the Blessings of Liberty to ourselves and our Posterity, do ordain and establish this Constitution for the United States of America.

Turn to Article II, Section I, Clause 8 of the U.S. Constitution and you will find the presidential oath of office that all presidents swear to on their inauguration day.

> I do solemnly swear (or affirm) that I will faithfully execute the office of President of the United States, and will to the best of my ability, preserve, protect and defend the Constitution *of the United States.*

Please do a search for 42 U.S. Code Section 265 regarding protecting American citizens from the introduction of contagious diseases from abroad. Diseases that may be introduced into the U.S. by either persons, foods, or organisms entering our country from abroad. All of us remember the mandates imposed on we Americans during the COVID-19 pandemic. The *restrictions* and the *businesses shuttered* in our country greatly impacted our daily life, livelihood, and our economy at large. Do you know that thousands upon thousands of illegals (undocumented individuals who have not gone through a legally required formal application process to be admitted to this country) have been entering the U.S. and have been shipped throughout our country and onto welfare rolls? Do you realize that many of these illegals were and are positive carriers of the corona virus? This spread of the virus by illegals has occurred and is still happening! This viral spreading by illegals is being allowed even after all of the drastic life-changing mandates the American people have adhered to during the pandemic. Why would any sane government allow this? And there are even more dangerous occurrences at the border that threaten "We the People."

Fentanyl and narcotics are pouring across our borders at an alarming rate. In fact, the overwhelming amount of fentanyl and heroin entering this country is coming across our southern border. By the way, fentanyl is being funneled to the drug cartels from China. Cartel "mules" are spreading across our country to expand the distribution network of drugs. Terrorists from countries that hate us are crossing the border undetected because our border agents are busy handling the large numbers of illegals, who are surrendering, once across the border. Our agents must then aid these illegals to be put up in hotels, in many cases, all at U.S. taxpayer expense! MS-13 gangs are spreading throughout our cities, and they are predators and murders. Americans are dying from overdoses each and every day. In fact, eighty-one thousand Americans died from overdose in twelve months. That is the largest number ever recorded.

The questions that beg for plausible common-sense answers from the Biden administration are both simple and blunt. Why was the border wall construction, much of which was already paid and contracted for, halted in January of 2021? Why was our southern border opened in January of 2021 to the onslaught of hundreds of thousands of illegals coming into our country from all over the world? Can you think of any plausible common-sense answers to these questions that point to a concern for the long-term good for America? I cannot!

Please remember, the preamble of the U.S. Constitution says such things as "insure domestic Tranquility, provide for the common defense, and promote the general Welfare." Ask the U.S. citizens who reside on our southern border if they are experiencing domestic tranquility and ask them if they think the federal government is showing concern for their general welfare.

We all know that before and since 09-11-2001, our country has been, and continues still, to be infiltrated by sleeper cells of terrorists who will be awakened when the call to do harm to America is raised by the Jihadists. Terrorists are coming across our southern border! Do you feel that the federal government's actions on the U.S. Mexican border is providing for the common defense of America? Additionally, we need to remember something else!

> I do solemnly swear (or affirm) that I will faithfully execute the office of President of the United States, and will to the best of my ability, *preserve, protect and defend the Constitution **of the United States**.*

All presidents have sworn to *preserve, protect and defend the Constitution **of the United States**.* The preamble to the U.S. Constitution is the thesis of the constitution. All that follows the thesis is an attempt to form a "more perfect union" replete with structure and methodology for governance. The president swears to preserve, protect, and defend the constitution in its entirety. This oath mandates that the laws passed by the legislative branch and signed into law by the executive branch, as per the dictates of the constitution, must also be enforced. It is unlawful to pick and choose which laws you do not want to enforce. It is especially unlawful if such a choice is made because of some nefarious political motivation. This applies to the federal immigration laws that have become code to regulate immigration into the United States of America!

I ask you, is enforcement of our laws on immigration taking place in 2021? You will have to decide for yourself. There are U.S. immigration laws that you can research. The surge of detected and undetected illegals at our southern border raises many questions that we should all be asking!

Why do you think the left is really pushing this agenda? What is the cause and effect of this radical agenda? Who in the world could possibly be supporting open borders for the United States and why? What are the socioeconomic problems that are being forced upon this nation by this invasion on our southern border? Are all of these illegal aliens poor, innocent immigrants? Did you know that illegals from countries all over the world are slipping through our southern border that the Biden administration has opened? Are we more susceptible to gang violence, the ongoing proliferation of drugs, and, yes, terrorist attacks as a result of the open border policy of the Biden-Harris administration? How do we pay for this increased economic burden? How do our low-performing public schools address the added challenges of hundreds of thousands of children who are uneducated and cannot speak English? These are the serious questions that all of the media should be asking of the Biden-Harris administration. Do not hold your breath for such questioning. The Biden-Harris administration has a pass when it comes to tough questioning. They have a "get out of jail free card!"

This disaster and crisis on our southern border is a direct result of the policies that were instituted by Biden in January of 2021. The crisis has continued to worsen, and there is no end in sight. The crisis on our southern border is a far greater travesty than the situation that would have been experienced by these illegals had they stayed in their native land. Joe Biden created this humanitarian crisis when he encouraged this mass immigration. The American people would like to hear plausible and common-sense answers to the questions I have asked, but concerned Americans will never get meaningful answers because there are no common-sense answers to explain this federal government-induced debacle. Biden's debacle will have a lasting negative impact upon our country far into the future. And may I add, does anyone think that law-abiding American citizens should give up their Second Amendment rights in the face of thousands and thousands of criminals, from all over the world, crossing into our country? I hope you will consider my questions that I posed above as you read what follows. But first we should debunk the self-righteous proclamations of the left.

Let's debunk the myth being put forth by the left and their media puppets. I am being kind by using the word *myth* rather than the three-letter word that you may substitute for *myth*. The radical left is telling Americans that they are rushing to help these poor suffering people from Honduras, Guatemala, El Salvador, Mexico, and any other poor nation that has a population looking to America for economic salvation.

One thing they are not divulging is the fact that people from countries all over the world are slipping across our border. These people are coming into our country from countries that do not like us! In fact, we Americans are being told that it is our duty to absorb these poor people into our country. We are, after all, a nation of immigrants, and to not admit these people would be against every value upon which America stands. It is our duty! The power brokers behind this myth tell us how much they care for these unfortunate people. They use the media to denounce those of us who ask questions and insist upon merit-based immigration. They categorize us as uncaring racists and people who do not care about suffering children. How convenient their argument is and how two-faced can you be? The sanctimonious statements made by the left about how much they care about the hundreds of thousands of immigrants crossing our border is a clever way to cloak their real motivations: for an open southern border.

So it seems we are being lied to. Additionally, there is another story taking place, as of mid-July 2021, that further illustrates the hypocrisy of the left.

My good friend, Austin, and I have had yet another interesting conversation. He asked me why it is that truly oppressed Cubans, who have suffered since the late 1950s under totalitarian communist rule, are not being welcomed to the United States, as are the millions of illegals crossing our southern border? And why is it that BLM supports the communist regime in Cuba instead of the thousands of Cubans taking to the streets seeking political and economic freedom from over sixty years of autocratic rule and the failed socialism of communist rule? These were two very good questions that generated a great discussion that pointed out, yet again, the sheer hypocrisy of the left and the Biden administration. I assure you that Austin knew the answers to the questions before he asked me! Please pause for a minute and answer the questions before you read on. It is this type of questioning that I might have posed to my students in order to engage them in some higher-level critical thinking.

So what say you? If my students did not make much progress answering the questions, I might have asked, "How do Cuban Americans, in Florida, typically vote?" And the answer is, republican, is it not? Why might any new Cuban refugees coming to Florida also vote republican? Could it be that they would easily recognize the socialism being pushed by the democrats and due to the suffering of Cubans for decades under socialism and communism they would run as fast as they could to register republican once they gained citizenship! What does BLM's decision to support the regime in Cuba say about who they really are, and just as important, who is backing them? Let me give you a moment to ponder these questions. I bet you know the answers! I will return to this subject in the next paragraph.

Here is another question, surprise! Why is it okay for BLM and other groups to protest in the streets of the United States, a right they clearly have as long as it is peaceful, but not okay for Cubans to protest? BLM must support socialism and communism, do they not? Their support for the Cuban regime tells me all that I need to know! Cubans in America hate socialism and the autocratic rule of communism. Obviously, Cubans in Cuba hate socialism and the autocratic rule of communism. Any Cuban refugee who might come to Florida is not ever going to vote for the democratic candidates who clearly are supporting socialism. The Cuban people know firsthand that socialism is, and has always been, a failure. They will have none of that! As always, you decide, but does this story not smell of socialism and hypocrisy? Would it not fit the agenda of the radical left to assure that Florida does not become an even stronger "red state"?

The position of the radical left power brokers' proclamation about how much they care and the humanitarian efforts they clothe themselves in is a myth. I will go ahead and say what you may be thinking: It is a lie and is straight from the methodology of Saul Alinsky. The truth of the matter is that this ruse being perpetrated upon the American taxpayer is, in fact, a well-designed move to change the demographics of this country. The left wants a demographic change that will be more likely to produce enough liberal democratic voters to keep the radical left in power into perpetuity.

Why do you think so many of the illegal aliens are being bused throughout Texas, Tennessee, and into Virginia? Could it be a well-designed plan to further tip these states to the left and change them to solid blue rather than the color of red and conservatism? Go count the electoral votes of these three states and see how quickly they would aid the current solid blue states to reach the required two hundred seventy electoral votes needed to elect a "left wing" president on the democratic ticket. New York, California, and Illinois are locks when it comes to electoral votes for the liberal blue count needed to reach two hundred seventy electoral votes. If the liberal left were to read this, they would shout me down and tell the world that I am a racist. "We care about helping these poor people," they would yell. I submit that they are disciples of Saul Alinsky's modus operandi.

My rebuttal would be a very loud, "No, you do not care!" You care about gaining power for the radical left and the agenda of the radical left. And in order to do that, you need to buy constituents. You are buying the loyalty of these poor people with taxpayer dollars of hardworking Americans. In fact, you are borrowing bribe money in the names of our children, our grandchildren, and the unborn.

If you really cared about these people, you would not encourage them to come here via the route they are forced to travel. More importantly, if you cared about the American people, you would not encourage illegals to come here, period. You do not care about their welfare. These people are subjected to the coyotes and drug cartels that use these people and charge them huge fees. Unaccompanied children coming to this country from central America are abused. Have you seen the video of infants dropped over the wall into the U.S.? Rape and sex trafficking goes unchecked. June of 2021 news claims that there are children detained on the southern border that are on "suicide watch!" What does that tell you about their harrowing experience? And these kids will be shipped out to various states?

Think about the criminal element that this administration is enriching with the open-door policy on our southern border. The drug cartels now control our southern border, and they are shipping "drug mules" into the U.S. on a daily basis. Yet the Biden administration insists that there is no crisis at the border! Are you kidding me?

The vice president waited ninety-three days after being appointed "border czar" before going to the southern border to view this crisis. Even then, Harris went to El Paso and not to the Rio Grande Valley, the epicenter of the illegal's surge. She did not get within hundreds of miles of the hot spot of illegal intrusion into our country. Why not, you might ask? Could it be that the administration could not continue to insist that there is no crisis if the VP actually traveled to the Rio Grande Valley? It would not play well for the VP or the president to appear on camera near the overcrowded and chaotic mess that exists at the epicenter of this crisis on the border. Heaven forbids that an American citizen in one of these border states came face-to-face with the VP or the president and asked, "Why are you doing this to our country?"

The VP then had the audacity to say that we have to consider the cause and effect of this immigration. The cause she claimed was the oppression and life's circumstances in Central America. Wrong. The cause for this surge of illegals is the policies of the Harris-Biden administration! The effect is chaos and putting America into an even greater financial crisis and at a greater risk for crime and terrorism. Have you ever been around people who refuse to look at or accept responsibility for the mess they have created?

We are, indeed, a nation of immigrants! We are a great "melting pot" of a mixture of all races, ethnic groups, creeds, and cultures that have made us a very diverse nation. But to utter the statement "we are a nation of immigrants" as an excuse for open borders and unlimited immigration makes no sense. Since there is no rhyme or reason for such a nonsensical statement, we must point out both the fallacy and motive of this statement.

There is a huge difference in the immigration invasion coming across our southern border today and the immigration waves in the early 1800s and subsequently in the third wave of immigration that came through Ellis Island in 1881 to 1920. Yes, this nation has been built as a result of and during massive waves of immigration.

When the European immigration to our Atlantic shores spilled westward, there were three thousand miles of wilderness to be settled before the Pacific Ocean was reached. In case you have not noticed, that three thousand miles of wilderness has been settled since the 1890s. This rush to complete our self-proclaimed "manifest destiny" resulted in great success but was also a great tragedy for the American Indians. I would be remiss if I did digress here and make the following statement.

There was a great negative impact, as a result of the migration of these pioneering Americans, in all waves of immigration. This "manifest destiny" of settling the continent from the American east coast to the west coast of America resulted in the sad displacement of the first migrants to this land, the Native Americans, who themselves migrated here from Asia. The stone-age culture of North American Indians fell victim to a more technologically advanced culture. These two very different cultures clashed over conflicting views about land utilization and land ownership. The impact of these differences led to the tragic conflict that ended a proud way of life. My motivation for discussing this tragedy is based upon sadness that this cultural clash followed the path that it did. And it is important to note this event of American History!

I have never lived the life of the American natives, and few people have. According to my family ancestry, I have been told that I have Indian blood coursing through my veins. If that is true, it is a very small amount, but unlike Elizabeth Warren, I have never tried to benefit myself with a claim that I am of American Indian descent. Guys, I just had to say that! It seems to me that such a false claim by Senator Warren is disrespectful to a group of people who have been subjected to far too much tragedy.

At the same time as the west was being settled by Americans, many of whom were recent immigrants who became U.S. citizens, the U.S. entered the era of industrialization. Factory workers, miners, steel workers, many other tradesmen, and laborers were needed, and they flocked to our shores. They came with hope and a desire to improve their way of life. They learned our English language, embraced our founders' ideals, swore allegiance to the United States of America, and were willing to die in defense of the goodness of their adopted country. They entered this country legally. They came in spite of the fact that there was no welfare line for them to crash. There was no Motel 6 waiting for them at the end of their journey, and certainly nobody was going to pay to take care of them!

Immigration circumstances up to the 1920s were far different from the circumstances of today. Today, immigration must be based upon merit. We are no longer a rural economy where 90 percent of the people can provide for their basic needs by cultivating the land. We are in debt way over our head. In fact, the continued viability of our financial stability is in deep jeopardy. If we can afford added immigration, it must be carefully scrutinized in order to provide for the common defense of our nation and people. Contrary to current practice and the common thought of far too many, we cannot just print money to pay for whatever everyone wants. Allowing massive immigration of illegals is counterproductive to the well-being of "We the American People" and the financial viability of the United States of America. Where is our protection?

We have immigration laws on the books, do we not? Therefore, when you take actions that have encouraged this massive illegal invasion, you are in fact encouraging foreigners to break American law. How is encouraging illegal invasion of our country not a violation of sworn duty to uphold the United States Constitution? Allowing hundreds of thousands and millions of illegals to enter our country, in violation of our laws, is a slap in the face to all legal immigrants and to those waiting in line to come here legally. How can you come here and have any standing for citizenship when your very first act of stepping onto our soil is an act of breaking our law? I do not know about you, but that illegal act does not place illegals in good standing with me when it comes to accepting them as law-abiding citizens!

Many of the poor people crossing our border are being horribly used, and others are coming here to use us in the most criminal of ways. How can you become a productive American citizen if you do not respect the concept of our citizenship? Citizens are expected to obey laws, and if they do not, there are supposed to be consequences of punishment. If we allow laws to be broken without punishment consequences, then we do not have a country. If you want to come to this country and you show such initial disrespect, then I have no faith that you will respect other duties expected of our citizens.

So what are the real motivating factors for coming illegally to the United States. Many of these people believe that the government of the United States is welcoming them. That is a cruel hoax with very nefarious motivations. It is also polarizing our nation and causing great divisions among our citizenry.

I acknowledge that the unaccompanied minors would not understand these concepts and nor should they. Yet those who sent *unaccompanied children* north and those U.S. government officials responsible for encouraging them to come do not get a pass from me. Their actions exhibit gross irresponsibility because they have subjected those children to much terror during their journey north.

States' Rights versus the Federal Government's Violations of Federal Immigration Laws

What happens when the federal government and the president of the United States refuses to enforce the established written federal laws on immigration? Supposedly, the American Civil War, 1861–1865, settled the question of the supremacy of federal power to enforce federal laws upon seceding southern states. Those southern states made claims that states' rights trumped federal laws on such issues as the expansion of slavery westward, protective tariffs, and the abolition of slavery. These issues divided the nation as the southern states claimed states' rights and the northern states claimed that federal law was supreme as per the dictates of the constitution.

The Confederate States seceded (left) from the Union, seized federal installations, and they fired upon a United States fort, Fort Sumter, in 1861. The North/federal government refused to allow rebellious secession from the Union and set about conquering the rebel states. After four long and bloody years, the North's Union forces defeated the Confederacy, thus solidifying the recognition of the federal government's supremacy. You can rehash that debate, but that is a story for another time.

Without question, the founding fathers wrote into the constitution's bill of rights, powers specifically reserved to the states. "The powers not delegated to the United States by the Constitution, nor prohibited by it to the States, are reserved to the States respectively, or to the people." See the Tenth Amendment to the U.S. Constitution.

Our constitution established a federal system of government. Simply put, that means that powers are divided between the central or federal government and the respective states of the United States.

Article VI, paragraph 2 of the United States Constitution presents what has been recognized as the "supremacy clause" of our constitution. Generally, this means that the federal constitution and federal laws reign supreme over state laws and state constitutions. Again, I ask, what happens when the federal government refuses to enforce the established written federal laws on immigration?

Whoa, hold the phone, the horses, or whatever you can latch onto in order to make sense of this mess I have just written. Everything I have stated is true and is well documented!

Please consider the title of this section, "States' Rights versus the Federal Government's Violations of Federal Immigration Laws," as you read about the call to action issued by various governors. Do states' rights for existence and preservation include and require states to protect themselves from an invasion when the federal government abrogates its duty to provide for the common defense, insure domestic tranquility, and promote the general welfare? Never, in my life, did I think I would ask such a necessary and ridiculous question!

Texas governor Greg Abbott issued a statement on June 11, 2021, that Texas would build the border wall that President Donald Trump started and President Joe Biden stopped. Why? Governor Abbott swore an oath when he took office to represent the people of Texas. His state is in chaos due to Biden's refusal to enforce federal immigration laws that would serve to protect the people of Texas, Arizona, New Mexico, as well as the rest of the country.

Then three days later the governor of Arizona, Doug Ducey, joined Governor Abbott in a request for help from other states to help in securing the southern border amidst all of the chaos that has resulted since the Biden administration took over in January 2021.

Florida governor Ron Desantis has pledged to send help and join Texas, New Mexico, and Arizona to do a job that Biden and the federal government is refusing to do. Namely, these states are trying to protect the U.S. citizens who live in the border states and subsequently the entire country. Not only has the Biden-Harris administration created a crisis on our southern border for illegals, drugs, gangs, and terrorists entering our country, they have created a constitutional crisis as well.

States are feeling compelled to take actions in defense of their state and the country as well. The federal government is supposed to do that job, but the Biden-Harris administration is failing to perform their constitutional duty! Will the federal government go to court to prevent the states from doing the job that the federal government is supposed to do but refuses to do? The irony of this situation makes my head spin; at the same time, it scares the "hell out of me!" Clearly, individual states care more about the preservation of this nation than does the federal government and the Biden-Harris administration.

The American people are by far the most generous and giving people on the planet. America and American capitalism, has provided trillions in foreign aid around the world to ease suffering, rebuild nations, and provide defense from aggressor nations. Our charitable gifts and humanitarian aid are unparalleled in the world. Do not accuse those of us with conservative values as being selfish when we insist on closed borders and merit-based immigration. The giver has a right to say when and how much they will give. We have given plenty! Enough is enough, and an "America First Agenda" is necessary to preserve America for Americans! Then, and only then, will we be able to help when we can.

In 2009 when the Obama-Biden administration took office, the U.S. National Debt was ten trillion dollars. When Obama left office in 2017, the debt was 19.5 trillion when President Trump took office. President Trump rebuilt our military to a position of second to none and eliminated the caliphate of terrorism in the Middle East. (That was two things that the Obama-Biden administration refused to do or take on as responsibilities.) Then in March of 2020, this nation began to assume tremendous debt as a result of the unprecedented corona virus shutdown of the nation. By September 30, 2020, the debt was twenty-seven trillion. As of March 2021, the debt had risen to twenty-eight trillion. Who knows what the debt will be by the end of 2021?

While businesses are begging for workers, Biden continues to borrow money we cannot afford in order to send out checks for people to stay at home. Is it not ironic that American businesses are forced to compete for workers with a federal government that is paying people to stay home long after the pandemic crisis is passing? When Biden was questioned about this, his reply was a sarcastic, "Pay them more!"

There is this thing called interest you must pay on money you borrow. Do you realize that the interest on the public debt of the federal government is 378 billion dollars per year? The federal government collects about 3.8 trillion dollars from all sources of tax collections. From that total, the government is paying one trillion per year into Social Security, three hundred eight billion into Medicare, and forty-three billion into unemployment insurance. Since our deficit spending is way out of control, our debt will increase.

What happens when interest rates go up? What will it cost to pay the interest on the national public debt, a debt that continues to rise due to deficit spending? Someone in Washington needs to do the math! Raise interest rates by only 1 percent on twenty-eight trillion in debt and see how much more it costs annually just to service the debt! Please, do not use new math calculations. Use the old-fashioned math that will help you to add and subtract with ease. You know the kind of math that I am talking about; it is the kind that adds up to the fact that you cannot spend more than you take in. That is something I learned in my household, but the federal government, unlike my state and many other states, is ignorant of Accounting 101!

We are not even talking about paying down the debt, are we? Does it sound to you like this nation can afford to continue paying foreign aid that gets into the hands of corrupt officials in countries all over the world? Can we afford to take in millions of illegals that we will have to add to public assistance? Our country has far too many people on the "dole" now. The last thing our national debt and our taxpayers need is millions more on the federal and state dole! You tell me! Can you hear the "fire bell in the night?"

10

American Education, Back Then versus Today

Without a doubt, the most difficult task you will ever undertake is that of being a good parent. In my sixty-eight years on this earth, I have never found any job to be as difficult and filled with the level of uncertainty of what is the best thing to do as is the job of parenting. But I must say, being a teacher runs such a close second, in today's America, that there is but a whisker of a difference. Teachers are having to teach and perform duties that absentee parents should be doing. Such an overburden on teachers, coupled with other problems in schools, is forcing many to seek tutors or go the homeschool route to assure that their children are learning the basics. Kudos to those dedicated teacher/parents who are forced to raise children at school and are also raising children at home.

There are many responsibilities of parents from the moment of conception until the day the child leaves home and begins their life as an independent person. Of all of the many parental responsibilities that include the necessity to feed, clothe, house, discipline, provide structure, teach the management of money, teach the duties of citizenship, and provide love for their child, I must add the responsibility of assuring that their children get an education that will allow that child to go out into life as a functionally literate citizen in possession of basic ELA and math skills. These basics must also be accompanied by a skill set that enables a young adult to work at a vocation that will allow them to be self-sufficient adults.

Too many students graduate, and they are not equipped with skills that allow them to be employed or to compete for employment. Educational data illustrates that far too many graduates are ill-prepared, in all of those categories of literacy, and for skill sets that enable them to attain economic self-sufficiency. Parents, who care, are bewildered at the low achievement scores of students, especially in light of the dollars spent for each child's education. Too many parents trust the school district, teachers, and curriculums to adequately educate their children.

Research the chaos that has erupted in Loudoun County, Virginia, public schools, between the school board and the parents who have recently learned of what their children are being taught by the liberal leadership of that school system. Parents in Loudoun County are objecting to policies in favor of transgender students using bathrooms of their declared gender preference. Add to that the fact that parents discovered that teachers were required to attend critical race theory training that would then be taught to their children and a scene of chaos erupted at the school district meeting. Seems to me that we need to review what the objectives for public education should be. Given the data on basic ELA and math literacy scores and job readiness, it seems to me that all available minutes of the school day need to be utilized for the teaching of the ABCs and the 123s. What say you?

For these reasons, and many more to be stated later, I wish to drill down into the problems that I have experienced as a public school teacher and as an adjunct professor of education at the college I attended from 1969 through 1973. Why? Because a sound education system is the basis for our children's success as well as for the success of our nation and democracy. I hope I have interested you enough so you are motivated to read more!

People who want to subvert our democracy and who want to fundamentally change the United States will give lip service to the importance of a successful educational system, but they will not agree with what I am about to present in this chapter. They will attack me as a racist and a white supremacist. I am neither! In fact, when you look at the false narrative being presented by the liberals regarding CRT, Project 1619, attacks upon capitalism, and other agendas of the left, I feel that a case can be made that they are, in fact, racist.

I believe that the leftists see public education as a vehicle for the delivery system of the radical left's agenda. Evidence for my position can be found in their effort to add critical race theory (CRT), Project 1619, and other nonfactual revisions in history into school curriculum. I find it particularly disconcerting that such a political faction would be willing to mislead our vulnerable children during their formative years, via a public education delivery or by any vehicle, for that matter. There are powerful entities in the federal government and in the teacher unions that are pushing the teaching of CRT and Project 1619 in our public schools! That is a travesty, and it is a page taken from the socialist playbook. This curriculum is an example of how lies and propaganda are used to brainwash children! All parents must get into the schools to see what is being taught. That is the right of all parents. These actions of the radical left are reprehensible, and I am leading the effort to prevent such an invasion of false narratives into a tiny school system in WV, where I serve as school board president.

Why is a well-educated citizenry so important? Upon what is a democracy dependent? Obviously, well-educated people tend to thrive economically. You may be quick to counter my statement with the assertion that you know many people who are financially successful without the benefit of college and perhaps without a high school diploma. I agree with you because it is a fact, and you are right! Yet our citizenry must have adequate ELA and math skills, not only to participate in our democracy but to be prepared to be functionally literate for the everyday needs of their lives. I can tell you that we are not being successful in that endeavor. And we need to assure that our citizens value and understand the basic functions of our government and the true history about events that built this great nation.

All of you have heard, and many of you may have said, "Kids are not graduating with as good of an education as I got when I was in school." Older parents and grandparents make this statement all of the time. Employers will tell you that the skills their young employees have, fresh out of high school or college, is unacceptable. All of these statements and the national achievement test scores begs answers for two questions, "What are the problems, and how do we fix K–12 education?" The questions may seem simple to phrase, but I assure you that coming up with answers is difficult, solutions are extremely complex, and there are many root problems.

Teaching K–12 students has never before been such a challenge as it is today! When I left public education, in June of 1989, for a fourteen-year business career in insurance and then reentered the teaching and coaching profession in 2003, I was shocked, angry, and ill-equipped to deal with the enormous changes and challenges confronting me.

I bet you have a question, and the question is probably, "What are the societal and educational problems responsible for the difficult challenges that teachers and students are confronting in today's schools?" The answer is, there is a myriad of problems confronting educators and students. The title of this chapter is "American Education, Back Then versus Today." Before we begin to assess the problems and seek answers, I want to discuss the "Back Then" era that I experienced in education.

I am going to begin this by presenting some personal thoughts about education in the 1950s and '60s and offer a comparison with the education of the 2000s. I hope you find my following statement about my educational experience, that began in 1958, interesting!

My earliest recollection of formal education was sitting on the sofa beside my mother as she homeschooled me for the first half of my first-grade year. There was no kindergarten or pre-K in those days. My mother taught me to read and count, and I was fascinated by the world of learning and knowledge that was opening up for me. My mother was a very good teacher, and I owe her everything! My maternal grandmother read to me, and she had a great love for teaching children. Toward the end of the first semester, we moved, and I began attending school in a most unique setting.

Few people even know about the one-room school concept, and even fewer ever attended a one-room school. However, there was a time when such schools dominated the educational landscape in America. I attended a one-room school, and I must tell you that compared to many schools of today, it was both a unique and rewarding experience. If you attended one of these schools, you will recall the memories with a smile; and if you did not, let me introduce you to a concept of education that has all but disappeared. (I realize that you would have to be rather old to have had this experience, and I hope that most of you are too young to have attended a one-room school.)

Elton School had but one room for instruction. The back of the building was at the base of a wooded mountain that faced Fisher Creek. This flood-prone creek flowed between the school and the one-lane road known as Lawn Road. I vividly remember the year 1958, my first year of school, and the school's site in Elton, West Virginia, of Summers County. Summers County is located in the Allegheny Mountains of southeastern West Virginia. Today, I am looking at one of my dad's old circular saw blades upon which an artist, Carl McDaniel, painted a picture of Elton's school. Though sixty-three years have escaped me, the picture creates a flood of memories that I wish to share with you.

You did not have to be very astute to recognize that this facility was short on amenities and built with a very lean budget. I remember a coal-fired, potbelly stove that sat in the corner next to the teacher's desk. Each of the five grades, one through five, had their own little round table encircled by oak chairs that had a shelf beneath the seat for books. There was a library that consisted of a couple of shelves, beneath the windows, for the few books that were available. The cloakroom had a water fountain that provided a small stream of water that tasted of iron. The small kitchen was my mother's workplace. She cooked the most delicious meals for the cost of a dime. We called those meals "hot lunch." If the question has not entered your mind, let me point out that the bathrooms were outdoors, and we sometimes called them "Johnny Houses." These privies were located next to the building that stored our heating supply of coal. The floors of the school were hardwoods and had been oil-treated for cleaning purposes and appeared quite dark. I am sure that in today's world, there would have been fire code and EPA violations associated with the coal smoke and oil-treated floors. But we seem to have survived quite well.

Some of these one-room schools and other school facilities were the products of Franklin Roosevelt's Civilian Conservation Corps (CCC) or the Work Progress Administration (WPA) organized in the 1930s in an attempt to stimulate the U.S. economy of the Great Depression era. There was no playground equipment, so out of necessity, we mountain kids became quite creative when it came to entertaining ourselves.

Recess, and the time before school began, was so much fun that if I listen closely, I can still hear the shouts and screams of ten to thirty mountain children having the time of their young lives. We ran through the field of honeysuckle and broom straw playing tag or chasing a rubber ball, that is, if someone had thought to bring a bat and a ball.

There was the occasional fight that would result in a knot on the head or a black eye, but mostly there were wrestling matches that ended in someone saying "uncle" and both parties glad it was over.

Building dams and ponds with roots, sticks, and mud for the containment of tadpoles and frogs in the little branch behind the school was enjoyed by both genders. Beyond the little branch of water, we ventured into the woods to climb trees, swing on grapevines, or find a patch of green moss that was as soft as carpet.

You might throw a ball over the roof and yell, "Annie Over." You would hear this shout just before the kid on the other side would catch the ball as it bounced off the roof and promptly yell, "Annie Over," as they returned the favor. This game might continue until you were hustled into a game of marbles.

A boy would produce a piece of yellow or white chalk for drawing a large circle or triangle on the concrete front porch or use the toe of his scuffed shoe for creating the same on the dirt surface of the playground. The best shooters always returned to class with a bulging pocket of multicolored marbles mixed with a few little steel balls.

The girls used chalk to draw boxes on the concrete walk for playing hopscotch. Boys and girls alike yelled rhymes as two students turned either a single long rope or two ropes that allowed for double Dutch jumping on the sidewalk or in the dirt.

And I can still hear the refrain, "Red Rover, Red Rover," we dare (a named student) over. Picture two separate horizontal and parallel lines of students linked together by holding hands as the two lines faced off. The challenged student would run as fast as they could and try to break through a set of linked hands. If the runner was successful, they could pick a player from that line and take them back to enlarge their team of hand-linked players. If you failed to break the chain of hands, you had to stay in that line.

There were other games and fun activities for fall, winter, and spring that always gave way to the more serious activities of study. Suddenly, our glee was interrupted by our teacher, Miss Daisy (Cozort) and, in later years, Mrs. Geneva Fitzwater. They would appear on the porch and ring a handheld bell while yelling, "Books." If it was the start of the school day, we formed a single file line on the walk, youngest to oldest, faced left, and crossed our heart as we said the Pledge of Allegiance to the flag that hung from a wooden flagstaff. I never knew anyone to be offended or to question our daily lessons of patriotism that often included the many different songs that praised America. After so many years, I sometimes look back and must admit I am amazed at what we accomplished and truly appreciative of the venue that provided for our education. I say this from the vantage point of having been a high school teacher for twenty-six years.

How fortunate we were that our teacher and our parents were so hardworking and dedicated to our educational success. Success was measured in our ability to read, spell, write, and do our arithmetic. From our ABCs, 1-2-3s, *See Spot Run*, multiplication tables, and that weekly spelling test, we drilled and drilled to gain the all-essential and basic foundational skills that allowed our education to expand to that of productive, lifelong learners. Imagine your teacher moving from grade level to grade level teaching and keeping students on task. The younger kids learned from the older kids as skills were repeated and repeated through classroom activities that included read around the room, go to the blackboard to work math problems faster than your classmates, to spelling bees, or writing those times tables over and over until you could give the answer faster than the bat of an eye. We read from a little red book of American History and learned the stories of struggle and triumph of our nation.

At the time, we did not know that outsiders thought of us as ignorant "hillbillies" or that they might have claimed that our educational environment put us at a disadvantage. We believed our school provided an educational experience with purpose and something to be valued. If we got in trouble at school, the punishment at home was worse than what we received at school. You see, my dad would say, "Boy, you get an education so you don't have to work the jobs I have had to work all of my life." I took that advice to heart!

When I told my students this story, they were amazed that I was not as old as Abraham Lincoln! In fact, one student asked me if I was as old as Abraham Lincoln. Seriously, he did! Somehow, I failed that student when it came to the time and place sequencing of a timeline for American History. Because of this very humble setting for the beginning of my formal education, there are people who are amazed that I was able to earn a Master's Degree in Education; have taught at five high schools in two states; was selected as the 2008 History Teacher of the Year for the state of West Virginia and competed for National History Teacher of the Year with the Gilder Lehrman Institute of American History in New York; or that I enjoyed a successful career in the insurance business as a salesmen, manager, and owner of an insurance agency.

All of my formal education was accomplished without air-conditioned schoolrooms, internet, calculators, computers, or cable television. I believe we accomplished so much with so little. May I say that I was fortunate to attend school in that era before liberal techniques, jargon, and ideology invaded public education and diluted the educational effort and wasted precious time for the educational process. We did not waste time in school. There was too much to learn, and time was short for learning the basics that we all use today and every day of our lives. It was a time before attorneys and teachers' unions began to circle around school districts like sharks looking for an opportunity to feast with frivolous lawsuits that served to tie up school systems and to hamper the educational process. This legal effort took place at the federal, state, and local levels. Also, this was a time era before teacher unions were guilty of protecting those teachers who were responsible for bad teaching!

I am thankful that our tiny local school system, in which I preside as the president of the school board, has many good teachers and very few bad teachers who do not take their job seriously! I feel rich for having had my one-room school experience, and if I could go back to those earlier years of my formal education, I would change little, if anything! Well, indoor bathrooms would have been nice!

Before I go on, I ask that you search through the above educational experience that I just presented for the purpose of picking out things that you feel could be explanations for any modicum of success that those educational venues may have provided. Consider what follows as well!

Let me be clear! I am not advocating for one-room schools to be reopened today. I will say that there is research available that points strongly to the fact that small schools can be very successful. I do think there are some things we can learn from this educational structure of the past. It should be pointed out that, first and foremost, there was strict discipline in the schools I attended. There was also overwhelming respect shown by students and parents for the school at large and the teacher specifically. The one-room school focused heavily upon arithmetic, reading, spelling, parts of speech, basic grammar, punctuation, and sentence writing. In those early grades, we spent very little time on social studies and science. With five grades, one teacher, all in the same room, there was not enough time for social studies and science per se. Teachers can teach reading, spelling, and writing while using social studies and science materials, and they should, in the early grades. Furthermore, teachers of social studies, sciences, and mathematics in the upper grades can, and should, employ the discipline of ELA in their engagement of students' learning of those particular disciplines of study. It can be done quite easily and very productively for all disciplines of study if you are willing to think outside of the box!

Students at the different grade levels in the one-room school benefited from the repetition of various skills. Because of the intense focus and repetition of these basic skills, we gained a solid foundation of basic and fundamental educational skills and knowledge that we would need for a lifetime of everyday usage. We spent so much time on these skills year after year through our first eight years of school that we really learned and retained those skills and knowledge. This foundation of education was strong, and it allowed us to become life-long learners, and we were functionally literate in English language arts and arithmetic. And yes, there are exceptions on both ends of the achievement scale. There will always be students who can master these basic skills more quickly than others, and they should receive additional challenges as they will be the ones who will seek and be successful in the venue of higher education. Others will need more and more help on the basic skills, and we should provide the needed interventions. In any case, there can be no allowance for the wasting of time. The skills I learned in those early years of formal education have served me well. I have used those skills for the sixty-three years since I began school at the age of five. So you may be asking, "Is that not what happens today?"

Go to https://www.pewresearch.org/fact-tank/2017/02/15/u-s-students-internationally-math-science/ to view the February 15, 2017, article by Drew Desilver titled "U.S. Students' Academic Achievement Still Lags that of Their Peers in Many Other Countries." The data in this article should be enough to bring into question the effectiveness of our education system when it comes to the ability of our country and our students being able to compete in the fields of math, reading, and science with the other major industrial nations of the world. And I quote Desilver's article, "Internationally, U.S. stands in middle of pack on science, math, reading scores." Desilver arrived at this definitive statement as a result of analysis of the scores on the Programme for International Student Assessment (PISA) that is given to fifteen-year-old students, each three years, in countries that are developed as well as countries that are developing. This is a cross-national test for reading ability, math and science literacy. Desilver's article points out that in 2015, the United States ranked thirty-eighth out of seventy-one countries that participated in this cross-national test! This lack of academic success is abysmal, and it is a harbinger that our country and workforce is faced with a very uncompetitive position in the world for things that rely upon skills in reading, math, and science literacy.

The future success of the United States, on the world stage, is dependent upon educational excellence, and we are not exhibiting that trait in our school systems. A math ranking of thirtieth and a science ranking of nineteenth just does not speak well for American education whether our students are in public or private schools. To be sure, there are always exceptions, but these underwhelming numbers and the prognostications of the data point to a downward slide for the United States' ability to outperform other countries of the world. This brings our world leadership position into serious question! Are we in trouble? You decide, but if you asked me, I would say, "You bet we are in trouble." This educational ranking of thirty-eighth out of seventy-one countries is unacceptable and does not represent "American Exceptionalism!"

The 2021 PISA assessment was cancelled due to COVID-19 restrictions. There are scores available from the 2018 PISA assessment. There was a slight growth in scoring in the United States between the years 2015 and 2018.

The United States' scores in PISA reading testing placed the U.S. at a rank of fourteenth among the countries participating in PISA testing in 2018. The total average score for all countries in reading was 487. The United States scored eighteen points higher than the average with a score of 505. China came in at 555, and Singapore scored 549. Not a stellar performance for our country, but we scored even lower in math.

There were thirty-three countries that outperformed the U.S. scores for PISA math testing in 2018. The test average for all countries in math was 489. We were eleven points below the average with a score of 478. Eastern Asia countries, including China, displayed dominance. We are not educating students to compete on the world stage. Our country is suffering for this educational deficiency! Science scores were some better, but still disappointing for the leader of the free world.

Seventeen countries scored higher on the 2018 PISA science testing. The average score was 489, and the U.S. scored thirteen points higher with a score of 502.

Overall, these United States' scores in reading, math, and science placed us in the unenviable position of fourteenth, thirty-fourth, and eighteenth respectively among the more than seventy countries of the world that participated in the testing. Do we want to import mathematicians and scientists from the likes of the Chinese communists for research and development? I think not! The future of America will be an unmitigated disaster if we depend upon countries like China. Has government and liberal policies so diluted our educational presentation that we have become middle of the pack performers in the fields of reading, math, and science? To be fair, government and liberalism are not the only problems that are negatively impacting our educational performance! But I assure you, they both are major contributors. Are our children becoming lazy and satiated without the willingness to set goals and then work to achieve those goals? The overwhelming majority of our doctors, dentists, engineers, researchers, etc. were and can be again "Made in America!"

The scientific and technological development of the United States has been, without question, the leader of the world during my lifetime. Actually, we have been a world leader in those areas since the late 1800s and the early 1900s industrialization of America. Can that continue when we lag so far behind in student achievement?

Once the products of the world had an all-important stamp upon them, "Made in the USA." A stable and productive future for the United States is dependent upon being a world leader in educational achievement. Manufacturing in the U.S. has dropped dramatically, and that is a weakness that we cannot tolerate. Our education system needs to put much more emphasis on training more students in the various vocational and technical fields in order to provide a skilled workforce that can rejuvenate manufacturing in this country. We need an even stronger commitment to career and technical education (CTE) programs! Our country cannot afford to be dependent upon other countries such as China for our source of steel, aluminum, medical supplies, and so many other products. These products need to be made in the USA. The American educational system needs to graduate more students with the skills and knowledge to assure that these products are once again, Made in the U.S.! Too many students go to colleges and universities and leave with a pile of student debt and no skills that allow them to enter the job market. It is important what field of study you choose.

Until we remove the liberal left control from our schools and liberal influence on curriculum, higher levels of critical educational achievement will not and cannot happen. We have no time to waste on critical race theory and things such as Project 1619! One of the things I noticed in that one-room school was that there were two genders. Some school districts are wasting time on things like multiple gender identifications! Graphic illustrations about the birds and the bees in elementary schools. Give me a break. Is it any wonder we have a lot of troubled youth who have been introduced to things that destroy and confuse their innocence? Kids are introduced to enough, outside of the school, without schools assisting in the confusion and destruction of innocence. That garbage destroys the sanctity of what schools are supposed to be. I am sorry, but I do not see that such things are part of the prime directive of education. And the prime directive is all we have time to do! What I have stated thus far and what I am about to say I will say loud and clear to anyone who wishes to engage in this conversation of "American Education, Back Then Versus Now." We need to wake up, roll up our sleeves, and get down to business without wasting time if we want to improve educational delivery.

Teaching, though difficult, does not have to be as complex as rocket science. We have to roll up our sleeves and go to work with a sense of urgency, common sense, be relentless in the pursuit and achievement of high and lofty goals for graduating well-educated students ready to succeed at life. This must be done by first building a rock-solid foundation in the basic fundamentals of ELA and math! These basic fundamentals of ELA and basic math must be reviewed and drilled over and over through the first eight grades from one year to the next in order to assure that students will carry those skills with them for a lifetime. That is the only way that we can be sure we have made the very best effort to graduate kids who are functionally literate in ELA and math so they have the necessary skills to function as independent adults! To do less is a travesty and an abrogation of our duties.

By first making the eight-year commitment and requirement that our students must gain a solid educational foundation in ELA and math, we will have prepared students not only for the necessary everyday life skills requirements but for the last four years of education in which some of our students will pursue the higher levels of ELA, math, science, or career and technical vocational schooling. Student success in high school suffers because too many students are not ready for the higher applications of reading, math, and science because they have not mastered the necessary rock-solid foundational skills. Any activities in school that rob teachers and students of the time needed to master these all-important basic skills must be eliminated. If we get this job done in the first eight years, larger numbers of our students will be equipped for and ready to succeed at the higher levels of these disciplines and thus be on a path to realize meaningful careers. And we do not have a second to waste on the curriculum and modus operandi of the liberals that have invaded and taken over education.

So much of what we have been doing in education does not work! It is time to look at things that were successful in the past and join them with those things that we now know work today. Teachers and school districts must evaluate every part of lesson planning and instruction in order to be sure that there is a high level of coordination between those things students are learning and those skills and knowledge that are required in the real world of work! Too often, teachers are unable to perform triage on the overall curriculum in order to assure that for the amount of time available, students develop a high level of proficiency in the most important skills as opposed to trying to cover the entire curriculum from A to Z.

Does the phrase "Jack of all trades, master of none" come to mind? It is wonderful to master the curriculum from A to Z, but that cannot always happen for all students. In order to get to Z, you must not sacrifice the links in the chain that are crucial for building the essential foundation from which students can continue to grow at the pace they can maintain. The very definition of insanity is "continuing to do the same thing while expecting a different result!"

Some years ago, there was a "buzz" going through the educational community that placed an emphasis on how we had to diversify our educational offerings in order that we produce a more well-rounded graduate. Sounds really good! I agree, provided we have the time to offer all of the fluff courses. What we have done in education is offer these time-consuming extras at the expense of the time needed to assure that students have mastered the essential basics. There should be strict rules that say you cannot engage in fluff until you have proven, via sound testing, that proves you are on track and on target to master the basics. First things first, and we should not deviate from those axioms.

We should not need something like the launch of Sputnik, by the Russians, on October 4, 1957, to propel us into action to fix our failing educational system. The launch of the world's first artificial satellite by the Russians drove a massive math and science educational emphasis in the U.S. Twelve years later the United States safely landed men on the moon in 1969. From 1969 forward, our country continued to benefit from that intense educational focus. During that era of the Cold War, with the Soviet Union, we understood that our very existence was dependent upon the intense focus we made in order to excel in education and R and D. Why is it that we do not understand that same concept today? It is just as important, for our survival, in 2021 and beyond as it was in 1957! Our scientific and mathematical know-how outpaced the world, and we were, once, second to none. We can, and we must, be second to none again.

Before you read further, please, take a few moments to reflect on some of the teachers, the classroom management styles or lack thereof, teacher engagement of students, and teacher preparation or the lack thereof for the classes you attended. Can you remember what seemed to work and what did not work? Can you remember the classes that were disasters and those that were real learning experiences? Can you identify what you think was the mix of ingredients that the teacher assembled into their daily presentation? I am trying to engage you, get you to recall those things you already know, and prepare you for what I am about to offer. My offering is the result of twenty-six years of classroom instruction that spanned the time era of 1973 through 2014.

There are many ingredients in the formula needed to assure academic achievement and success in the classroom for all of the students that you can get to buy in to the task at hand. Sacrifice even one ingredient, and the achievement level drops. Several of the ingredients are so important and interdependent that it is difficult to rank them in importance. What we seek, as educators, is a sound learning environment that allows intense focus by students. To achieve the optimum learning environment requires both classroom discipline and skilled teachers.

We teachers must find ways to engage students and to communicate to them that learning is paramount for a successful future for themselves, family, and our nation. Our chance of reaching that goal would be easier if the government would quit giving away money that stifles initiative and clouds the necessity for working hard to prepare for your own individual financial responsibility and self-sufficiency!

We must reconnect the concept of hard work and relevance of subjects studied within the minds of our students in order to get buy-in for achievement that leads to academic success and ultimately to self-sufficiency of more young adults. To do this, we need to avoid wasting students' time on those subjects that educators cling to as their "sacred cows of education." Students will need help in order to explore what they can do and what puts a sparkle in their eyes. They must recognize that success in a chosen specialization in education is the key to a productive future and that the government is not going to take care of you!

Our government, which means "We the people," is broke to the tune of twenty-eight trillion dollars in debt. The federal spigot that has poured forth dollars will go dry! That fact is a mathematical certainty. Both teachers and students must come to understand that a high level of intense focus on teaching and learning are necessary for the kind of success that will help you land on top of your endeavor.

More students and some teachers must work harder than they are currently working.

If you are a teacher reading this, I know that some of my statements may have offended you! That is not my intention, and I freely acknowledge that we have, in most districts, a majority of our teachers who are working extremely hard! Only you are able to do the necessary self-evaluation required to determine if you are in the category of teachers who work extremely hard or if you are a teacher who just shows up and does the minimum necessary to keep your job. I trust that if you have read this far, you are one of our great teachers, and I applaud you!

Students need a laser focus on subject matter that will help them reach the attainable academic goals necessary to assure a productive future for that individual. Can you even imagine how many people in this country are getting cell phones that are paid for by the government? I do not know who is paying for the phones, outside of the parents who can afford them, that every kid in America takes to school, but I can tell you that cell phones in schools are problematic and a serious distraction that is detrimental to the learning process! Good school systems do not allow students to use cell phones during the school day! Cell phones, turned on and used in schools, prevent the laser focus needed for optimum learning.

Some students cannot master great volumes of subjects and material. They need a great deal of time to master the basic and essential materials, and we must not overwhelm those students with too much! These students who need the extra time, and who may lack the ability for extremely difficult math and science subjects, will get lost in the avalanche of materials and subjects they cannot do and do not need. There has to be recognition of how much a student can master, and we must help them to become functionally literate and not dilute their achievement by pushing them into subjects they cannot do and will not ever use. We must help students determine what they are suited for and what they can be successful doing.

Do you not find it ludicrous that in order to graduate from high school, students in most districts are required to take and pass algebra II? Are there numerous students who should take algebra II and who are successful in passing the course? Yes! And they will need that course for their future endeavors. We need to meet their needs! But to force students who want to work with their hands as carpenters, plumbers, secretaries, hair dressers, and a plethora of other vocations to take algebra II or chemistry is asinine!

Time is precious, and students have no time to waste. Those students wasting their time in algebra II or chemistry need more time in basic and/or vocational math. Would you believe we have students graduating high school who have no concept of business math, budget creation, or how to calculate interest as protection from those who push credit upon those challenged in math? But I guess it is unreasonable to expect citizens to balance the checkbook since the federal government refuses to balance their books. Please accept my apology for making such a bad joke! There are only so many instructional minutes in a day, week, month, and a school year. We must be frugal with and cognizant of just how we spend those precious minutes for the most essential building blocks that leads us to graduating students in possession of higher levels of academic achievement in skills they will need for their working lives and their daily needs!

Before we go on, I must share a true story! My friend John was the head varsity football coach, and I was his assistant. A strong and well-built freshman approached us with a sincere desire to play football. I will not use his name, and he will never read this book. To make the story short, let it suffice to say that he was not eligible to play his sophomore year because he could not pass algebra I, and he would never be able to pass algebra I.

This is what the young man said to us: "If they would give me some kind of a test, they would find out that I can't do that algebra stuff. I used to do good in math when we had numbers. But now, they have put letters with the numbers, and I can't get it!" Let me say that the young man never played football. The worst thing is that he became so disenchanted, like millions of other kids, that he dropped out of school. I must confess that I do not know what happened to the young man. What I do know is that the system failed this kid! We wasted his time in algebra I rather than spending more time teaching him basic skills in necessary math literacy. Perhaps if we had put him in a math class in which he could achieve, and one that he truly needed, he may have enjoyed some success and learned the skills necessary for some endeavor while gaining self-esteem. We will never know! So not only can he not do the unnecessary algebra I, he cannot do the basic math needed to function in life. So what creates a sound learning environment and provides for a wise use of instructional minutes?

As discipline and a sense of urgency erodes in the classroom, so does the environment that is conducive to learning. Too many classrooms in the United States do not have a sense of urgency, and the teachers do not have the "command presence" necessary to provide and maintain the disciplined classroom that is so necessary for the optimum learning environment. Without discipline, there can be no intense focus, no sense of urgency, and learning is greatly diminished. Teachers who have to suffer with unruly students simply cannot focus on teaching. Even worse, students who want to learn cannot learn in an environment of chaos. I had an emphatic and simple rule in my classroom: *I will not allow you to disrupt the learning environment for students who want to learn, and you will not create chaos that prevents me from making my best effort at assisting learning!* And I assure you, I did not allow chaos in my classroom. Motivated students appreciated that about me and is amazing how many of the unruly students stop and talk to me years later. Students want discipline and structure, and when none is present, there will be enough students go with the flow of chaos so that nobody will learn and you cannot teach.

Too many teacher colleges are not teaching teachers how to manage classrooms with discipline. I know; I have supervised student teachers, and they are ill-prepared. This inability to create a disciplined learning environment is one of the major reasons so many young teachers leave the profession. School boards, superintendents, principals, teachers, parents, and state departments of education must bite the bullet and fight the battle to assure a disciplined learning environment. We must stand up to all of those organizations and individuals that weaken our ability to provide the most optimum learning environment. Fail to do that, and student achievement will continue to falter and the doom and gloom we are experiencing now, will continue. In addition to discipline, there are many other interdependent factors necessary for success in the classroom.

Many people would now assume that my next ingredient for success is teacher knowledge of subject matter. While you cannot be successful as a teacher, without that subject matter knowledge, it is useless without the skills necessary for the art of teaching. First, there is discipline that must be coupled with a teacher's ability and skill for creating daily lessons that engage students, challenges students, and helps students connect success in the class with the concept or dream of a fruitful life. These lessons must be based upon sound educational objectives for the curriculum at hand. A teacher's real work begins long before class meets.

The difficult work is creating engaging lesson plans that keep student's attention and helps them focus on the essentials. Teachers and school districts must also recognize the achievement level of skills and knowledge that their students have when they arrive in their classrooms. Teachers must know what foundational skills the students have and what is most important to teach from the curriculum at hand. If students are not ready for the new curriculum, it is the job of the district to provide the instructional assistance needed to get the students ready for the next curriculum's objectives. All too often the district and the teacher just say "all aboard" and off they go into the class without the targeted intervention that is necessary to bring students up to the level needed to perform. And so the merry-go-round of failing or ill-prepared students continues to turn through grade level after grade level until we turn students out into the world without functional literacy skills in ELA and math.

Teachers must allow students time to discover, ponder, struggle, fail, and ultimately succeed on activities. Teachers need to be facilitators of learning and not lecturers that seek to demonstrate all of their knowledge on the subject. Lecture, lecture, and lecture some more and you run the risk of a dull stare from your students because they have tuned you out! Learning requires student involvement with much repetition and a constant reapplication of skills learned as students move forward in the study of the subject or skill being studied. Students forced to listen to lectures or view films never learn how to engage in meaningful dialogue that sharpens speaking and questioning skills. They are not exercised in the processing of materials in order to participate in higher-level thinking that is truly critical. They never learn how to formulate arguments and defend a position based upon a sound factual presentation.

By the way, there has been, for several years, an intense effort to help improve students' self-esteem. Granted, self-esteem is very important, but too many systems are trying to confer self-esteem upon students. That does not work! High self-esteem cannot be handed out to students with low self-esteem. Self-esteem must be earned, or it will be as bogus as counterfeit money! I contend that promoting children into a higher grade or into even more demanding curriculum without the basic skills is a major culprit for the creation of low self-esteem.

Teachers who routinely pass out mindless worksheets and tell students to temporarily memorize the info presented and then give them a test based upon that worksheet are slackers who will never know if their students can think critically, solve problems, or if they are mastering required curriculum concepts or not. To be fair, some worksheets, if used at a minimum, are useful for introduction of the basic facts of new material provided they assist in developing summarization and writing skills that require the development of critical thinking skills. It is the manner that teachers engage students that is so important. Students who are asked on a regular basis to only regurgitate materials from a worksheet are not getting an education.

Can you imagine, given the low scores on testing performance of students in ELA and math, that there are teachers out there who say, "Okay, you can have a free day today"? I know this is true because students would ask me, once, if they could have a free day. I would say, "A free day?" They would answer, "So-and-so teacher gives us a free day!" There were no free days in my class, just like there are no free lunches in real life. The free day is for the teacher, and student achievement is the loser! We are so far behind that the minutes we have in school may not be enough, and they are too precious to waste!

A teacher who engages pupils in a dialogue that occurs as a result of questions that the student is motivated to answer are those teachers who really facilitate learning. Careful lesson preparation requires that teachers, during preparation of lessons, keep in mind the desired ending results of skills and knowledge that we want students to achieve. Teachers must have prepared ahead of time the activities and appropriate essential questions that facilitate engagement and achievement of the desired ending results of the lesson. Such sound and careful preparation in lesson planning will force students to continuously reuse fundamental skills and knowledge they possess as they are actively engaged in learning and mastering new curriculum objectives. Repetition upon repetition of basic skills, year after year, is most necessary for those skills to be learned and recalled as automatic as the learned skill of tying one's shoes! This is a concept that the one-room school had to follow, out of necessity, and I believe it was a working formula that we need to employ more and more in all elementary and middle schools as we move from grade to grade. Practicing fundamental skills and using knowledge previously learned, in order to do higher-level thinking, leads students to the most effective learning. Students who use this process for reaching fact-based conclusions are lucky students who are realizing real educational benefits. Do this proactive lesson preparation and you will find that more students are engaged, and you may discover you have less discipline issues. Will this type of teacher preparation improve achievement? I think so, but what do you think?

I read a third-grade math curriculum that stated students should be able to multiply one- and two-digit numbers. That was all the objective said. Were the students supposed to commit the times tables 1–12 to memory as we did in the "back then days"? A young teacher might look at that objective and say his/her students can multiply 1 by any two-digit number or any one-digit number and feel the objective had been achieved. Or the student may have learned how to key in a number, push the (x), add another number, push =, and what do you know—they can multiply any two numbers. Mission accomplished. *Wrong!* Such shortcuts are a farce, and they are a travesty for the education of children. Children must develop what I call numbers sense, and until they do, the light bulb for being able to be proficient in math will never happen. The only light bulb that will come on will be the one on the calculator.

Failing school districts may not have teachers who are properly teaching students the necessary foundational fundamentals of ELA and math. These districts may not have enough teachers who teach students how to do higher level thinking in order to solve problems. Or these teachers may be seriously hampered by administrations that are unwilling or unable to affect the necessary discipline for an optimum learning environment. Or their students may come from home environments that provide no motivation for learning. Or there could be a combination of all of these failings in our failing school districts. The problems that school districts and teachers face are daunting!

Good administrators and well-prepared, caring, and dedicated teachers are worth their weight in gold. We need to pay teacher salaries accordingly in order to attract the best and the brightest into this crucial vocation. Do not say to me that we cannot afford to pay the price to secure good teaching. The all-important question is, how can we afford not to pay the cost for good teachers for our children's education and for our country's future success? By the way, paying for well-trained and highly motivated teachers may be as simply as readjusting the spending of the huge amounts of money we throw at education! Merit-based bonuses are controversial and a no-no in districts with teacher unions, but we should not deny payment to those who prove to be highly successful by rewarding mediocrity as we do when we pay everyone the same rate of pay.

All too often, too many teachers create assessments that do not assess the depth of knowledge that the objectives of the curriculum require. The tests are too simple and are not driven by the standards or objectives of the curriculum. The students get a passing grade or a grade that does not reflect what the student should have mastered. That is what I call teaching without rocking the boat. The level of the "depth of knowledge" (DOK) must not always be a DOK 1 or 2. Students have to be challenged with the higher levels of DOK materials and questioning. The result of not rocking the boat is that students pass on to a higher grade, or they graduate as cripples for life when it comes to literacy in ELA and math life skills! This passing them on takes the heat off the administration and the teacher. Parents and grandparents are proud right up to the time they get the first semester grades from the college, or they learn that the so-called graduate does not have any discernable skills to enter the job market.

Too many parents and teachers feel it is their responsibility to assure that students do not know what it is like to be out of their comfort zone. Sorry, but life has a lot of discomfort, and students need to learn to cope with the realities of life. Providing safe zones, teddy bears, and giving everyone a trophy with the premise that nobody fails simply makes our kids cripples for life! Do not baby students, and do not just pass them on. To stand firm and not be bullied into making life easy for students necessitates teachers are supported by the principal, superintendent, and the school board!

Education is serious business, and it requires the commitment of many different stakeholders. I submit there is not enough commitment, just more and more money thrown at a problem in a way that shows the powers in charge do not understand what the problems are and, therefore, cannot fix the problems. The liberal element that has invaded our school districts is far too willing to give a pass to both students and teachers. Expectations are not high enough, and the sense of urgency is quite lacking. Look at the positions taken by the teachers' unions and then tell me if those positions are conducive to improving achievement.

If you think that I am exaggerating the problems in schools or if you think the things that I am suggesting just cannot be the case, then I urge you to google this site, https://www.educationviews.org/13-baltimore-city-high-schools-students-proficient-math/. Read for yourself, but according to this article, in a 2017 study, it was found that in thirteen of the thirty-nine high schools in the city of Baltimore, Maryland, thirteen schools did not have a single student that was proficient in math! Let me say that again! Not a single student proficient in math. Six more high schools had only 1 percent of their students proficient in math. Are you curious to know if this abysmal performance is duplicated in countless other districts across the country? If you are curious, I bet you have the skills to research other school districts to determine how they compare!

As you read, please ponder whether my offerings are plausible reasons to explain what could possibly be causing such failures of systems that have so many students who are failing. I assure you, the Baltimore, Maryland, high schools are not unique regarding low math scores! When you learn of the dollars spent for each student, you will recognize that money spent is not the problem in this system or in many other districts that are failing. There are so many problems in education to be discussed. By the way, I speak to educators from all over the country, and the discussions regarding problems are so similar that it is amazing!

Time after time I witnessed students coming to my class so sleepy that there was no way they could focus on learning. Why is that the case, you may be wondering? Unfortunately, there are many reasons for sleepiness in class. One reason that I found was that students were talking on their cell phones until the wee hours of the morning. Parents and guardians, that is your fault! Do something about that now. It does not have to be cell phones because televisions and more likely computers or games are the culprits. Again, parents or guardians have to parent, and you have to limit and/or take devices away from your kids. Are there parents who want to be their child's best friend rather than the parent who requires kids to be disciplined in order to have a chance for achievement success? You decide this one!

Students are used to being entertained by television, phones, computers, and games. Even the best teachers cannot compete with that type of entertainment all of the time! Learning can be hard, and it certainly is not always as fun as the latest electronic game.

While we are speaking of devices that so many Americans, especially students, are addicted to, it is time to speak about the need to decrease screen time. I spoke earlier about how I felt students of my era had accomplished so much without all of the devices we use today. Could it be that companies and big tech had a vested interest in convincing educators that computers were the absolute answer for improving education? Can computers be used in ways that augment learning? Yes! Can they be used in ways that produce negative results? Yes!

The challenge in education and in good teaching is to plan lessons that derive the greatest educational advantages possible from the use of computers based upon the stated curriculum objectives. There must be strict guidelines for their use, and their educational value must undergo continuous evaluation for determination of whether they are improving achievement. Parents, do not allow any device to become a babysitter. Do not allow devices to prevent the development of interpersonal communication skills and meaningful relationships. Do not allow devices to replace the physical activities that our children need as they grow into adulthood.

Our educational system has not been achieving at high levels, when we are compared to countries around the world. Earlier, I presented evidence that clearly proves this point. And if that is not bad enough, COVID restrictions placed on public schools have further retarded the learning process, and our students are now more behind than ever. Is it not curious that so many parochial schools' students attended school in person all during the pandemic when we would not allow in-person learning in so many of our public schools? The teachers' unions saw to that! I find it amazing that this in-person learning did not cause sickness from COVID for those students. I know a public school district that sent their K–5 students to school all during the 2020–21 school year with no negative impacts. Even with that success, they were eventually ordered to cut back on in-person learning.

The remote learning, for most students forced to stay at home, was a disaster. So much for the presentation that we can replace teachers with computers. There is no substitute for in-person learning in a classroom directed by a highly motivated and well-trained teacher! To be sure, there are many wonderful educational sources developed for use on computers. They can be most effective, but most students also need the teacher to facilitate the use of those programs and provide feedback and additional instruction.

Go anywhere in our country and you will find kids of *all* colors having kids! These kids are born into poverty and on government assistance. Kids who become pregnant are doing so without being involved in a committed relationship. Fathers are all too often nowhere to be found, and if you can find them, they do not have a value system that adheres to the belief in the parental responsibility for rearing their children. These absentee fathers are also representative of *all* colors! Does anyone think that these "kid parents" are reading to their children or that they have any vision, whatsoever, for the disciplinary control and overall parenting of these children? I suspect not. This is a major problem because too many children enter school who have not developed to a stage of readiness for learning. They have not been read to, have not been taught the ABCs, shapes, colors, or numbers. If you are a parent, grandparent, guardian, or about to become one of these, it is your responsibility to feed these children's minds, just as you must feed their growing bodies.

I am not sure how we lost the value system of the "nuclear family," the basic social unit we identify as a couple who are responsible for their dependent children. I do know that the basic social unit has been so dramatically weakened that our educators are dealing with more and more discipline problems in school, dealing with more students that enter school having never been read to, and more students who cannot focus due to their uncontrolled chaotic home life. So many students come from homes in which their daily environment includes drugs, violence, abuse, or broken homes.

What I also know is that the government rushed in years ago and said we must pay for all prenatal care, provide for the cost of child birthing, provide housing, food, etc. for all of the young and unmarried mothers. These pregnant kids may then get out on their own and into government housing or stay with parents. Once this door was opened, more and more kids were sucked into this endless cycle of poverty and government aid. Some couples never marry because the unwed mother gets more federal and state aid by not being married. One child leads to two children born into poverty, and all too often the numbers of children rise above the number two. Or if the couple gets married, it is after the government takes care of all birthing costs.

There are exceptions to all situations, and some of these unfortunate children and parents somehow climb out of this mess. Education is an important key for those who seek to end this cycle, and there are success stories. Children who come from homes of poverty all too often have a greater struggle in school. Sadly, there are far too many who never get out of this poverty cycle, and their children grow up expecting the government to continue sending the handouts. So the children will, in many cases, repeat the same mistakes as their mother and absentee father did. And the government will rush in!

News flash! Does liberal government policies and handouts cause more harm than good? One day the checks will stop because the economic system will implode as a result of insurmountable debt, and that is a mathematical certainty. Then this nation will witness chaos and the final breakdown in society. What, I ask, will be the liberal solution to that social volcano?

So the American taxpayers are getting the shaft. The problem is, the shaft is getting bigger and bigger, and this problem cannot be allowed to continue. This nation's deficit spending and debt is spiraling out of control and has been for decades. The radical left will grab more and more power and demand more and more taxes of those who are producers. One day the overtaxed producers will simply lay down and die an economic death. The party or parties that support this socialism and lack of responsibility gain temporary political support from those who benefit from such finite aid. Our impoverished and uneducated people fall into the line of march orchestrated by our "Pied Piper" government that is leading them and all of us into economic doom and the destruction of life as we know it. This has gone on so long that people have come to believe that government actually owes them sustenance from cradle to grave! This belief is being sold by the "left's political and community organizers" all over the country. It is being sold in our schools as well. That is one reason why the radical left is viciously attacking capitalism.

I find it easy to defend capitalism and the entire free enterprise system. Capitalism has raised millions upon millions of people around the world out of poverty. Socialism has never raised anybody out of poverty. Socialism drags more and more people into poverty until that system implodes.

You might be called a racist if you suggest this cycle must stop. Remember, all colors of Americans game the system. Again, there are exceptions, and I freely recognize that there are many who are deserving of our help. It is those able-bodied people who should be held responsible for getting off the dole. Far too many politicians, from all parties, are reluctant to stop this system that has contributed to the destruction of the family unit. Children from broken homes all too often struggle and fail in school!

God knows, we need to fix our education system and teach more people to think critically! That there are problems in education is irrefutable, but far too many people cannot identify the causes, cannot offer workable solutions, and many more cannot or will not look into the future to see what the impacts of a broken educational system will be on our country and society. Can you hear the "fire bell in the night"? Stay with me. I have to digress, but I promise to tie this all together!

Study American History and you will discover that this country was not built via the socialist platform we are now climbing upon. This country will not survive this expanding socialism. No country has ever survived socialism! We must educate our students about the truth of capitalism in order to defend capitalism from the fraudulent attacks being made by the proponents of socialism. We must have more young students who understand fiscal responsibility and why we must balance our budget. What does this have to do with education? We must improve education to the point that our students are fluent in ELA and math, can think critically, question the propagandists, demand facts, and be able to analyze facts and data. Students must be taught real history and government so they understand how we became who we are and, for that matter, who we really are. Students must understand how our government functions in order to gain respect for the system of governance and values that have made us great! These basic educational skills that I have just outlined are fundamental to a highly functional democracy. We cannot continue to function as a society, nor fix our problems, with an ever-growing number of uneducated citizens. The uneducated, and the victims of brainwashing, are too easily led. The left seeks out those people; in fact, they seek to create people with that mindset, and they are purchasing Americans' support by addicting them to a stay-at-home mentality dependent upon the government dole. COVID-19 has proven to be a most useful tool for the left! This simply cannot end well unless there is an immediate and rapid change in the modus operandi of those in charge. I hope you see the connection. Back to more specific problems in education.

Teachers cannot be a student's buddy. You exhibit interest and caring, but from a position of the person of authority. Next to failing at the command presence authority needed for discipline, I see too many teachers, young and old alike, who become too familiar with students. Ultimately, they fail! Some are forced out of education, and those that remain are not as productive as we need for them to be when it comes to creating the most optimum learning environment! But what is taught is sometimes questionable!

Children go to school, and once they arrive at school, they are under the direct supervision and control of the school administration and the classroom teachers. That is the way that is supposed to work! We parents have always trusted that arrangement. All goes well with that arrangement almost all of the time. Because our children become a captive audience while at school, it is very important for parents to visit schools and to keep a close eye on curriculum taught and what individual teachers are teaching our children. Again, that happens in a correct fashion almost all of the time, but ask yourself, is there an opportunity for a tiny fraction of the teachers, with an agenda, to teach values and interpretations that you do not want taught to your children? Be on guard!

Unfortunately, given the myriad of problems of broken homes, too many school districts, principals, and teachers are forced into a position of "in loco parentis." Schools provide, at no cost to students, breakfast, lunch, and even send food home in the evenings and during the summer months. Schools search for clothing for disadvantaged children. Schools provide the paper, pencils, etc. that students need. Teachers must always be on the lookout for signs of abuse and must contact Child Protective Services if they even suspect that the child is in a setting that puts the child at risk for a myriad of different issues. Schools must make parents aware of medical needs. So many children are coming from chaotic homes that districts are always seeking more and more mental health counseling for children. I thank God that I and my four brothers had two parents that were in the home and who looked after our needs. I was lucky, and I hope you were as well! Too many children are not that lucky, and that necessitates that the responsibilities of teachers and school districts must go far beyond the intended duty of teaching students. Such challenges make it more difficult to create the optimum learning environment and to improve student achievement. We owe the children and the future of the nation to step up the effort for this essential task!

Beware of school districts, administrators, and individual teachers who intentionally take it upon themselves to assume a role of in loco parentis for the wrong reasons! One of the many impacts of COVID-19 on school systems was the discovery by many parents around the country of some curriculum being taught that many parents found objectionable. Let this be a lesson to all parents; you have a right to know what is going on in your child's school. My best advice to you is trust, but always verify. You are the watchdog!

Too many parents have discovered, in the last year, that some in education have an agenda with nefarious purposes. Captive audiences of innocent children, in their formative years, are being targeted by some who want to provide presentations such as Project 19, critical race theory, numerous gender identifications, sexual experiences, and various nonfactual revisions of our nation's history. As a social studies teacher, I was placed in a powerful position. It is incumbent upon teachers to accept that position of influence over children with the highest respect for the limitations on things we should not impose on children. There are teachers, and I have met them, who seek to impose their individual values and preferences on children. That is dangerous and unacceptable! Most parents are unwilling to confer that power upon any teacher.

From my study of the United States Constitution, I have always believed that the jurisdiction of overseeing public schools was a power held by the states, not the federal government. Goggle https://www.ecs.org/wp-content/uploads/2016-Constitution-al-obligations-for-public-education-1.pdf for the "EDUCATION COMMISION OF THE STATES' 50 STATE REVIEW" article written by Emily Parker in March of 2016. The article clearly points out the fact that the jurisdiction over public schools rests with the state governments and not the federal government. The findings of 1973 Supreme Court decision of San Antonio Independent School District v. Rodriguez serves as proof that states should have local control. Recently the federal government's various agencies have pointed to parents' protests about curriculum as something that should be investigated to prevent domestic terrorism of school boards. US Attorney General Merrick Garland is involving the FBI to potentially investigate the harassment of school boards by protesting parents! What I have seen on television regarding some school board meetings certainly points to anger and chaos, but unless there are documented threats of murder or abduction of school board members or school officials, I do not see the necessity of FBI involvement. I admit that there may well be events taking place that I and the public do not know. Could this be a tactic of the left designed to scare and deter legitimate protest? If this is just a scare tactic, I would ask you if you have ever heard of the KGB tactics. Does this sound like an attack on the freedom to assemble and to petition government for a redress of grievances? Does this sound like a potential curb on free speech? Seems clear to me that the states should be in control and that parents in the districts have rights when it comes to the education of their children. What is the motivation for the federal government's position on this issue? We must fight to save American freedoms! Parents have the right to peacefully protest and question curriculum and school boards!

It was not my responsibility or right to make good little democrats, republicans, atheists, or followers of a particular religious doctrine of the students entrusted to me by parents! Period! It was, my responsibility to teach manners, rules, civic responsibility, an appreciation of laws that protect society, respect and tolerance for differences of opinions, the cause and effect impact of historical events, predictions of expected outcomes based upon study of history, the growth and development of the American story as it has evolved over time, the story of the effort to change practices in America as we have strived to come closer to the ideals expressed in our founding documents, and to encourage respect for the rights of all Americans regardless of their race. That is a long list, but it is just a few of the responsibilities.

My job necessitated that I put students into activities that forced them to seek facts and positions on both sides of an issue and then require students to evaluate the data and state positions that they could support and defend with facts and real events.

My social studies classes included debate, discussion, summarization, reading comprehension skills, writing skills, and, yes, mathematics. I accepted the responsibility of teaching factual American History. I introduced my students, as I have done in this book, the good, the bad, the ugly of the American story. What I did not do was to selectively take negative events and present them as the total story of America in order to shape minds to fit an agenda set upon destroying America. When you selectively take events out of the total context and leave out the counterbalancing facts and events, you are being deceitful, and you cheat students. I have always trusted the overall rightness of the American story, and I believe that when you present the whole story, the goodness and wrong of the story come forth. We continue to improve on America. We do not throw out the baby with the dirty bathwater.

In summary, you must trust but verify when it comes to child's education. Be on guard and watch carefully what is taking place in your schools. Continuously assess your child's mastery of ELA and math. They are the essential foundations for all future learning and for being able to function as a self-sufficient adult.

Turn the page to chapter 11 titled, "The Declaration of Independence and the Constitution of the United States of America." I am sure you have the necessary ELA skills for understanding chapter 11 and for the study of these two documents. Hopefully, I can share something on the subject that will be relevant to the thrust of this book.

11

The Declaration of Independence and the Constitution of the United States of America

I am of the opinion that we Americans are indeed blessed to live in a country that was founded by the unique and bold positions expressed in the both the Declaration of Independence and the Constitution of the United States. Are we perfect, have we ever been perfect, or will we ever be perfect? The answer to those three questions is an emphatic *no*! The philosophy and basis of these two documents were astounding to the world of 1776 and 1787, not because they were something new on the world's political stage but because their radical nature placed great emphasis upon the rights of individual's freedoms and governance. Until this time, most of the world was governed by forces of great strength that were maneuvered by would-be autocratic rulers. That we and our creed will never achieve perfection is not a reason to abandon a system of governance that is still second to none that the world has ever seen.

Under autocratic rule, mankind suffered through great trials and tribulations of persecutions directed toward religious practice, political philosophy, how economic activity would be structured, as well as the unalienable rights that many Americans have taken for granted in recent decades. Because of this abuse, which lasted for decades and centuries, the human spirit thirsted for freedom.

Suffering humanity, under autocratic rule, began to dream of a better way of life, and millions were ready to seize an opportunity that might provide for freedom. This nation's birth based upon the 1776 Declaration of Independence, the self-governance achieved by the 1789 ratification of the Constitution, and the passage of the 1791 Bill of Rights all combined to eliminate so much of the denial of unalienable rights that were commonplace throughout the history of the world, prior to 1776 and 1791. Not perfect, in practice, but still a keeper! Without question, this nation and its principles must be preserved. Our nation has the best system of governance that any group of imperfect humans can ever hope to create!

The ideas expressed in the Declaration of Independence, when compared to the norms of rule by the so-called royalty of the European monarchies, were extremely radical and the antithesis of the realities of governance in eighteenth-century Europe. Suddenly, the world's political landscape, so long shrouded in darkness by autocratic rule, was flooded with a light of hope. What a novel idea, individual's unalienable rights might be secured via self-governance or democracy. Such an illumination of potential freedom was like a magnet that attracted the heart and soul of the oppressed. This shining illumination was first emitted by the Declaration of Independence. The 1776 Declaration of Independence paved the way for eventual "rule of law" provided by the writing of the Constitution of the United States of America in 1787 and by ratification of the constitution in 1789. All of this was made possible as a result of the desperate struggle of the American patriots, with a little help from our friends in France, when together we successfully defeated the power and wealth of the British military forces.

We study history in order to determine the causes and effects of the great historical events of the world. We should analyze the present and couple that analysis with our knowledge and perspective of recent and much older historical events. A clear understanding of the causes and effects of historical events, both those of our distant past and more recent past, coupled with an analysis of the present, can help us predict where we are going in the future. It is paramount, due to the attacks being made upon America by the radical left, that we combine our knowledge of our past with an analysis of the present in order to project what will happen in the future. This is the only way to protect the freedoms, goodness, and functionality of America far into the future. The historical events that necessitated the writing of the Declaration of Independence must be understood because those devastating events and effects must not be allowed to happen again, lest we lose the "joy of life" provided by the Declaration of Independence and our Constitution!

Are there far too many Americans who do not appreciate the "joy of life" provided by our foundational documents? I believe there are, because they have not been taught the facts of our real history. Also, they have never experienced anything but the goodness of the American way of life. They do not understand the horror of life under autocratic rule; therefore, slick salespeople can convince them that America is bad and has always been bad. The "destroy America as we know it" agenda, of those people who seek to vilify this nation, employs the use of such tools as revisionist history, division, racism, critical race theory, politically correct speech, and a socialist philosophy of spread-the-wealth syndrome. These people are identifiable as socialists by the nature of their modus operandi which is continuously demonstrated by their actions of giving away the money of hardworking American citizens to illegal aliens and to those who want something for nothing. Not only do they give away the money we have today, they are also giving away borrowed money that belongs to our children, grandchildren, and great-grandchildren. If too many American citizens, along with the illegals that are being inserted into our interior, receive and buy into what the radical left is seizing and offering, then there will be a seizing of power that will doom the "joy of freedoms" and economic vitality that our founding documents have provided.

So take a look at the provisions of these two wonderful documents that have freed so much of the world by spreading the light of freedom and hope!

The Declaration of Independence

When in the Course of human Events, it becomes necessary for one People to dissolve the Political Bands which have connected them with another, and to assume among the Powers of the Earth, the separate and equal Station to which the Laws of Nature and of Nature's God entitle them, a decent respect to the opinions of Mankind requires that they should declare the causes which impel them to the Separation.

We hold these truths to be self-evident, that all men are created equal, that they are endowed by their Creator with certain unalienable Rights, that among these are Life, Liberty, and the Pursuit of Happiness—-That to secure these Rights, Governments are instituted among Men, deriving their just Powers from the Consent of the Governed, that whenever any Form of Government becomes destructive of these Ends, it is the Right of the People to alter or to abolish it, and to institute new Government, laying its Foundation on such Principles, and organizing its Powers in such Form, as to them shall seem most likely to effect their Safety and Happiness. Prudence, indeed, will dictate that Governments long established should not be changed for light and transient Causes; and accordingly all Experience hath shewn, that Mankind are more disposed to suffer, while Evils are sufferable, than to right themselves by abolishing the Forms to which they are accustomed. But when a long Train of Abuses and Usurpations, pursuing invariably the same Object, evinces a Design to reduce them under absolute Despotism, it is their Right, it is their Duty, to throw off such

Government, and to provide new Guards for their future Security. Such has been the patient Sufferance of these Colonies; and such is now the Necessity which constrains them to alter their former Systems of Government. The History of the present King of Great-Britain is a History of repeated Injuries and Usurpations, all having in direct Object the Establishment of an absolute Tyranny over these States. To prove this, let Facts be submitted to a candid World.

He has refused his Assent to Laws, the most wholesome and necessary for the public Good.

He has forbidden his Governors to pass Laws of immediate and pressing Importance, unless suspended in their Operation till his Assent should be obtained; and when so suspended, he has utterly neglected to attend to them.

He has refused to pass other Laws for the Accommodation of large Districts of People, unless those People would relinquish the Right of Representation in the Legislature, a Right inestimable to them, and formidable to Tyrants only.

He has called together Legislative Bodies at Places unusual, uncomfortable, and distant from the Depository of their public Records, for the sole Purpose of fatiguing them into Compliance with his Measures.

He has dissolved Representative Houses repeatedly, for opposing with manly Firmness his Invasions on the Rights of the People.

He has refused for a long time, after such dissolutions, to cause others to be elected; whereby the Legislative powers, incapable of Annihilation, have returned to the People at large for their exercise; the State remaining in the mean time exposed to all the dangers of invasion from without, and Convulsions within.

He has endeavoured to prevent the Population of these States; for that Purpose obstructing the Laws for Naturalization of Foreigners; refusing to pass others to encourage their Migrations hither, and raising the Conditions of new Appropriations of Lands.

He has obstructed the Administration of Justice, by refusing his Assent to Laws for establishing Judiciary Powers.

He has made Judges dependent on his Will alone, for the Tenure of their Offices, and the Amount and Payment of their Salaries.

He has erected a Multitude of new Offices, and sent hither swarms of Officers to harass our People, and eat out their Substance.

He has kept among us, in Times of Peace, Standing Armies, without the consent of our Legislatures.

He has affected to render the Military independent of and superior to the Civil Power.

He has combined with others to subject us to a Jurisdiction foreign to our Constitution, and unacknowledged by our Laws; giving his Assent to their Acts of pretended Legislation:

For quartering large Bodies of Armed Troops among us:

For protecting them, by a mock Trial, from Punishment for any Murders which they should commit on the Inhabitants of these States:

For cutting off our Trade with all Parts of the World:

For imposing Taxes on us without our Consent:

For depriving us, in many Cases, of the Benefits of Trial by Jury:

For transporting us beyond Seas to be tried for pretended Offences:

For abolishing the free System of English Laws in a neighbouring Province, establishing therein an arbitrary Government, and enlarging its Boundaries, so as to render it at once an Example and fit Instrument for introducing the same absolute Rule into these Colonies:

For taking away our Charters, abolishing our most valuable Laws, and altering fundamentally the Forms of our Governments:

For suspending our own Legislatures, and declaring themselves invested with Power to legislate for us in all Cases whatsoever.

He has abdicated Government here, by declaring us out of his Protection and waging War against us.

He has plundered our Seas, ravaged our Coasts, burnt our Towns, and destroyed the Lives of our People.

He is, at this Time, transporting large Armies of foreign Mercenaries to compleat the Works of Death, Desolation, and Tyranny, already begun with circumstances of Cruelty and Perfidy, scarcely paralleled in the most barbarous Ages, and totally unworthy the Head of a civilized Nation.

He has constrained our fellow Citizens taken Captive on the high Seas to bear Arms against their Country, to become the Executioners of their Friends and Brethren, or to fall themselves by their Hands.

He has excited domestic Insurrections amongst us, and has endeavoured to bring on the

Inhabitants of our Frontiers, the merciless Indian Savages, whose known Rule of Warfare, is an undistinguished Destruction, of all Ages, Sexes and Conditions.

In every stage of these Oppressions we have Petitioned for Redress in the most humble Terms: Our repeated Petitions have been answered only by repeated Injury. A Prince, whose Character is thus marked by every act which may define a Tyrant, is unfit to be the Ruler of a free People.

Nor have we been wanting in Attentions to our British Brethren. We have warned them from Time to Time of Attempts by their Legislature to extend an unwarrantable Jurisdiction over us. We have reminded them of the Circumstances of our Emigration and Settlement here. We have appealed to their native Justice and Magnanimity, and we have conjured them by the Ties of our common Kindred to disavow these Usurpations, which, would inevitably interrupt our Connections and Correspondence. They too have been deaf to the Voice of Justice and of Consanguinity. We must, therefore, acquiesce in the Necessity, which denounces our Separation, and hold them, as we hold the rest of Mankind, Enemies in War, in Peace, Friends.

We, therefore, the Representatives of the United States of America, in General Congress, Assembled, appealing to the Supreme Judge of the World for the Rectitude of our Intentions, do, in the Name, and by Authority of the good People of these Colonies, solemnly Publish and Declare, That these United Colonies are, and of Right ought to be, Free and Independent States; that they are absolved from all Allegiance to the British Crown, and that all political connection between them and the State of Great Britain, is and ought to be totally dissolved; and that as Free and Independent States, they have full Power to levy War, conclude Peace, contract Alliances, establish Commerce, and to do all other Acts and Things which Independent States may of right do.—And for the support of this Declaration, with a firm reliance on the protection of Divine Providence, we mutually pledge to each other our Lives, our Fortunes, and our sacred Honor.

Thomas Jefferson of Virginia is credited as being the main author of the Declaration of Independence, but he was assisted by a committee that included John Adams, Benjamin Franklin, Roger Sherman, and Robert Livingston. There were edits of the document by the committee prior to the final passage. A total of fifty-six colonial delegates signed this birth certificate of the United States of America. The birth of our nation took place during the meeting of the Second Continental Congress in Philadelphia's Independence Hall.

It has long been accepted that the birth date of the United States of America is July 4, 1776, and that this was the date the document was signed. July 4, 1776, appears at the top of the document. There is some historical dispute about the actual signing date. Some historians claim that the document was not signed until August 2, 1776. Regardless of the date signatures were affixed to the original document, this Declaration of Independence, by the thirteen British colonies, shocked the world. How dare these colonial rebels challenge the sovereignty of King George III. And by the way, the birth of the United States of America was not in Virginia in 1619, as the proponents of Project 1619 falsely claim!

We hold these Truths to be self-evident, that all Men are created equal, that they are endowed by their Creator with certain unalienable Rights, that among these are Life, Liberty, and the Pursuit of Happiness.

Without a doubt, this line of the Declaration of Independence is the one that is targeted most frequently by those who want to sully the greatness of this nation and our founding.

The first object of contention is the phrase, "that all Men are created equal." This phrase is chastised and ridiculed because it does not say all men and all women are created equal. That is a fair complaint, when you attack the exclusion of women from the phrase created equal, based upon a perspective that originates after the passage of the Nineteenth Amendment that was ratified in 1920. The Nineteenth Amendment gave white women the right to vote, if they were citizens! The Declaration of Independence was written and signed in 1776. Life, culture, and accepted norms were quite different in 1776 versus 1920. The fact that women were not mentioned as equal in the Declaration of Independence does not make the document less earth-shattering or less valuable to humanity. The document was radical and a game changer for humanity. No place in the world, that I am aware of in 1776, would have recognized the equality of women with men. That fact does not take away from the importance of the document. Because of the accepted culture of the era, the statement of "all Men are created equal" was the norm that would have been expected. Gender roles of the eighteenth century were different.

The document did, however, set a high standard for individual rights. The radical idealism proclaimed to the world by this document did, over time, disturb the conscience of America. After a very long period of challenges and suffering, this document's wording did not deny all races and both genders the right to sit at the "table of equality" in America. Sometimes radical change, especially when it is change for the better, can only take place in increments over a long period of time. While such slow change is not excusable, there are societal norms and reasons that delay justice, unfortunately.

President Abraham Lincoln said, regarding a different subject, "A house divided cannot stand." I believe his statement is appropriate for the subject of this discussion as well. History shows us that America has become even greater over time! More people have been gathered under the protective umbrella of our creed! Also, in addition to this discussion, we should look at another phrase that seems to be read incorrectly by those who wish to put forth a perverted agenda.

"Life, Liberty, and the Pursuit of Happiness" does not entitle anyone to "cradle to grave sustenance" by the government of "We the people!" There are many citizens in our society that a kind and generous society can and should help! I say this to all of those who game the system and for those who seek to bribe citizens with the public's money, "You cannot have it both ways!" "All Men, all women, and all races are created equal." Therefore, we are all equally responsible for our own individual struggle to provide for our own sustenance, as unequal as our achievements may be. Created equal does not mean that the fruits of labor of all are to be divided equally. That is socialism, and the writers of the Declaration of Independence and the Constitution of the United States of America did not subscribe to socialism.

The final phrase of the Declaration of Independence is quite noteworthy, in that all who signed the document subscribed to that document with the full knowledge that their signatures made them part of a frightening reality: "We mutually pledge to each other our Lives, our Fortunes, and our sacred Honor." I cannot explain this statement as well as Benjamin Franklin did after they all signed the Declaration of Independence, and I quote, "We must all hang together, or most assuredly, we will all hang separately." What does this statement mean to you? Think about the commitment and the reality of what this statement says regarding the actions taken by these fifty-six delegates to the Second Continental Congress who signed this world-famous document! Because of their belief in the rightness of their cause, a fight for freedom and liberty, these men committed treason against Great Britain's King George III! Such an act of treason would result in the loss of their greatest possession, their lives, if the cause failed. Failure or capture would result in being hanged until death! What does such commitment as that mean to "We the people" in 2022 and beyond? Though many take our freedoms for granted, I assure you the signers of the declaration demonstrated that they did not take freedom for granted. They risked everything in their pledge and quest for freedom for themselves and for their posterity. We are their posterity, and we must preserve these blessings of liberty for our posterity!

The successful execution of the American Revolution of 1776 through 1781 was a desperate cause embraced by roughly one-third of the colonists who wanted to rid themselves of what they perceived as tyranny and autocratic rule of a king thousands of miles across the Atlantic. The reason for the false attacks made against our institutions and about our foundational documents by the radical left is quite simple. The radical left wishes to destroy the sanctity and validity of all documents and the history of America. To do that, they take events of history out of context.

To fully understand history, you cannot just project and talk about incidents out of context, and then point to a document such as the Declaration of Independence and proclaim, "We must change America because America is and always has been evil and wrong." One of the best distortions and examples of taking a story out of the total context is what the radical left is seeking to do with the legacy of George Washington. Yes, I know that he was a slaveholder in Virginia. I have also read accounts that our current vice president's father has written that he is descended from a family of slaveholders! George Washington, our first commander in chief, was the "Father of our country!" Read the history of George Washington's unfaltering perseverance and leadership during the American Revolution. Without his leadership, it is doubtful there would have been a United States of America. His courage was unquestionable! Because he lived in a time and place where many people owned slaves, as wrong as that institution was, are we to deny all of the good qualities and contributions he gave to the cause that created this country? Unfortunately, the eighteenth century was a time in history in which slavery was an accepted norm that slaveholders had been born into. Nobody has the right to own another person, but that statement was not accepted in the eighteenth century, and it had not been accepted in all of world history prior to 1776. The radical left tries to deny the protections of freedoms and unalienable rights that the Declaration of Independence and the Constitution of the United States have clearly provided us for generations. Those who seek to destroy respect for this nation by intentionally misleading our citizens and especially the young with negative propaganda are as dangerous to America's future as any foreign military that hates us.

These activists attack the founders and the documents they produced, American values, and traditions as examples of systemic racism and extreme hypocrisy. They are teaching our children, in both public schools and in institutions of higher learning, that we are systemically racist. I denounce that assertion with the upmost vigor. Has racism existed, and does racism continue to raise an ugly face in this country? Absolutely, but that is not the fault of our documents and our ideals; it is the fault of the individuals, of all races, who refuse to judge people by the content of their character rather than by their skin color! We will not solve such despicable acts of racism by tearing down the country and attacking different races of people.

The opposite of what we enjoy and stand for in America is autocratic rule! We freely admit that there are freedoms promised in these documents that were not provided for all Americans for many generations after 1776 and 1791. We have already discussed that the norms of the eighteenth century did not recognize rights the same as we began to recognize them during the late 1860s and later in the 1900s. These "destroyers of America" selectively point to dark stains of our past and ignore the progress made, over time, to provide more freedoms and rights to more Americans. First, there were the foundational documents, and with the changing times, Americans began to more fully live up to our creed. These attackers will not improve American life by destroying our system of governance and the economic functionality of free enterprise capitalism. They will, however, lead us into a dark future that will not allow the light of freedoms, provided to us since 1776 and 1791, to shine!

> We the People of the United States, in Order to form a more perfect Union, establish Justice, insure domestic Tranquility, provide for the common defence, promote the general Welfare, and secure the Blessings of Liberty to

ourselves and our Posterity, do ordain and estab-
lish this Constitution for the United States of
America. (Preamble to the Constitution of the
United States of America)

Have you read the preamble to the Constitution of the United
States of America that was written in 1787 and adopted in 1789?
Seems to me that this is a very good thesis statement for the most
outstanding document ever written for the purpose of structuring a
system of governance. The outline of goals put forth in this opening
statement not only tells the world the intentions of the document,
but it addresses the failings of our first plan of central government,
the Articles of Confederation. While I find it difficult for anyone to
argue against these goals of the preamble, I do think that prudence
requires that we briefly discuss some specific points that you just
read. By taking this approach, I feel I can rebut the attackers of our
way of governance!

Please read again the first phrase of the preamble!

No one person nor group of people will ever be perfect. From
that understanding, we should all recognize that the works and the
performance of any one person or group of people will never be perfect. To attack performance and actions of individuals throughout
history is okay, but that does not mean the overall structure of our
governance should be discarded or radically changed by an action
such as packing the supreme court to achieve a political agenda for
extreme and radical change. We, the imperfect people, are very telling and are correct for this discussion! This opening phrase of the
preamble, "We the people," was an announcement to all Americans
in 1787 and the world that our system of governance would be very
different. People, not a king or dictator, would, with all of their
imperfections, seek to secure the blessings of liberty for themselves
and for posterity. Pretty big order, don't you think? With this system,
it was the goal of our "founders" that no single person would be so
powerful that they alone would make all decisions for the citizenry.

The phrase "in Order to form a more perfect Union" is telling
in that the goal is clear, but nobody claimed we would achieve per-

fection. "We the people" have worked toward that end and the spirit of freedom of this nation has, over time, helped to keep us on the path of becoming a "more perfect Union." That effort needs to continue, but the actions of divisiveness being put forth by the "radical left of change" does not seek to create a more perfect union. Rather, their actions and agenda seem intent on making it impossible to even maintain a union!

Consider the following actions of the radical left and/or the Biden-Harris administration's actions, silence, or lack of action that are creating a more imperfect union: 1) defund the police; 2) allow the rewriting history; 3) allow millions of illegal multi-national aliens to come into our country; 4) allow the drug cartels to send mules carrying drugs and weapons into our country across our southern border; 5) create a labor shortage in this country because the federal government wants to pay people more to stay at home than they would make if they had to work; 6) borrow and spend our country into financial oblivion; 7) stand by while anarchists loot and burn our cities; 8) tell Americans and our school children they must wear masks while the Biden-Harris administration allows thousands upon thousands of illegals, who are positive with the COVID virus, to be shipped all over our country; 9) using the public's money to bribe citizens and encourage illegal aliens to come here and subscribe to the socialism that is being pushed with the slops of freebies that are being handed out; and I could go on and on about the insanity of what has taken place in this country since January of 2021! If these things were not so tragic for America, the insanity of these occurrences would be laughable.

Do you believe that anybody could be so devoid of common sense as to allow these things to be taking place? I find it hard to believe that common sense escapes these people, but maybe it does. Is there another possibility? Could it be that there are nefarious goals that are well served by allowing this insanity to continue? As always, you decide! I will say this: I am opposed to whatever the cause of this insanity is! And the American people need to prepare for 2022 and 2024, or the insanity or nefarious purposes will take this nation over the edge and to the "point of no return!" Wait, I have more phrases to discuss.

The next phrase for discussion is "insure the domestic Tranquility." This one is short and sweet. Without police, the evil and criminal elements of society are emboldened to prey upon defenseless citizens. That is exactly what happened in the spring and summer of 2020 as our cities were looted and burned. That is not insuring domestic tranquility. Enough said, but I must go to the next two concepts that appear in the thesis, preamble, of the constitution.

I have chosen these two phrases and goals of the constitution's preamble for discussion: "provide for the common defence, promote the general Welfare." When I was a young boy, growing up in rural southeastern West Virginia, we knew all of our neighbors for miles, and they knew us just as well. It would shock you to know that we never locked the doors of our homes. We never had to. Today, we all think about defending our homes and being safe. I no longer feel safe without locking the doors of my home. I have other protections in my home that neither I, my brothers, or our parents would have ever felt we needed. In short, our common defense and our general welfare seem to always be in question today. Do you feel safe in your country? I must confess that I do not.

We the people of the United States of America have, in the past, felt like we were protected from enemies, both foreign and domestic, but no longer. Criminal gangs from south of the border have invaded our cities. The drug cartels are killing our people with their poisons of deadly chemicals. They have an army of distributors and dealers in our country. They, not the Mexican government, are in control of what goes on along the border between the United States and Mexico. Sadly, the Biden-Harris administration is not in control of our southern border. Biden and Harris are responsible for the chaos that exists there. The cartels are well armed. The policy of open borders and the socialist offerings of the Biden-Harris administration, as directed by the radical left, are further enriching the drug cartels who are transporting foreigners across our border.

These illegal and criminal aliens are coming from countries all over the world, and they are a clear and present danger to "We the people of the United States of America." They do not share our values! Based upon these facts, do you believe that our president and vice president are embracing the directives of "We the people" as stated in our constitution's preamble? The premise upon which the constitution was written outlined the purpose of our federal government. Both the president and the vice president swore an oath to defend the constitution of the United States. Please, read again the preamble to the Constitution of the United States.

> We the People of the United States, in Order to form a more perfect Union, establish Justice, insure domestic Tranquility, provide for the common defence, promote the general Welfare, and secure the Blessings of Liberty to ourselves and our Posterity, do ordain and establish this Constitution for the United States of America.

I submit that I do not see much, if any, adherence to the directives of the preamble by any elected officials in Washington! We are not seeing the creation of "a more perfect Union," nor the assurance of "domestic Tranquility," providing for "the common defence," nor a promotion of "the general Welfare." In fact, I believe we are witnessing just the opposite. That must end in 2022 and in 2024!

Does it seem to you that those in control in Washington seem more concerned about foreigners than they do about you, your children, grandchildren, and future generations of Americans? Who is truly concerned about Americans who work, pay taxes, those who have worn a blue uniform to protect our neighborhoods, those brave men and women who have defended this country on foreign soil and who stand ready to do so again, or just the people who work and obey the laws of the land? I propose, as did President Donald J. Trump, that we put America first! I also say that we must start putting "We the people," the American people, first.

The beliefs put forth in the Declaration of Independence, the outline for the purpose of our Constitution as expressed in the preamble of the Constitution of the Unites States, the framework for a successful working form of government provided for in the Constitution of the United States of America, and the Bill of Rights are a shield against tyranny and autocratic rule. The umbrella of protection for our unalienable rights that these documents have provided since the eighteenth century is second to none in world history.

Join me in Chapter 12, "Does the Bribery Purchase of American Citizen's Votes Doom America?" Before you turn to chapter 12, I want to say that I believe we are doomed if votes can be bought. The purchasers of votes will stop at nothing to achieve their goals, and their goals spell disaster for "We the people!"

12

Does the Bribery Purchase of American Citizens' Votes Doom America?

(Google https://quotes.thefamouspeople.com/alexis-de-tocqueville-659.php to view the following article, "67 Enlightening Quotes by Alexis De Tocqueville, the Author of Democracy in America.")

The American Republic will endure until the day Congress discovers that it can bribe the public with the public's money. (Alexis de Tocqueville)

Alexis de Tocqueville was a French historian and political scientist born on July 29, 1805, in Paris, France. He traveled in the United States during the year of 1831–32 observing American culture, government, and religion throughout various regions of the country. As a result of travel and observation of America, he wrote *Democracy in America*. The book is still prominent today and continues to be studied and quoted. Tocqueville is remembered for his numerous quotes that illustrated his philosophy and observations about America. One of his quotes, that I read many years ago, that is particularly interesting to me is, "The American Republic will endure until the day Congress discovers that it can bribe the public with the public's money." Was Alexis de Tocqueville a clairvoyant, or did he have a magic crystal ball? I think not, but this quote has interested me for many years, and I often wondered if his statement, which seemed to indicate an inevitable future circumstance, would ever become reality in America. I thought, surely not; the American people are far too smart for that, and surely there would never be enough American politicians who would be so corrupt and power hungry that they would risk the survival of the nation. Was I wrong? As always, you decide, but we should discuss this issue to determine if what I once considered as a possibility is now reality.

As you read this chapter, may I suggest the following guided reading question for which you should seek an answer and examples of proof? Are American citizens being bribed with public money, by Congress, and does this irresponsibility spell doom for the American republic as Alexis de Tocqueville suggested?

The U.S. constitution established a representative democracy. We the people, in modern America, cast votes for members of both the House of Representatives and for the U.S. Senate. The Seventeenth Amendment to the constitution was passed in 1913, and from that point forward, the elections of U.S. senators would take place in the voting booth rather than by appointment by state legislatures. The combination of these two legislative bodies make up the United States Congress.

"The American Republic will endure until the day Congress discovers that it can bribe the public with the public's money." Has Alexis de Tocqueville's 1830s statement become reality in 2021 America?

Twenty-eight trillion dollars, and counting, of national debt is due in large part to politicians who refuse to cut back on wasteful spending that would permit the balancing of the federal budget. Elected representatives in Washington routinely tag on "pork barrel" spending measures to necessary spending bills in exchange for support of the original bill! This way, the constituents in the home district receive funding for pet projects, and the cost of the needed spending bills rockets upward and the debt increases. Without term limits for congress, we see members who are reelected for decades because they have "brought home the bacon." Spending bill after spending bill that favors special interests in the home state seem to assure that the public's vote can be bought with the public's money through the bribery process. One thing I bet Tocqueville would not have envisioned is that the bribery would be carried out with borrowed money! Money borrowed on our grandchildren's future is a travesty and an abomination! Most states and most households balance their budgets! Failure by the federal government to stop their criminal spending will cause the destruction of this nation as surely as if a thousand hydrogen bombs were dropped on the country. Would you agree that this fiscal irresponsibility is evidence that proves Tocqueville's prediction? What say you? Perhaps we should discuss some more specific details! As you read further, I am confident you will be able to answer the question!

Google https://www.foxnews.com/politics/ilhan-omar-guaranteed-income-1200-monthly-checks?yptr=yahoo to read an article by Brie Stimson of Fox News titled "Ilhan Omar backs 'guaranteed income,' pitches bills to send $1,200 monthly checks to most Americans."

Google https://www.yahoo.com/lifestyle/why-andrew-yangs-universal-basic-113000216.html?fr=sycsrp_catchall to read an article by Luke Darby on 8/23/2019 titled "Why Andrew Yang's Universal Basic Income Proposal Has Been Gaining Ground" to view another ridiculous policy of socialism that will destroy America.

Have you heard of the concept of guaranteed income? Free monthly income with no strings attached. I have been looking for free money all of my life, but with the exception of a few nickels, dimes, or quarters dropped on a sidewalk or left in the change return of the old-fashioned telephone booths or a vending machine, I have not found free money. Have you? Does such a thing as free money actually exist? Free money, is that an example of an *oxymoron* put forth by morons or at best by people who are ignorant of natural law and the reality of production necessary for surviving on planet Earth?

Apparently, this moronic concept does in fact exist, because there are pilot programs in force in some of the large liberal cities of

America that would provide a guaranteed income. In fact, Ilhan Omar, U.S. House of Representatives of Minnesota's Fifth District supports sending guaranteed income of $1,200 monthly to most Americans according to the articles I have read and cited. Andrew Yang, of New York, has proposed universal basic income. Rashida Tlaib, a member of the U. S. House of Representatives from Michigan, proposed that illegal aliens get a preloaded debit card with $2,000 and a recharge of $1,000 a month until one year after the economy recovers. Again, these proposals are well documented on the internet. Google their names and you will see their statements! I did not see any mention of the criteria for determining what would be the identification of a recovered economy. You know, come to think of it, most of those giveaways never seem to terminate, do they? A proposal was put forth in August of 2021 to fund forty-two billion to pay utility bills for citizens who have not paid utility bills since the onset of COVID-19. I could go on and on because there are so many of these ridiculous proposals being put forth by the radical left! Is this the "equitable distribution" that the left keeps talking about?

The left has become very adept at using the English language, in creative ways, to cloak old verbiage that may not be too popular. Equitable distribution is nothing more than redistribution of the wealth of hardworking people and successful entrepreneurs. In short, it is pure socialism! Socialism that is couched in a way that is supposed to make us feel guilty for not going along with the concept of helping people they say are in need. To be sure, there are people in need in this country, but not nearly as many as the left would have you to believe. Nor do they need as much help as the left wishes to provide. If you give enough to make them comfortable, there would never be any incentive for self-improvement, would there? My question to you is, "Can or should the people of the United States be responsible for all of the people around the world in need? How many people are looking for a free ride? With whom and to whom should we be responsible?"

The jobs report for July of 2021 indicated the economy had added some nine hundred thousand jobs. Great news, according to the Biden administration who would contend that the country is heading in the right direction. Wrong! The problem with figures is that liars figure how to use figures. What was not mentioned is the fact that there are, as of July 2021, nine million unfilled jobs in America. What they also do not tell you is that they are working to determine how to continue extending unemployment benefits under the guise of "need for COVID relief."

As of August 2021, leftists have fought and succeeded in extending the moratorium on evictions by landlords of tenants who are not paying their rent. So the entrepreneurial landlords get no help to pay their ongoing bills, taxes, mortgage payments, and maintenance costs, but we have people in the congress who want to provide guaranteed income and payment for utilities of the tenants. That is how government creates slums of abandoned properties by landlords. Could this be a way to destroy ownership of rental properties and have the government rush in to run these properties for the poor? Sounds like something that was done in the Soviet Union. I don't know! Just wondering what their reasoning might be, but I can assure this will not end well, and it cannot be sustained. Wait, I have a novel idea and suggestion!

How can there be such a need for such a large amount of unemployment benefits when there are nine million unfilled jobs? My novel idea, stop the free money handouts of borrowed money we cannot afford, end the moratorium on tenant evictions, and stop the flow of unemployment compensation and tell people you have to go back to work.

You will see signs saying, "Now Hiring or Help Wanted," during every walk down the street or trip taken. Prices are soaring because of demand for limited products that are not being produced because people are sitting at home on the dole. Employers are competing with the federal government for workers that the federal government is paying to stay home at a higher income than they would make working. That is *nuts*! The left has used COVID-19, that has killed Americans, including friends and relatives of mine, to their advantage to not only place their man in the White House but to bribe the citizens and buy the votes of the benefactors of free money. This has been a successful "end run" to addict millions to the concept of living off the dole. Do it long enough and people come to expect and demand that it is their right to be taken care of from cradle to grave.

The "dole" is being paid for on the backs of hardworking men and women and entrepreneurs who carry the weight for all of this "inequitable distribution" of stolen money. Also, the borrowed money is theft being perpetrated on our children, grandchildren, great-grandchildren, and the future existence of this country. Some will say that I am uncaring and that my assertions are ridiculous and a right-wing conspiracy. They are wrong! I will let you, the objective thinkers, decide based upon the facts, not on rhetoric.

People who want and get something for nothing don't care where the money comes from. I freely acknowledge that there are people who are truly in need, and we should help people. The problem is, the system is being gamed by millions, and the unaffordable giveaway of money is being offered by those with nefarious motives. Politicians know that the benefactors of this money know the source of this money! So before the next election, the political bosses of every district will remind these people who they should support in the election. The bosses will remind these benefactors of just who it was that got them the money they are addicted to as a result of the easier life of living on handouts. If you need another fix, you must go out and vote for the dealers! These voters, whether they are American citizens or illegal aliens, will vote for those elected representatives guilty of bribery using the public's money.

This American form of Marxism is actually worse than what we saw in the Soviet Union, see in North Korea, China, and in other places around the world today! Why? Make no mistake about it, at least those proletariat comrades of those failed socialist societies were, and are, forced to work. Mark my word, all in this country will one day work again. The question is, who will the taskmasters be at that time? I prefer to vote for people who will strive to protect the freedoms associated with free enterprise capitalism. I like the freedom to excel and work at the vocations of my choosing, whether it be a business I own or a job I choose. How about you? You will get a say-so in the matter. You get a choice to decide our fate when you cast your next vote in 2022. Please, cast your vote wisely.

> The American Republic will endure until the day Congress discovers that it can bribe the public with the public's money. (Alexis de Tocqueville)

What say you?

Perhaps I should be more direct with the left! I believe we should provide an opportunity for debate. I want to give the left a chance to be forthright and to come clean with the American people. Americans deserve transparency! I am going to ask questions that all of the GOP should be asking of the radical left and the entire democrat party for that matter. Seems like almost all of the democrats are sticking together! There are a couple of exceptions in the Democratic Party.

While I have not agreed with all of the votes that WV Senator Joe Manchin has cast over the last couple of years, I must say that he is showing great statesmanship with his refusal to give in to some of the left's most radical desires. He has indicated that he is against the wishes the left has regarding the "filibuster," "packing the supreme court," and "statehood for DC and Puerto Rico!" He stands strong on the Second Amendment. We all know why the left is pushing so hard for these items and why they wish to accomplish those agendas before 2022! As a former governor of my home state of WV, Senator Manchin understands the necessity for balancing budgets. He balanced the budgets during his tenure as governor of West Virginia. The production of steel requires that the materials be processed with high temperatures. Like steel, political resolve has to stand up under the great heat of political pressure that Senator Manchin is experiencing. What is it like to work in the hot kitchen of the Democratic Party in Washington? I can only imagine!

I have often thought that Senator Manchin would make a great representative for WV as an Independent. And for that matter, I believe his values are more in tune with the party platform of the Republican Party. After all, WV is a solid red state, and over 70 percent of the votes cast in WV in 2020 went to Donald Trump. If Senator Manchin holds true to these stated positions that I have heard him state numerous times, he will exemplify the highest level of statesmanship that an elected official can model on these issues. Refusing to do what the radical left is pressuring him to do and standing strong regarding what he has said he will not do illustrates a position to do what is best for the country regardless of the personal political cost. That type of courage and political resolve is what President John F. Kennedy looked for when he wrote the book *Profiles in Courage!*

Where is the leadership in the GOP, the Grand Old Party, the party of Abraham Lincoln, aka the Republican Party of today that can pull that party together and demand answers from the Dems. Before I begin asking the questions all members of the GOP should be asking, let us first set the stage for the reasons why we must be asking serious questions. *Time is running out for the sustainability of our nation.* To do that, we will take a quick trip back in our history to November 19, 1863.

> Four score and seven years ago our fathers brought forth on this continent, a new nation, conceived in Liberty, and dedicated to the proposition that all men are created equal. Now we are engaged in a great civil war, testing whether that nation, or any nation so conceived and dedicated, can long endure.

Another line of this speech says, "That this nation, under God, shall have a new birth of freedom—and that government of the people, by the people, for the people, shall not perish from the earth."

What you just read, as you already know, is the Gettysburg Address given by Abraham Lincoln on November 19, 1863, when he dedicated the Soldiers' National Cemetery in Gettysburg, Pennsylvania. The battle of Gettysburg took place during the first three days of July 1863 and was considered the high tide of the Southern Confederacy. Lincoln was dedicated to the task of preserving the "Union" that was brought forth on Independence Day in 1776. Are there points made in this primary source historical document that are fitting in 2021? Read it again and think of the many things you are witnessing in our country today. Consider what was at stake in Lincoln's time and consider what is at stake today. Time for some serious and demanding questions for the radical left!

There are many questions that all members of the GOP should be asking the radical left. And the GOP should be blasting the airways with those questions. The Republican Party should specifically describe, for the American voters, exactly what is going to happen if this country continues to spend money we do not have. Since they are not asking the questions, I will ask the questions.

Since the debt clock of "We the people" is at twenty-eight trillion and counting, I ask you, the left, what is the indebtedness number at which the United States' dollar becomes as worthless as a grain of sand taken from the beach? I assure you there is a number, and it is not far down the road. Any student of Economics 101 knows that the spending taking place in Washington is criminal and insanity! Let me remind you people, who seek to give away trillions, the government of the United States does not and has never had any money! No money! The money and wealth belongs to "We the people!" Period! It is not yours to give away and to waste. The dollars I have earned since I began working at the age of thirteen have been hard-earned. Should the dollars that you are sending out not also be hard-earned? The people who pay the taxes and who will be called upon to pay the debt will do so with hard-earned money! I wish to ask you another question.

What is the debt number at which our entire economy implodes and we become a Venezuela or a Soviet Union? Surely you know, but if you do not, I suggest you resign and go home to your district or state because you are not competent enough to represent "We the people." What you are good at is bribery of the voters, with the money of the public. Newsflash, it is not your money! I and the American people are waiting for the debt number.

This question is for the people who no longer want to work and stand on their own two feet, the people who are gaming the system and accepting the left's false promises of an easier life. I am talking about the people who could not possibly be related to the Pilgrims and immigrants who worked and struggled to build this nation! When the left's big giveaway has forced the absolute bankruptcy of our country and the country can no longer pay the interest on the debt, has no money to send checks to anyone, or cannot afford to defend us from foreign enemies, where will you get your daily bread, housing, clothing, utilities, and protection? Perhaps we should all work and live within our means before we reach the point at which we can no longer survive life's daily challenges for sustenance.

Would Chuck, Nancy, Joe, Kamala, the squad, and other representatives in congress, who support this leftist agenda, please tell the American people what your plan will be when this assured and imminent catastrophe takes place? The truth is, they do not have a plan for taking care of America! They may have another plan for America, and if so, I can tell you I do not like the alternative, and I do not believe you will either. Please tell us what your plan is or what you have in store for us! I just thought of another question.

Would someone in Washington please ask for national airtime and tell the American people what life will be like when the world no longer accepts our currency as the petrodollar? Life can get very nasty quickly! I have several related questions for the Washington leaders. What is the current interest rate that the government has to pay on the national debt? At our current debt, how much of our annual tax revenue has to be used to service the national debt on an annual basis? Give or take a billion or two will be close enough? The estimate of the monthly cost of interest that the federal government pays on our twenty-eight trillion dollars of debt is, according to this cite, https://www.treasurydirect.gov/govt/reports/ir/ir_expense.htm, approximately forty-seven billion dollars! The annual tax revenue for the federal government in 2020 was about 3.42 trillion dollars according to this site: https://www.statista.com/statistics/216928/us-government-revenues-by-category/. According to the data found on this site, https://datalab.usaspending.gov/americas-finance-guide/revenue/, the 2020 deficit spending was over three trillion dollars! This total lack of fiscal responsibility is not sustainable, and I do not care which party is in control in Washington. There are many threats to American freedom, but this lack of fiscal responsibility is huge, and it will steal our freedom.

My suggestion, to the American people, is that we should all be calling our elected representatives and asking all of these questions I am asking. Should our leaders in Washington be telling all of the American people the answers to these questions? It might be a great motivation for the American people to show up and vote for sustaining America. The overwhelming majority of "We the people" still want that! There are others who need to hear the truth, and it will be a wake-up call for them to join the rest of us. Tell the truth and start a statesman-like crusade to fix the problem. The American people, who really care about this country, may vote for you! There are other important questions that the American people would like answered! By the way, many of us can calculate the answers to the math problems I have presented; it is basic math. However, I think you should tell us. Do you know the answer? If not, I am even more worried.

By how much does the interest amount we must pay each year on the national debt increase if interest rates go up by 1 percent? What is the amount of national debt, and what is the interest rate combined with that debt that will eat up all of the current tax revenue in order to service the national debt? Does anyone have any idea what happens to your spendable income after the leftists deduct the majority of your earnings for taxes? At that point, we will all truly be equal, and the dream of equitable distribution will have been achieved. And the overwhelming majority of Americans will not like what they have left. We will then experience the standard of living of many third world countries.

I will not hold my breath for the radical left to answer these questions, and I advise you not to either. If ever, in our long history, there was a time for honest statesmen to step forth and lead this country, this is the time! The barbarians are at the gates! Americans throughout our history have always stepped up in such perilous times! Trust me, it is time to step forward and be heard at the ballot box for economic freedom.

"The only thing that is permanent is change." Supposedly, this is a quote from a Greek philosopher, Heraclitus, from about the year

500 BC. Such an axiom as this should tell us that society and government must constantly deal with change. And we do! The question becomes, when is change too much and detrimental to sustaining functionality of a system in ways that the system can no longer continue to exist? Can the radical left change the foundations of our society and government so much that our way of life and democratic government are destroyed? Are we on the precipice of becoming a nation that will not be able to sustain itself? I fear so, but what do you think? I believe there are multitudes of examples of the dangerous activities of the progressive left that threaten our nation's survival. This philosophy is being implemented and practiced all over our country today. The left has invaded our public schools, colleges and universities, Hollywood, and the social media platforms. Adults, teens, and children are being bombarded daily with the destructive stimuli of the *progressives*. Our traditional values and the rule of law are under constant attack. Our history is being rewritten with the focus being an emphasis upon the negative events of our history as if that is all we should know about America. That is wrong! There is a much bigger and brighter picture and story that needs to be presented. This modus operandi of the left in America today is exactly the tool that was used in the early days of every movement of one-party autocratic rule around the world throughout history. The enticing honey was socialism and the "spread the wealth" slogans. Stop the evil practice of free enterprise capitalism! We must stop this madness with votes that will stop the madness we are witnessing!

The essential foundation upon which our democracy stands is the power derived from "we the people" by the votes cast by the citizenry. We have always stood proud on the fact that our right to vote is one of our most valued defining characteristics! If votes can be bought through bribery by elected officials or stolen at the ballot box, then the very essence of what democracy stands upon can be the methodology for the doom of our democracy. We are in real trouble, if what Tocqueville said is correct, and I believe it is happening as I write. Can the American voters be prudent and thoughtful with the votes they will cast in 2022 and beyond? I hope so! That is why I write.

Every election is important, but I believe this one is as critical as any in our history. We have to get more voters to realize there is a bribery issue, look back in history, see the present for what it is, and to act to protect the future of a country and governance that has provided well for Americans. The alternative, if we do not come to this realization, is a darkness that too many never see until someone turns out the "lights of liberty" or destroys the ability and the opportunity to thrive financially while providing for your family! The *vote* is the key, and the integrity of the vote and elections is paramount, else we do not have a republic, and then you will not have a vote or a say. Autocratic rule replaces democracy.

Since you have begun reading this book, I am sure that you have recognized that my message has become more direct and more challenging. To be honest, that was not my intent. My directness and my stern position is the result of a growing alarm for the survival of our country. Every day, of the first eight months of 2021, I am witnessing more and more events and actions that are making the "fire bell in the night" grow louder and louder in my ears. My fears and cognitive dissonance are growing! I began writing this book on December 26, 2020, and it is now August 19, 2021.

Recently, a friend of mine read an excerpt of the book in which I was in a very direct and stern mood. He asked me, "Do you think your style will allow you to change the minds of the people who were sitting on the fence of this?" The debate, as I am sure you are well aware, is whether or not our country is heading in the wrong direction! That was a fair question. I went home and thought about whether a softer approach in my presentation would be more successful for encouraging change.

My answer to his question, you guessed it, would be kind but direct and strong. We have "tiptoed through the tulips" of political correctness for far too long. Time is running out! How much time do you think we have left? I must confess that I do not know. I am banking on the intelligence of those who are sitting on the fence. I hope my presentation has encouraged and helped the majority of the readers who are fence sitters to analyze the facts and to take a position they can defend. I believe the history presented, coupled with the facts, will lead people to what I consider to be the only decisions we can make, if in fact we want to preserve this nation. My opinion, but as I have said numerous times in this book, you decide because that is one of the beautiful things about the country that we all want to preserve! These are serious and dangerous times that require serious and direct talk as we debate the actions that must be taken ASAP!

Thank you for staying with me! The next chapter, chapter 13, is titled "A Hostile Takeover?" It is the final chapter, and I hope it makes all readers analyze recent events and come to a conclusion about where we are heading as a nation. As you have noticed, the chapter title is a question. Read closely! You will know what to do, and you will reach your own conclusion.

13

A Hostile Takeover?

Understanding current events debates and the current socioeconomic discussions in the U.S. mandates a working knowledge of the vernacular used by politicians and the news media. Otherwise, you cannot comprehend or participate in the debate that is taking place. I am sure that the majority of you already possess good working definitions of the following terminology. If not, I hope the review is helpful.

1. Orwellian and the novel *1984* will be discussed in great detail in this chapter.
2. Saul Alinsky and the "Reveille for Radicals" will be discussed later in this chapter.
3. Dystopia is the opposite of utopia. Dystopia is a society that experiences great suffering with much injustice. Initially or ultimately, such societies are ruled by a totalitarian government.
4. Politically correct speech is, according to the following quote taken from www.yourdictionary, "Politically incorrect is when something is considered disrespectful or objectionable to a particular group of people." I do not know about you, but I see this as a weapon that is being used by the left to silence debate and legitimate questioning by all who oppose the radical left. As an example, nobody likes

being called a racist. So if you dare to question the fairness of "affirmative action" by suggesting that the merit of academic achievement or a successful résumé of experience should be the determining factor for acceptance, regardless of color, you would be labeled a racist because it is not politically correct speech to question "affirmative action" by saying it is a form of reverse discrimination. Honestly, I can understand how those who have witnessed discrimination due to skin color might think that "affirmative action" was an answer.

Without question, there have been racists who have discriminated and persecuted American citizens for no other reason than the pigment of their skin. That is sad, and I find it reprehensible. Judge people based upon merit, résumés, and the content of their character, and I do not give a damn about the color of their skin! However, when you use the quota system of affirmative action, you become discriminatory based upon skin pigment, and that is equally wrong. Such a system, as affirmative action, can and does deny the acceptance of innocent people of a different color who have never been guilty of any racist act. Such a system is racist by its very nature of application. That is wrong, and you cannot fix racism by utilizing a system that is also racist. Period!

The real racists take it as a compliment when they are called a racist, because they are racists. But for most who are not racists, the vitriol and the falseness of such charges often leads to silence. I suggest that if you remain silent and do not defend yourself, then the left has succeeded, and they win. Please note, being a leftist is not something that can be identified by the pigment of one's skin!

Critical race theory is identified by the following direct quotes taken from www.britannica.com on April 02, 2021.

> Critical race theory, intellectual movement and framework of legal analysis based on the premise that race is a socially constructed category that is used to oppress and exploit people of

color. Critical race theorists hold that the law and legal institutions in the United States are inherently racist.

This is another weapon of choice being used by the left. I want to expand upon my example offered in (4), regarding politically correct speech.

Does a white person have the right to question the fairness of the use of affirmative action? A white person might claim that the regulations of an institution using affirmative action are representative examples of reverse discrimination. A white person may be denied a merit-based position because a quota for non-whites has not yet been met. Does this denial, based upon a need to fill a quota, then become a racist act directed at a white person purely because of the whiteness of their skin pigmentation? I suggest that this might well be a racist and discriminatory practice by virtue of the left's very definition of critical race theory. Critical race theorists hold that the law and legal institutions in the United States are inherently racist. I know they say this only applies in the case of "people of color," but the white person denied the position based upon an unfilled quota may well be a victim of racism! Seems plausible to me, but what do you think? I believe others might agree!

The language of the left and their actions are divisive and counterproductive to solving problems. We should be one nation under God, and I do not care if you are white or a person of color. It is past time to stop judging any American citizen by their race or skin pigment of white, black, brown, red, or yellow, period! It is time to quit dwelling on past failures to live up to our creed. It is time, today in the present, to come together in ways that will provide a better future for all American citizens based upon the protections of our rule of law, the Constitution of the United States!

The speech given by South Carolina senator, Tim Scott, following President Biden's first address to a joint session of congress on April 28, 2021, was particularly revealing to me as I think about critical race theory. Senator Tim Scott said, "It's backwards to fight discrimination with different discrimination. And it's wrong to try to use our painful past to dishonestly shut down debates in the present. I'm an African American who has voted in the South all my life. I take voting rights personally." For his right of a free speech presentation of his opinion, Tim Scott was chastised as "Uncle Tim" or an "Uncle Tom." I encourage you to read about the life story of Senator Tim Scott and of his mother. I would then ask you if the success of Senator Scott is not a representation of all of the good things possible to those who work hard to achieve in America. Character, whether good or bad, always stands out. In this case, Tim Scott deserves a great deal of respect. He has great character, and I admire the work he does.

Remember this definition:

> Critical race theory, intellectual movement and framework of legal analysis based on the premise that race is a socially constructed category that is used to oppress and exploit people of color. Critical race theorists hold that the law and legal institutions in the United States are inherently racist.

The left's positions, simply put, have no logical basis of argument. They spin and contradict themselves at every turn when challenged! This poison that is being uttered all over our country and taught to our children by the left is destroying our nation. I have come to believe that is the intent of many in the radical left's camp! What say you?

I like and respect what Dr. Martin Luther King said: "I have a dream that my four little children will one day live in a nation where they will not be judged by the color of their skin but by the content of their character." I believe that he would want his desire for his children's rights to also be a right that would be granted to children of all races. And but for the murder of this great man, by an evil coward, the message of peace and courage practiced by this man, our country might well have enjoyed the benefits of much more of his righteous wisdom. Sadly, the assassination of Dr. King was wished for by far too many people! Those people were truly racists. I call them like I see them.

Systemic racism is a charge that is being leveled at our American system on a daily basis. Indeed, both the newly elected president and the vice president of the United States have being saying this since they took office in January of 2021. Are there racists in America and all over the world? *Yes!* Systemic is defined as relating to an entire system or all parts of the system. If it is not systemic, then it is localized to a specific part of the system.

So was and is the KKK a disgusting group of racists? *Absolutely!* Is the "white congregation" of my family's church racist? *No!* This church recently hired a minister of God. He and his family are among the nicest people our community is privileged to count as citizens. He routinely visited my elderly mother and brought her chocolate milkshakes. This man of God just happens to have a skin pigment that is dark brown. He does not have a racist bone in his body, and neither did the congregation that hired him! I tire of hearing the adjective African American. How about we just say "a good American citizen" of our neighborhood and leave color out of the statement?

I have said it before and I will say it again: Being identified as an American is not determined by skin pigment. This church judged this man by the "content of his character!" Remember, I live in the mountains of Southeastern WV, and that is further south than Richmond, Virginia. Racism is not systemic in America, but the false narrative of the left seeks to make you believe we are. And might I ask, is the left systemically racist?

Do the activities of the activists and their propaganda, on the left motivate nonthinkers into becoming racist? If so, please ask yourself, why would they do such a vile thing?

Corporate "woke" or the state of being "woke" is relatively new to me. If you are so minded as to be "woke," then you are on the alert for examples of racial injustice. By definition, you should be angry, and you should stay woke. I agree with this point of view. What I do not agree with is the propagandized weaponization of this concept. The radical left is using this concept as a means to divide our society and promote injustice and chaos for the purpose of imploding society. There is no justice to be found in killing, looting/stealing, and the destruction of public and private property. Those who engage in these activities are not protesting; they are looking for an excuse to steal and act out their criminality.

Indoctrination is perpetrated upon the very impressionable young, the uneducated, the angry, and the nonthinkers or those susceptible to following the herd. Indoctrination is, as per the dictionary, a process whereby groups gain members by teaching a person or group to blindly accept beliefs without any critical questioning of the dogma. In short, people are brainwashed with propaganda of lies, omissions, or the presentation of stories without critical facts.

The media is very good at this activity. And by engaging in this total lack of real journalism, the media is guilty of a violation of freedom of the press. They are owned by those who seek to spread a false narrative that America is a bad place. Their goal is to find support for a particular narrative to force violence and or change. Those who love real freedom should be on guard. Remember, Ronald Reagan warned us that freedom is but one generation away from extinction and must be defended. The best weapon against indoctrination is to ask "why." Give me the facts! I would say, do not trust, and be sure to verify before you become trusting.

Project 1619 curriculum is a perspective put forth by Nikole Hannah-Jones, a staff writer and investigative reporter for the *New York Times Magazine.* Nikole Hannah-Jones wrote the lead essay to kick off the project. Other writers added additional essays. This is a revisionist perspective about the founding of the United States of America that is an assertion that the founding of this country actually began in 1619 rather than 1776.

Why 1619, you might ask? Because it was 1619 Virginia that was the time and place the first Africans were brought to the land of what was to become the United States of America. Not surprisingly, this curriculum is being used on a broad scale in such cities as Buffalo, New York; Chicago, Illinois; Winston Salem, North Carolina; Wilmington, Delaware; and Washington, DC. In fact, some four thousand five hundred classrooms across the country have used the materials.

I would like to ask you to close this book at this time and google the article, "A Review of the 1619 Project Curriculum," at https://www.heritage.org/progressivism/report/review-the-1619-project-curriculum. The article was presented by the Heritage Foundation and written by Lucas E. Morel, PhD. Lucas E. Morel, PhD, *is the John K. Boardman* junior professor of politics at Washington and Lee University. He is the author, most recently, of *Lincoln and the American Founding* (Southern Illinois University Press, 2020). Lucas E. Morel's review and rebuttal of the 1619 Project curriculum cannot be bested by this author. Please read this man's work!

I hope you are rejoining me after reading the article I recommended to you. For my purposes, I wish to provide the following excerpts from Professor Morel's article. And I quote, verbatim,

> According to the 1619 Project's lead essay, there is no tension, no debate, no struggle by the white Framers of the 1787 constitution in their efforts "to form a more perfect union." In fact, the historical record does not show that the Founders were uniformly dedicated to preserving slavery. To leave out this significant element of the Founding era is to miss an incredibly important aspect of American History—namely, that America is a nation born of debate and has developed through argument and, for the most part, peaceful resolution of its political conflicts. If there is any "framing" of history, and "narrative arc" that should be taught in K–12 schools, it is this broader account of the nation's Founding and history. It is at once truer to the facts and a more engaging account to teach youth. The resulting civic education will ultimately be more constructive as they learn about the noble ideals and leading actors of the nation's history alongside the ways they fell short of the ideals of the nation's true Founding, the Spirit of '76.

Wow, I wish I could write so eloquently on this subject as Professor Morel has written!

Slavery has always been, is, and shall always be a despicable denial of unalienable rights and is just plain wrong, period! The 1619 Curriculum Project would teach our children, falsely I might add, that the basis of the founding of the United States can be traced to Virginia soil in the year 1619 due to the introduction of slavery at that time, and it was then that our country was founded. Virginia was a colony that was fully controlled by the British empire in 1619. Virginia would not be a state of the United States until 1776, 157 years after the tragic introduction of slavery in Virginia. The birth of the United States of America, according to real history, was July 4, 1776! It was this date that thirteen British colonies in America declared themselves free and independent states, the United States of America. The colonies declared that they were free and independent of any further control by King George III and the British Parliament in London, England. Any other interpretation of the birth of this nation is a complete distortion of American History that ignores factual history.

The 1619 Curriculum Project is aimed at the most vulnerable in our society, the children of our schools. In the previous paragraph, I presented two narratives about the founding of America. Which narrative do you believe? What do you want taught to your children and grandchildren? I want unadulterated facts to be taught to children. I always taught the introduction of slavery to 1619 Virginia. What is the motivation for this 1619 narrative, and what are the impacts on children who are taught such a false curriculum objective?

This false narrative of history is causing divisiveness in our society. These false statements of history lead to more racism, on all sides. Young and impressionable children face enough challenges without a curriculum of false statements that claim the birth and foundation of our country was based upon the advent of slavery in the British colony of Virginia in 1619. This false premise is so baseless and without merit that I can only assume there is some nefarious motivation behind this effort to mislead children. Could it be that the replacement of the true historical facts with false statements is really an effort to inflame groups of people to become angry with America? Starting children's education about America with false information will make it impossible for children to recognize both the good and bad experiences of our history. Such a false introduction to American History would prevent children from ever being able to see the real ideals that America was founded upon. Is the goal of this activism a concerted effort to disillusion segments of our society for the purpose of preventing all Americans, of all races, from working together in order to improve the American dream? Please, offer another plausible reason.

We should teach the dark story of slavery in America. Why? Because slavery was wrong before it came to the North American shores; it was wrong from 1619 to 1776, wrong from 1776 to 1865, and, my friends, slavery is just as wrong today in the countries outside of the United States where it still exists! Do you think it is important to discuss the places of origin for this evil institution?

Unfortunately, slavery existed many places in the world prior to the conclusion of the American Civil War in 1865. We could identify the White European countries that participated in the slave trade with Black Africans who sold their enslaved captives of war into bondage. But would such identifications really matter or change the past? Duh, *no*! What could we do with this wasted energy of activism that insists upon rehashing a story that ended in 1865 and that we cannot change? If activists are truly concerned about doing something good for humanity that will make a difference, I suggest they pursue bringing an end to slavery in African and Asian countries where the tragic practice of slavery still exists. Just a little research into this modern-day slavery will horrify you. Tell me where I am wrong.

One of the most powerful arguments made by Professor Morel is a point I have already made in this book. It is that the ideals of our founding are remarkable. And the fact that we often fell short of perfect is understandable. The left knows that, but their goal is to divide the nation, weaken our nation, and create mistrust that makes it impossible to solve problem. The left does all of this via a false narrative so they can break the county down and seize power.

Yet the ideals presented to us by the founding fathers are a guiding light and moral compass that has improved the condition of millions of all races up to and including today! We are faced with far too many pressing problems that must be solved for the good of all Americans. Do not waste the precious time we have to solve real problems by causing baseless problems!

"White Privilege," as per the dictionary, is "inherent advantages possessed by a white person on the basis of their race in a society characterized by racial inequality and injustice." Racial inequality and injustice? The very nature of humanity is one in which we all recognize the reality that we are imperfect beings! Does anyone think there has been any inequality and injustice perpetrated on poor, white, and uneducated people?

I do not believe in white, black, brown, red, or yellow privilege. I believe we should rise based on merit. We will not rise or progress as a society with the concept of affirmative action. If all Americans could embrace color blindness, the better off we would all be. Yet we will never be perfect.

I have no doubt—in fact, I would bet all that I own—that the success of Dr. Ben Carson and Justice Clarence Thomas was achieved in spite of numerous unfair and unnecessary obstacles of prejudice and racism. I would also bet that these two men and countless other Americans of color have had to climb over mountains of discriminatory barriers! I have the upmost respect for both of these men, but they do not require my respect. They are Americans who have earned their way and position!

Cancel culture is a convenient tool of big tech or the left. If you become a prominent political or public figure who gains a following on a social media platform and begin to take a position that the left sees as counterproductive to their narrative or goals, they simply kick you off their platform. They cancel you out of the picture, off the stage, or out of the news. Classic example of being canceled, President Donald J. Trump.

Cancel culture is a powerful way to make someone irrelevant, especially when you consider how many people get their only news or information from the social media platforms. Do you remember how the social media tech giant cancelled the *New York Post's* article on Hunter and Joe Biden's connections with China? The evidence presented on the laptop was too powerful and damning to be allowed for massive public consumption. They stopped it because it was coming out before the November 3, 2020, presidential election. Block Donald J. Trump from posting on Twitter or block the *New York Post's* article on Hunter and Joe Biden, and you are canceling them out, thus the term cancel culture. Such actions are censorship with the purpose of denying the American people the truth. The result is you can alter an election via unscrupulous means!

Sex education today is more than just a parental enlightenment of their children to the facts of the "birds and the bees!" Go to https://www.welcomingschools.org/pages/affirming-gender-in-elementary-school-social-transitioning/ to read the article entitled "Affirming Gender in Elementary School: Social Transition." Wow, no wonder kids in liberal school districts may struggle with their ABCs and the 123s. What a trip to lay on a child. Teachers and schools barely have enough time to teach ELA and math curriculum. According to the sores on achievement, there is little to brag about for the scores on ELA and math. Leave the "birds and the bees" to the parents.

So if a student of fifteen with male genitalia says he feels female, then it is okay for him to compete with the girls in track team competitions. Does this motivate parents to want to remove their children from that school district and then send their kids to a school of their choice?

We have completed our review and illustration of key terms. Your understanding of these terms is crucial to your ability to see today's social turmoil for what it really is. This allows us to discuss actions being taken in our society and government, thus allowing us to speculate if we are witnessing a power grab that is determined to destroy the system in which we live.

A hostile takeover? Obviously, the question implies confrontation. Is there a movement in the USA that can be categorized as a hostile takeover? A hostile takeover that has the expressed goal of seizing power in order to change the nation into an entity that would be the antithesis of what we have aspired to be since 1776, 1787, and 1791? Will the citizens of this great country experience great suffering and totalitarianism? What confrontations are taking place in our country? From where does the impetus for these confrontations originate? Who are the forces, both within and outside of our nation, that are orchestrating and funding these anti-American groups in our nation? Are there countries that would benefit immensely if the USA became an impotent and divided nation stripped of its vision, leadership, and economic vitality on the world stage? When you consider the stakeholders and the viability of our nation, one is compelled to wonder, who will be the winners and the losers in these confrontations? What is the modus operandi of these powerful forces? Given all of these questions that I have posed, it is imperative that we master all of the working vocabulary necessary for an intelligent discussion and clear understanding of the revolution taking place in our country. Time to discuss the term *Orwellian*, which was number one on my list of terminology that we must all understand.

George Orwell's Novel, 1984, and Orwellian Identifications of Totalitarian Activities

Orwell's novel, *1984*, was first published in 1949, and it depicts life in a dystopian society that experiences great suffering and injustice while being ruled by a totalitarian regime. The United States of America is not, yet, a dystopian society. I say this due to the fact that we are not experiencing great suffering and injustice in America, no matter what the radical left and the left-wing media are saying as they attempt to brainwash large segments of our society during a great power grab. These anti-American groups would have you believe that we are now a dystopian society of great suffering and that our citizens are being subjected to injustices. They sell this false narrative all over the segments of media that they control. Also, for sale is the myth that they can and must fix America! That is, simply, not true! These power seekers have created this false narrative, and they want you to believe that they have the answers or cures for ending what simply does not exist. Is it not ironic that these false cures the left is putting forth will create a society of dystopia that will be ruled by totalitarianism? When someone or a group destroys the free and open society that we have enjoyed, we will then live in a dystopian society ruled by totalitarianism.

I believe you would be intrigued by reading Orwell's novel, *1984*. There was a movie made about Orwell's book that you might find enjoyable. The movie is available on YouTube. Could we become a dystopian society such as the fictional one that George Orwell depicted in his novel, *1984*? Let us answer that question at the end of this chapter. What is this "Orwellian" scenario all about?

I am referencing this URL video, presented on YouTube (https://video.search.yahoo.com/search/video?fr=mcafee&ei=UTF8&p=orwellian+meaning&type=E211US752G0#id=4&vid=f5f968bdddfbb3bd160d8d20ac912b59&action=view), for brief analysis of Orwell's 1949 novel, *1984*. His novel depicts life in the futuristic and fictional dystopian society of 1984. Also, I want to present the methods of social controls utilized by that totalitarian government.

Accordingly, the narrative of this audio-video states the following descriptors of what we now recognize as Orwellian. And I quote the statements made about Orwell's book, "It denotes an attitude and brutal policy of draconian control by propaganda, surveillance, misinformation, denial of truth, double think, and manipulation of the past." The presentation goes on to explain how Orwell's fictional totalitarian regime endeavored to remove from public records the evidence of certain persons' past existence. Accordingly, the book uses motifs (reoccurring themes) to depict life in the Soviet Union. Finally, the video narrative leads you to understand that these practices introduced in Orwell's book are "practiced by modern repressive governments." End of quote. *Wow!* Do you need to read the above statement again or listen to the audio-video in its entirety? Perhaps you are motivated to first read the book, *1984*, and view the movie. While you contemplate, I have some comments to make. Have you witnessed any of these Orwellian currently taking place in our country?

Again, I say "Wow!" Can you imagine any society falling victim to such activities, or have you ever witnessed the use of such deplorable manipulations to seize power? I will answer these questions From my perspective. Of course, you can imagine such activities, and of course you have personally witnessed such events! While Orwell created a fictional and futuristic society suffering through life in dystopia, he did not just imagine it. Evidently, he witnessed dysfunctional and repressive regimes. He was able to witness and view the perfect model for repressing any opportunity for a free and open society to exist. He knew what life was like in the Soviet Union. His book provided a warning to all free societies that the socialists and communists were hell bent on infecting the entire world with their deadly contagion of socialism and the autocratic rule of totalitarian communism. And it takes very little research to discover that life can get really distasteful very quickly. We have a really good deal in the United States. Thanks to George Orwell, we have been made aware of some very nefarious activities that have and are being employed to seize control to fundamentally change America. These described activities of subversion and manipulative controls are the same methods that have been used by the communists in the Soviet Union and continue to be used in Red China by the "Chicoms" (Chinese communists).

You often hear someone say, "This sounds Orwellian!" When you hear such a statement, you will now know that they are categorizing activities or events, based upon what Orwell has illustrated, as tactics used by totalitarian regimes or power seekers attempting to destroy free and open societies. Freedom-loving people must always be on guard for deliberate and calculated moves designed to seize control of free societies! Are you on guard? Can we identify Orwellian activities in present-day America? More on Orwellian later, but now we need to develop what I call the anti-American "ism" of Saul Alinsky. Once I complete my discussion of this dangerous "ism," we will see if we are now experiencing what George Orwell was predicting way back in 1949.

Rules for Radicals by Saul Alinsky 1971

Are we Americans falling prey to a mad rush toward a dystopian society that is controlled by a totalitarian, one-party rule by Neo-Marxists? In my lifetime of sixty-eight years, I could never have imagined that I would ever have to ask such an alarming question. "Say it ain't so, Joe!" Some will go "ho hum," another McCarthy conspiracy theorist. To whom I issue this challenge, refute my factual presentations with facts and prove me wrong! To quote U.S. Ambassador

Adlai Stevenson during the 1962 Cuban Missile Crisis when he confronted Soviet ambassador to the UN security council, Zorin, regarding the question of whether the Soviets had placed offensive nuclear missiles in Cuba, I offer Stevenson's quote: "I am prepared to wait for my answer until hell freezes over, if that's your decision." What are the unbelievable events that we have witnessed in recent years that suggest that Orwell's examples of dystopia are now being perpetrated upon our "free and open society"?

Google https://www.crossroad.to/Quotes/communism/alinsky.htm to find the article that presents quotes and excerpts from Saul Alinsky's 1971 book, *Rules for Radicals*. If you do not read another word of this book, I beg you, please go to this URL. The revelations of this article, written with explanations of direct quotes from Alinsky's book, will first astound you and then horrify you. Why will you be horrified? It made me cringe with fear, because it is as if Saul Alinsky has risen from hell to orchestrate the madness we are witnessing in America today. You must read the article!

You may be wondering and asking yourself, what is at risk? Let me say emphatically, *everything is at risk!* All of our hallowed freedoms, our free and open society, and our economic system is under attack. The Neo-Marxists' intention is to conquer us from within, via infiltration of all of our institutions. What are some of their specific goals? Liberals, radical left, and Neo-Marxists—whatever you wish to call them or however you group them—want to add two more states, add more justices to the U.S. Supreme Court, and increase illegal immigration. They are giving away money like it grows on trees. They are constantly talking about gun control and defunding or abolishing the police. Yet all of the powerful leftists have bodyguards and demand either police or national guard protection.

To accomplish the legislative ends of their agenda, they want to end the filibuster in the U.S. Senate while they have a fifty-fifty split in the Senate and have a majority in the House. With four more liberal senators, as well as more liberal representatives, they could control the legislative branch indefinitely, free to pass any liberal agenda they want. They would appoint four or more left-wing justices to the supreme court. And with more democrat voters, compliments of illegal immigration, they could potentially flip some red states to blue states. Additionally, it is unfortunate, but there are votes that can be bought if you pass out enough handouts. What happens then?

Then, the left becomes the majority, and they will have completed the power grab. A major power move happened on November 3, 2020, when they somehow snatched victory from defeat when Joe Biden was declared the electoral vote winner in the presidential election. If the power grab continues in the midterm elections of 2022, well, it is game over for the United States as we have known it. The radical changes will be unstoppable, will erode the basic values and freedoms for which we have stood for so long. Even worse, the country will implode financially. There is no way that their fiscal irresponsibility will allow this nation to continue as an ongoing concern. In an effort to sustain the country financially, they will have to take more and more of the wealth for redistribution. And they will, and they can do it, if they win in 2022. In the end, we will be yet another Soviet Union.

The following is but a synthesis of the article. The article is, in fact, a synthesis of Alinsky's book, *Rules for Radicals 1971*. It is far beyond the scope of this work to provide you with in-depth analysis of Alinsky's work or, for that matter, in-depth analysis of the site's article that interprets and discusses Alinsky's book. What follows is my brief synthesis of Alinsky's dogma that has been so ably presented on the site, https://www.crossroad.to/Quotes/communism/alinsky.htm.

Alinsky was a Neo-Marxist that influenced both Hillary Clinton and Barack Obama! Go to an online dictionary and you will find that Neo-Marxists are defined, and I quote,

> Relating to forms of political philosophy which arise from the adaptation of Marxist thought to accommodate or confront modern issues such as the global economy, the capitalist welfare state, and the stability of liberal democracies.

How about that? In fact, Clinton's topic for her political science thesis, in 1969, was "There is Only the Fight," which is, according to the above-referenced article, a reference to Alinsky's earlier training manual.

Surprise, surprise, surprise, as Gomer Pyle used to say. Obama is an Alinskyite! Obama spent years teaching the Alinsky model. In 1985, Obama went to work as a community organizer for an Alinsky group in Chicago known as the Developing Communities Project. I wonder if Harris and Biden ever had a relationship with Alinsky. They certainly had a relationship with Secretary Clinton and President Obama. Bet you did not know about Alinsky's influence on these people of power. If you did not, do not feel badly; I did not realize either. Read on. There is a highly sophisticated method being employed to attack American values and institutions from within. The madness may make you angry when you see the "big picture."

As I have said, what follows will be a synthesis of the major points that Saul Alinsky crafted. From that springboard, I will present the examples of Alinsky's dogma that you will readily recognize as being employed by those who have seized power in America. And they are employing Alinsky's teaching!

Alinsky taught his disciples to stay camouflaged. Put on a suit and cut your hair was the best camouflage. Then, you were ready to do the organizational work necessary to build the movement to take over the establishment. I do not believe most people in the country ever connected the dots that indicated the liberal positions of Clinton and Obama were linked to the dogma of Saul Alinsky. Did you know they were students of Alinsky's movement? I did not! Since Alinsky was a disciple of the Italian communist, Antonio Gramsci, Alinsky followed the example and ideology of Gramsci when he preached the concept of "gradualism" rather than a violent revolution to take over the West. Gradualism requires time and patience. Members of the army of Alinsky and Gramsci would first infiltrate the organizations of western society. Additionally, according to the writers of the article, "Quotes and Excerpts from *Rules for Radicals* by Saul Alinsky—1971," found at https://www.crossroad.to/Quotes/communism/alinsky.htm, the goal and modus operandi of the movement would be to take over the United States from within! So the disciples of Alinsky infiltrated the West's workplace undercover. They became educators, community organizers, politicians, Hollywood producers, actors, or just disgruntled protestors of everything American. They began their work in our colleges and universities. Once they gained a foothold there, they moved into curriculum manipulation in our public schools. Anti-Americanism has become a theme of many curriculums adopted throughout our school systems. They seek to rewrite history to fit their narrative. If you do not already know that there are many Alinsky disciples in power, you will soon, because you will recognize their employment of his tactics. And what were the weaponized tactics of Alinsky?

Time for us to put on our thinking caps and do an analysis of current day events and dilemmas in order to see if these events and dilemmas can be categorized as Orwellian. You can decide whether you believe that these events are textbook examples of Alinsky's methodology for grabbing power to take down the establishment.

For years, and more and more in recent months, when I hear of a new policy or action that makes no sense to me, I have screamed you cannot make this stuff up! I have done this each time I have witnessed the actions, policies, and rhetoric put forth by those in power. My responses have often labeled those people as insane, stupid, or just plain idiots. What do you think? You live in America and have every right to think as you darn well please. Grudgingly, I admit, so do they! Please, just be smart and evaluate facts and history. You can even be more polite, if you choose. My anger, research, and reflective analysis of what I see happening in America has ushered in an illumination about what is going on. Am I right? You be the judge as you read more.

I must profess that my analysis of what has been going on, prior to writing this book, has been wrong. I have come to realize that the people in power, the leaders of these many anti-American groups, and the media are not stupid at all! In my opinion, they are misguided and corrupt! But they are anything but stupid. They are well organized, patient, and employ very skilled deliveries of oratory and deception. They profess to love democracy and America. These and other things, I will point out, are straight from Alinsky's playbook.

And I would be guilty of a gross misrepresentation of the democratic process if I did not acknowledge that the *legal* casting of a majority of the votes, in favor of the changes being proposed by the radical left, is in fact democracy in action. But the acid test for a real democracy is one based upon free and honest elections! Do you have any questions about the integrity of the 2020 presidential election process? I do!

The will of the people is what a republic is based upon. That is why I write. Voters must be well informed of the critical factual information. Voters need to be skilled thinkers as they evaluate campaign promises of political parties. Voters need to be well schooled in factual history and need to think about what the long-term impacts of policy might have on the country's ability to survive. All of the planks of a party platform should be carefully analyzed before voters cast their vote. It seems to me that far too many voters have been brainwashed by media that employs less than honest reporting. In fact, they deceive and they lie.

When the radical left puts on their sheep's clothing, smiles, and offers new programs such as free college for all and their "cradle to grave" care from the government, they are offering you socialism. Once they addict millions to free stuff, and logical people know that nothing is free, they are really buying future votes to keep themselves in power. Friends, I must say again, search history forever and you will not find a single success story for socialism and communism! Do you not think that their millions of followers are being used for purposes of the overall movement? Their way, if they win, is an inevitable death knell for this country!

The radical left's movement is premeditated to weaken our values, change history, weaken our institutions, create dissatisfaction, make us feel guilty, and spend us into oblivion so our financial system will collapse. They are buying the minds and souls of millions with handouts of borrowed money; creating chaos and anarchy in our cities, push to defund and abolish the police to create more chaos, and they employ devious methods that threaten both our First and Second Amendment rights. Success in those two nefarious goals will make it is easier for leftists to control any opposition.

All of these moves have a singular purpose, and that is to grab total power before the 2022 midterm elections and then the 2024 election. Once they have total power, their *used* followers will be shocked when they realize that promises made could not and were never meant to be kept. Most of those followers will feel stupid, used, and hopeless. How can I say these things? Because real historical study reveals that this has happened time after time! It was done to the Russian people, the Cubans, the Chinese, and many more. Will we let it be done to we Americans? That is up to all of us, but first we must wake up! I hope my writings are the alarm clock we need to awaken and look at the evidence we can find in history. It has all been done before; take a look at what follows.

The 1917 Bolshevik "October Revolution" was led by Vladimir Lenin. The Bolsheviks were successful in overthrowing Russia's ruling Romanov dynasty, royal family, that had ruled Russia for over three hundred years. The overthrow of the government was swift and would ultimately lead to the execution of Czar Nicholas II and his family on July 16, 1918. As a result of this coup, a civil war would develop in Russia between the Reds and the Whites. The Reds were the Lenin socialists, and the Whites sought to regain control of Russia. The civil war would end in 1923, and Lenin's communists would establish the Soviet Union. Lenin and his associates represent the "old guard" of violent socialist revolutionaries. The Italian communist, Gramsci, and his follower, Saul Alinsky, represent quite a contrast to Lenin and the Russian revolutionaries because they chose to employ "gradualism" as a means to take over a government.

Employing the philosophy of Gramsci and of the influential American organizer, Saul Alinsky, Neo-Marxists infiltrated the United States. The goal was to seize power and take down the establishment via the concept of gradualism. Once they seized power, the work to fundamentally change America would accelerate to warp speed. The infiltration has been successful. The power grab, as of November 3, 2020, election night, is almost complete. The changes that the radical left has desired are now, as I write, taking place at a very fast pace. How far will it go, and how quickly the total transformation of American values, traditions, economic freedom, and institutions will take place is dependent upon seizing additional power?

Since January of 2021, as a result of the 2020 election and the run-off senatorial elections in Georgia in 2021, the Dems control the White House, have a slim margin in the House of Representatives, and have a fifty-fifty tie in the Senate. The kicker is that the VP has the tiebreaker vote, and she is a Democrat. What are the goals that they want to achieve before the midterms of 2022? They still have a tough nut to crack before they can achieve the total power grab that will put them in control into perpetuity.

First in their sights is achieving an end to the filibuster. Secondly, they want to pack the supreme court with four more justices, all of whom would be radical leftists. Thirdly, they want to add Washington, DC, and Puerto Rico as the fifty-first and fifty-second states. With the adding of two more states, the country would have four more liberal senators. There would be assured gains for the liberal house as the two states would elect more liberal democrats. When you consider the number of electoral votes that come from liberal California, Illinois, New York, and other rock-solid "blue states," our country would become a nation ruled by one party, radical left-wing rule. Do you think that the 2022 midterm elections for the U.S. House of Representatives and the U.S. Senate are going to be hotly contested battles? I would bet the farm on that one!

Why will the election battles of 2022 be so vital? If the radicals cannot achieve the final power grab before 2022, they will be desperate to win overwhelming control of both the House and the Senate in 2022. If the Democrats win in 2022, then it is game over for the U.S. as we have known it since 1791. To block this final power grab, the Republicans know they must take back the House and the Senate in 2022. And then the Republicans know they must win the White House in 2024 so that in January of 2025, they can begin to reverse the radical changes made by Biden's unprecedented use of executive orders since January 2021. Regardless of which side of the political fence you live, everyone knows that the outcome is unpredictable. It is that close! All it takes is for one or two senators to defect to the other side, and it is game over for the party that loses senatorial votes.

Are there moderate Democrats in the House and Senate that will break caucus with the radical left? Who knows?

How did our country get to this stage of socialism? People had to be gathered into *the radical camp*. That is where multitudes of "community organizers" began the slow but sure changes that have proven detrimental to our sustainability as a nation. Organizers like Barack Obama! They had to find people who were *dissatisfied with their life's situation*. They had to create more chaos and division. They had to create a resurgence of racism because that would get people into the streets. Then these organizers began to preach their "pie in the sky stories" of how there was a better life for all if they could *rid the nation of the evils of capitalism*. Their sermon was, "Your life would be so much easier if we force the people higher up the economic ladder *to pay their fair share*." Are they talking about *redistribution of wealth*? There is no question about that!

The left will never admit that it is the prospect of achieving the reward of economic gain by risk and hard work that propels people to become successful. Let us be clear, with higher and higher tax collections, the resulting revenue is being used to fund more social programs of giveaways that have an abysmal record for success. Worse still is the fact that money spent on failed programs is, in fact, borrowed money that adds to the national debt.

I have wondered, for years, how government could be so irresponsible as to run up trillions of dollars of debt. That debt will destroy our nation's financial viability. Financial collapse has to be the radical left's plan, is it not? What other possible answer can you offer? You can only print funny money for so long before the dollar collapses and is worthless. As of today, May 17, 2021, we are seeing inflation and stagnation. The value of your hard-earned dollars is shrinking rapidly. I do not see how anybody could be so naïve as to not realize the impending financial doom. Have you noticed that nobody, and I mean nobody, is talking about the astronomical debt and deficit spending that is a for sure a death knell? They must want the financial collapse to happen on their watch! At that point of financial collapse, what would the radical left do? Will that be the excuse they need to seize total power? Would they declare a state of emergency, blame the establishment, and prescribe Marxism to save society? The Chinese, big tech, and certain American-hating billionaires would rejoice.

There would be little about which we could rejoice! If the radical left took this route, I would predict a civil war just like the one between the "reds" and the "whites" in Russia after the 1917 October Revolution in Russia. Only this time, it would be a civil war of the "red, white, and blue patriots of America" versus the "socialist reds." God help us if it comes to that! Pray that never happens because if it does, we all lose! I am more fearful of such a tragedy today than ever before.

I have been noticing flags flying that appear as normal American flags, but they are not. Have you seen the flags that are divided, diagonally or horizontally, with one side being the stars and stripes and the other half is a Confederate battle flag? The sight sent a chill through my body, and it was like dagger in my heart. We have a democracy that has flourished under the rule of law of our constitution before 1861 and since 1865. Let us use our rule of law to right the American ship. We cannot allow the history of 1861–1865 to repeat itself! Could all of the issues we are discussing have anything to do with the radical left's attack on our Second Amendment rights and their desire to seize the guns of law-abiding patriots? Think about it!

I encourage you to go to this Heritage Foundation URL, https://www.heritage.org/marriage-and-family/commentary/the-war-poverty-50-years-failure. There you will find factual information in the article, "The War on Poverty: 50 Years of Failure," written on September 23, 2014, by Robert Rector, senior research fellow of DeVos Center for Religion and Civil Society. The article was originally distributed by McClatchy-Tribune News Source. The subject is President Lyndon Johnson's January 1964 declaration of unconditional war on poverty. There has been much criticism about Johnson's War on Poverty. Robert Rector's opinion is clear, and I quote this passage in Robert Rector's article:

> When President Johnson launched the War
> on Poverty, he wanted to give the poor a "hand

up, not a hand out." He stated that his war would shrink welfare rolls and turn the poor from "tax-eaters" into "taxpayers." Johnson's aim was to make poor families self-sufficient—able to rise above poverty through their own earnings without dependence on welfare. The exact opposite happened.

The poverty level in this country in 2014 was 14.8 percent after trillions spent on the war on poverty. According to Robert Rector, the 2013 U.S. Census Bureau's report, points to the facts that 14.5 percent of Americans were poor. Compare that data to data supplied by reports in 1967 and the level of poverty in America is virtually the same. Did some people take the "hand up" and go on to be self-sufficient? Yes! I did, along with others! I went to college on a "War on Poverty Loan." And I repaid every penny back. Many did not pay back their loans, and that is what separates me from them—I needed a "hand up," and I did not want a "hand out!"

While driving through the mountains of southeastern WV, before dawn, and en route to a favorite trout stream, my good friend Austin and I were discussing my progress on this book. During this fishing trip, April 24, 2021, in between sips of coffee and dining on sausage and boiled eggs, we began talking about things that were Orwellian as well as details and examples of things that Saul Alinsky had suggested as a methodology for seizing power and radically changing society. Our conversation took an interesting turn when Austin related our conversation to a very worthy example, a recent event that was all over the news.

Austin pointed out some very key thoughts germane to the subject of the discussion we were having regarding the killing of a teenager in Columbus, Ohio. I wish to share the conversation with you, but first I need to describe what happened in Columbus.

You may recall that on April 20, 2021, in Columbus, Ohio, a girl of fifteen or sixteen, Ma'Khia Bryant, was shot to death by a police officer responding to a 911 call. Ma'Khia, the girl that was shot and killed, was holding a knife threatening to stab one of the other two girls involved in the altercation. You should research the police body cam recording of this tragedy in order to verify my previous statement. Both the girl being threatened and the girl the policemen shot were black. The death of any person is tragic, period! The grief of the family and friends has to be horrible due to the loss of life of their loved one.

Every time one of these tragic events happens, there is a rush to condemn police before the facts are presented. Each time there is a shooting, the media, celebrities, and people who get on social media rush to spin the event in order to whip the public into a frenzy. All too often they spin the story with false statements and incomplete stories that omit crucial facts in order to establish a narrative they want to create. This is absolutely deplorable. Is there a motive behind this spin?

The vitriol of the attacks on the Columbus, Ohio, policeman was both swift and unfounded. Some of these attacks appear to ignore the facts of the police recorder that captured the event. You cannot help but wonder why there is such a rush to condemn those who rush to a scene of violence in order to protect and serve. Consider the left's assertion that we need to reimagine the police!

Without law enforcement, all societies devolve into chaos. Does that not go without saying? Sure, it does! This chaos is a contrived method to further divide us, create more dissension, and to convince the country the system is bad and that change is needed. And you know who is in waiting to step in with "change you can believe in." This is Alinsky's and his community organizer's nirvana. It is what they have been working and waiting for. And the army of misguided is everywhere, and they are eager to step forward in front of the microphone and further tear down the law and order of the nation.

You should form your own opinion as to whether the following direct quotes of statements made on the TV program, *The View*, by Joy Behar and Sunny Hostin are creditable or not. The following direct quotes were taken from an article posted on the internet at https://www.washingtontimes.com/news/2021/apr/22/joy-behar-columbus-cop-should-have-fired-gun-in-th/ and written By Jessica Chasmar—the *Washington Times*, April 22, 2021.

And I quote Ms. Behar,

> "I've looked at the tape and I still can't fig-
> ure it out," she said. "Shoot the gun in the air
> as a warning, Tase a person, shoot them in the
> leg, shoot them in the behind. Stop them some-
> how. But if the only solution is to kill a teenager,
> there's something wrong with this. There's some-
> thing very, very wrong with the way these things
> are being conducted. Even if the cop had to do it,
> there's something wrong with it. I can't explain it
> any better than that."

I also quote *The View's* cohost Sunny Hostin. *The View's* cohost Sunny Hostin also disagreed with CNN's Don Lemon's take on the police video cam, Sunny Hostin argued that police incidents go from "zero to execution when there is a Black or brown person involved."

I suggest you do research to get the entire and unedited video recording of this incident as recorded by the officer's body cam. You can then make your own judgment. May I say that bullets fired in the air always come down and a projectile of lead in free fall can cause a lot of damage. What is the purpose for making a statement, such as "zero to execution when there is a Black or brown person involved"? I do not know, and I do not claim that the statement inflamed or caused further problems. Are such statements potentially dangerous when emotions are already out of control, as evidenced by the burning and looting in American cities? Statistics do not bear out the false narrative that policemen and women are going out hunting minorities.

I call your attention to another posted article that you should examine and analyze for purposes of this discussion. You can access the article, "Why It Matters that the Officer that Killed Ma'Khia Bryant Had a Military Background," written by Lydia Wang on Thu, April 22, 2021, 2:49 p.m. and posted on the URL https://www.yahoo.com/lifestyle/why-matters-officer-killed-ma-184928496.html. The following are direct quotes taken from the article referenced above.

The Columbus Police released Reardon's bodycam footage on Tuesday, but they did not initially name him as the shooting officer. The next day, the department shared a recording of Ma'Khia's original phone call and further video footage of the shooting. "We need a police officer here now," a girl says in the 911 recording, according to NPR. "We got these…grown girls over here, trying to fight us."

In the footage, Reardon arrives alone at the scene and repeatedly asks what is going on as Ma'Khia fights with two girls. "Get down," he shouts, before shooting Ma'Khia four times until she falls to the ground. Bystanders begin shouting that he didn't need to use his gun and that Ma'Khia was just a child. Reardon responds, "She had a knife. She just went at her."

The entire incident took place over the course of just ten seconds.

"A Black girl is dead because the cops brought a gun to a damn knife fight. If you don't know how to deescalate teen girls who are fighting, you should not be a police officer," Dr. Brittney Cooper, an author and Rutgers University professor, wrote on Twitter. "This is why our movements keep asking us to reimagine public safety and to defund the police. Because the cops act like the only tool they have is a goddamn gun. And that's a failure of both competence and imagination." This seems to be a classic example of vitriolic and inflammatory speech that just happens to be an incorrect representation of the facts I see on the camera.

There is a question that begs answering. What would have happened if no policemen were available or willing to come to the scene of this violence?

The following observations made by my friend Austin, which I also support, are presented below:

1. Would the shooting of a white teen by a black cop get this type of coverage from the drive-by media that seems to have a questionable agenda?

2. Would the shooting of a white teen by a white cop be presented with such vitriol?

3. Would the shooting of a black teen by a black cop also get this type of media attention?

4. Had the white officer merely fired shots in the air, and the knife-wielding teen then stabbed and killed the other black teen, would the white officer's failure to act be vilified? Would he have then been charged with a crime? I cannot help but believe that he would be charged and vilified. Seems like a terrible catch-22 for law enforcement officers whether they are male, female, black, or white clad in a blue uniform.

5. There has never been a society, that I am aware of, that can function in the inevitable chaos that would develop when there is no law enforcement. Abolish the police, are you kidding me? Did we not witness the violence and looting in the summer of 2020 when mayors and governors ordered law enforcement to stand down? By the way, these elected officials who are charged with protecting citizens and property allowed this violence while much of our media ignored the violence and claimed the right of people to protest injustice. Would a factual media presentation of what was being allowed in cities, under control of liberals, have cost the democratic presidential ticket votes? May I wonder out loud, if such an example of ignoring real news events is in fact a form of censorship by the media, that might make one question if we have a free press or a press that serves to protect and perpetuate a political agenda?

If ever there was a classical example of violent civil disobedience, the rioting protests of 2020 were exactly that. Yes, the Boston Tea Party was an example of violent civil disobedience. But it seems to me that there is, in force today, a constitution and rule of law that should be enforced in order to protect citizens and property from such wanton acts of violence and theft! What we witnessed in 2020 was not justifiable protest, and there was much violence associated with the protest. I am amazed that there are still policemen and policewomen that are willing to serve. We had better hope that they do not all quit and go home. And who could blame them?

Why does the drive-by media, such cities as Chicago or New York, and President Biden and VP Kamala Harris not scream to heaven about the "black on black" killings in Chicago? And the answer is, they do not talk about that crime, and the mayors do not address the crime aggressively because it does not suit or fit their narrative. So what continues to happen? Innocent black children and adults are routinely gunned down in that city because of drive-by battles of gangs. By the way, many of these gangs are representative of illegal aliens pouring through our southern border. That is a tragedy that should not continue to happen anywhere in America! Would someone in authority in the city of Chicago please provide equal protection under the law for the innocent black children, women, and men who are being gunned down in the streets of Chicago? The MS-13 gangs are murdering innocents and involved in gun battles with rivals for control of turf in our cities! I like what President Trump says on many occasions, "Get them the hell out!"

Defund or abolish the police and see how many more innocent children and adults of minority communities are murdered. The leaders in these cities and states need to increase funding for added police protection in these minority neighborhoods. These gangs need to be rounded up, given a fair trial, and if they are proven guilty, they should be imprisoned. If they are illegal aliens, they must be deported and not allowed to hide in "sanctuary cities." Mayors and governors took oaths, and they need to fulfill their sworn and moral obligation to protect all citizens. People in these cities should not have to live in fear, afraid to take their children to a playground. Do black lives matter? Yes, they do! And by the way, in America, all lives matter! Again, I call it like I see it.

By the way, going fishing was great! The catch was very poor; in fact, we did not catch anything, but the conversation that took place on the way home was interesting. We discussed examples of Alinsky methods that have been employed in recent years. The conversation was a game of questions with answers that were examples of Alinsky's methodology for taking down the establishment and seizing power and control.

The ride home debate began with the following question: "Was the 2020 election fraudulent?" Alinsky and his teachings were all about taking down the establishment by seizing power and control of the government. The Soviet premier, Joseph Stalin, was said to have made the following statement: "It is enough that the people know there was an election. The people who cast the votes decide nothing. The people who count the votes decide everything."

To say that the November 3, 2020, presidential election process and outcome was controversial is an understatement. To question the integrity of the election may garner you much criticism. Just ask the U.S. senator from Missouri, Josh Hawley. Senator Hawley is apparently a very good student of constitutional law. I am positive you do not need a constitutional lawyer to explain the following excerpts from our U.S. Constitution, because if you did, I would not be able to point out the following.

> The Constitution of the United States of America
>
> Article I, Section 4: Elections
>
> Clause 1: The Times, Places and Manner of holding Elections for Senators and Representatives, shall be prescribed in each State by the Legislature thereof; but the Congress may at any time by Law make or alter such Regulations, except as to the Places of chusing Senators.
>
> Article II, Section 1
>
> Clause 5: The Congress may determine the Time of chusing the Electors, and the Day on which they shall give their Votes; which Day shall be the same throughout the United States.

I have presented specific articles, sections, and clauses from the United States Constitution, verbatim, for a specific reason. One of the many reasons that the framers of the constitution, 1787, wanted the country to be governed by "rule of law" was to prevent such controversies as the one that erupted on the night of the presidential election, November 3, 2020. The founding fathers' goal was to prevent future officials from engaging in nefarious election activities that would assure a desired election outcome, one that suited their purpose rather than allowing the democratic process of fair and free elections to take place. Really, it is very simple when you contemplate how you want to be governed!

You can live by a set of rules and laws that govern society with a democratically approved rule of law, a constitution, or you can fall victim to the whims of those who desire to usurp power and avoid the democratic will of the people. The latter is how autocratic rule springs to life! The inevitable evolution of an autocratic power grab is that "We the People" are no longer the source from which government derives power. Unalienable rights can no longer be exercised.

The following referenced article will take you through pre-election changes in election laws, procedures, and rules governing the acceptance, collection, and counting of votes in numerous states, including the battleground states. Governors and other state officials outside the purview of the state legislatures made changes in election laws that were illegal because the constitution of their state, and the U.S. Constitution specified such changes had to be done by state legislatures! You will discover that battleground states were venues for pre-election maneuvering by Democrat governors and other Democrat officials. Why, you may ask?

These changes were made under the pretext that such changes in election law and procedures were made necessary because of the COVID-19 pandemic. I emphatically reject that premise. COVID-19 provided an illegitimate excuse for unnecessary and illegal manipulation of election laws by Democratic Party state officials or appointees. Seems to me that the only reason for such activities was that it made it much easier to stuff ballot boxes with ballots to assure Biden would appear to have won the election. I have been waiting for months for someone to show me creditable evidence that proves my facts-based conclusions are wrong. I need something other than the scorn presented by the media that sullies the name of anyone brave enough to ask such questions about potential fraud in the election. COVID-19 simply did not require such illegitimate and radical restrictions and creative changes for the ways votes were allegedly cast, especially when those changes were unconstitutional based upon both our federal and state constitutions.

These state officials, elected or appointed, were not empowered by the constitution to change state election laws. The right to change elections laws is expressly reserved for the state legislatures, according to the U.S. Constitution. The state legislatures did not make changes in these election laws; therefore, the changes were unconstitutional. Do these facts give credence to President Trump and his followers' claim that the election was stolen? I cannot think of a better way to steal an election and disenfranchise voters. What facts can anyone offer that legitimately proves that these actions were not a successful attempt to steal the election? This election was "Orwellian," and it employed many tactics taught by Saul Alinsky.

I refer you to the article, "Fraud & the 2020 Presidential Election," that you can find at https://www.discoverthenetworks.org/organizations/the-2020-presidential-election-fraud. If you desire to understand the constitutional arguments that were made, claiming election fraud, you should read this article. The article will take you step by step through the events of each of the battleground states prior to and after the election. The logic and rule of law that this article presents seems irrefutable to me, but as always, you decide. *You must read parts of this article! The facts presented will shock you!*

Note, the facts you just read in this article is a classic example of the methodology used by Alinsky and by totalitarians. They have been taught and have learned that you create a lie and say it over and over until people accept it as truth. When questioned, you either ignore the question or tell another lie. In addition, they attack the character of the questioner. Dare to question them and they will employ big tech to remove you from social media, or they will scorn you with attacks of being a disloyal American seeking to disenfranchise voters. They will shout you down! They will cancel you! The creed of America says that the individual has rights, and certainly the right to question has always been valid. The radical left does not want to be questioned. Why? Because the questioning might well expose their fraud! The truth might come forth as a result of the questioning.

Their lie, simply stated, was that the COVID-19 pandemic made it necessary to conduct the 2020 election differently. You tell me, did they "weaponize" COVID-19? They repeated and repeated the statement that the pandemic required the election to be handled differently. The pandemic gave them the platform to do what they had been trying to do with elections for a long time prior to the COVID-19 pandemic. The casting of votes in 2020 could have been conducted as elections had been conducted previously, with little or no changes. As of May 2021, those same people who said the election had to be conducted differently have continued to tell people they must still wear masks, even if they have had COVID-19 or who have been fully vaccinated. I question that position! I had COVID-19 in October of 2020, and I am also fully vaccinated.

Democrat governors knew it was useless to call the state legislatures back into session to change election laws because the legislatures were mostly Republican majorities in the battleground states. So unauthorized officials changed the laws, and they got away with their unconstitutional acts under the guise of necessity created by a pandemic. Why did they get away with the "big steal" even when cases chock-full of evidence of voter fraud and unconstitutional actions were presented to the courts? The Supreme Court of nine justices refused to hear the case when it was brought before them.

Most people can read and understand the excerpts I presented from the constitution. For that reason, it is fair to say you do not have to be a United States Supreme Court justice to read and understand that only state legislatures are empowered to change election laws. Here is where the "unfree press," that is and has to be controlled by leftists and totalitarians, comes into play. The press must repeat the lies or rhetoric over and over while chastising those who dare question the actions of the left. The press plays to their audience who has been trained not to question or think; they just accept. Controlling the press is a vital method used by those who seek to overthrow and seize power.

Here is the crux of the argument made by those who claim voter fraud and a stolen election. Five of these states had Republican-led state legislatures. Now, read again the U.S. Constitution's clauses I have presented, and you tell me who has the ultimate and final authority in the states to revise election laws and procedures. And you will find that those states in question also have state constitutions that mirror the U.S. Constitution!

One more point, I cannot condone the U.S. Supreme Court's refusal to hear a case brought before them. The attorneys presented clear evidence of violations of the U.S. and state constitutions. I have presented you that evidence. When you read the article that I referenced, you will clearly see the evidence.

What do you think about the Supreme Court standing on the sidelines during one of the greatest election controversies in American History? What was the duty of the United States Supreme Court? Chief Justice John Marshall must have screamed from the grave at what appears to be dereliction of duty. Still, I must note that the Supreme Court is an independent branch of government. They only listen to the cases they choose to hear. Could it have been as simple as the fact that they were afraid to do the right thing? I would not have wanted to be in their shoes, but they have taken an oath and been appointed for life to rule on just such constitutional controversies!

I want to spell out some specific actions taken in the battleground states and many other states that raised questions regarding possible fraud in the election? One thing that seems very questionable is the fact that these activities seemed to be most prevalent in the key battleground states and in major "blue cities." And these actions were planned months before the election. Since these actions were taken months before the election, does it not stand to reason that there was ample time to follow the constitution by having state legislatures take up the issues? Such actions caused eyebrows to be raised. Suddenly, and without the approval of state legislatures or state assemblies, voter ID was no longer important in some precincts; voter registration was allowed on election day. Unmanned drop boxes for ballots were allowed. Considering that absentee ballots were mailed out by the millions, there was no way to verify that the ballots stuffed into these boxes were placed there by legitimate voters or by voters who voted only once. There was no control of custody for ballots. This was insane, at best, and a criminal violation of the law in the worst-case scenario. Perhaps it was both, but more of the latter seems more plausible. Signature requirements meant to assure properly registered people were casting the ballots were eliminated as were postal markings in many cases. Photo identification, not necessary; just go ahead and vote. To the media and illegitimate controllers of the election, I must say that these election activities were not representative of American values.

Brave men and women did not fight, suffer, and die for such an abomination. The handling of the 2020 election is not the way a republic must operate in order to guarantee and protect the right of suffrage of those who followed the law as they cast their ballots. Such illegalities disenfranchise citizen voters. These actions are the means by which real freedom and democracy are lost! It is imperative that states move to secure election integrity before 2022. If they do not, the republic is lost!

Austin and I are still on the road home from our unsuccessful fishing trip. To be completely transparent, I must say that it is extremely rare that he experiences an unsuccessful fishing adventure. Lack of success, unfortunately, is a more regular experience for me. We felt gratified that we had solved the problem regarding the 2020 election, and we were ready for a new topic of debate. We were still not close to home.

The subject for discussion, disinformation! What do you think are classic examples of how the progressive left has used this method in recent years? We need a sound definition of the concept of *disinformation* so that we are all on the same page of understanding about this nefarious activity. According to the *Merriam-Webster Dictionary*, disinformation is defined as "false information that is given to people in order to make them believe something or to hide the truth."

Can you believe it, the term disinformation (*dezinformatsiya*) was first coined by Joseph Stalin and associated with the KGB? I can, and I also believe there are users of disinformation techniques who are thriving in our politics and within vast segments of our media. Those who use disinformation regularly employ this concept when they present lies in order to "sow seeds of doubt" within society. This is their method of attack upon leaders and courses of action they oppose.

Russian Collusion?

Do you recall the Russian collusion accusations directed at President Trump? The claim was, in simple terms, Donald Trump was a Russian asset and that he colluded with the Russians to get help to defeat Hillary Clinton in the 2016 presidential election. That had to be the case because the anointed one, Hillary Clinton, could not possibly lose to Donald Trump! The appointment of Special Counsel Robert Mueller would get to the bottom of this scandal. The investigation began in May of 2017 and lasted until March 2019. The American people were told the smoking gun against Trump would come out in no time at all. We heard that for almost two years.

After this alleged "Russian Collusion" was first introduced, it came to light that this charge was based upon the "Steele Dossier." Many news sources claimed that the dossier was paid for by the Clinton campaign and that the Steele dossier was a "disinformation tool" that was fabricated for the purpose of bringing down Donald Trump. Other media sources sung the praises of the Steele dossier as if it was gospel. Finally, Donald Trump was going down. Some news anchors boldly suggested Trump had better get his lawyer. Do you know that the vast majority of the investigative attorneys on the Mueller investigative team were democrats? Go to the internet and google the Steele dossier and you will find that major media sources continue to defend the authenticity of the document. Read the actual text of the dossier and see what the FBI did with the document. Keep researching and you will see what the FBI finally had to admit about the Steele dossier. Others flatly deny any validity to the document. Regarding the Steele dossier, some may say it would be difficult for everyday people like you and I to certify the truthfulness or lack thereof. I do feel that outcomes often speak volumes about authenticity. I have concluded that the Steele dossier was "disinformation" and was just such a tool as Saul Alinsky would have devised.

Finally, Robert Mueller, the man who was surely going to slay President Donald J. Trump, was ready to make his report public. Before I go further, let me say that all during the investigation, I said something is really weird here. The investigation dragged on and on. Millions of tax dollars were spent on the investigation that would surely take down Donald Trump. Did this whole thing turn into a convenient way to fleece the taxpayers of America? Or was it a convenient way to continue casting a negative light upon the president? Was it a way to take Americans' thoughts away from the roaring economy that Donald Trump ignited by removing unnecessary regulations that harmed businesses or to overshadow his leadership that lowered taxes and his mantra of always putting America first? The left needed to create negativity, and it did not matter that they fabricated a lie to do it. I think I know the answer to the why of the Steele dossier, but what do you think?

So I said that the Mueller investigation was a hoax! It was a hoax because if there was any merit to the accusations, there would have been an impeachment of President Trump long before the investigation dragged on for twenty-two months. They wanted the president that badly. As a result of the investigation, absolutely nothing was proven, and Robert Mueller looked like a deflated life-size clown in what was surely a circus of disinformation. After twenty-two months and millions of dollars spent, they had nothing! Why? Because there was nothing to be found! It was a hoax.

History was made when President Trump was impeached two times by the U.S. House of Representatives. He was acquitted two times by a trial in the U.S. Senate, where a guilty verdict would have removed him from office. I also know it is difficult to remove a president from office when he is, in fact, already out of office as he was during the second Senate trial and second acquittal. Not enough votes, either time, to get the man out of office. Remember, these two impeachments had nothing to do with the Russian collusion story. Are you aware of any pressing problems in the United States that the

House and the Senate should have been working to solve? I do! So why did our elected representatives waste time on two impeachments that had no basis for impeachment? If you understand Alinsky, I believe you may have some idea.

What did all of this "much to do about nothing" mean? Nothing has ever scared the left quite as much as Donald Trump and the followers of Trump. President Trump was proving that the left's story line about where America had to go on foreign policy and economically did not have to be. Regarding American foreign policy, America did not have to stand for terrorist attacks and the growing caliphate in the Middle East. The caliphate had to be destroyed, and it was! America would not send crates of cash to Iran. Iran would not be allowed to proceed with their nuclear program to gain nuclear weapons. North Korea was not going to be able to "blackmail" the U.S. or threaten Japan. China was going to be held accountable. NATO members were going to pay their fair share for the defense of Western Europe. Our military would be second to none and prove that "peace through strength" was the best chance of preventing war.

Regarding the economic forecast for America, was it not Barack Obama that said manufacturing jobs were not coming back to America and that we would transition into different types of economic production? Did Obama and Biden have some reason to want China's manufacturing to continue to increase and replace more and more American jobs? President Trump proved Obama was wrong. In fact, the fabricated legacy of Obama and Biden was being refuted by none other than Donald Trump. Under President Trump, manufacturing in America was on a significant rise. Corporate tax cuts were bringing factories back to our shores and keeping factories from leaving. Who would not want that for America? Trump wanted all health care products including medications to be made in the U.S. Steel and aluminum were on President Trump's agenda as products that had to be produced in America rather than allowing America to be dependent upon foreign sources. Only a fool would want to see America dependent upon the Chinese for health care products, medications, steel, and aluminum or anything else we would need.

President Trump would have corrected that dependency in his second term. Now, you know which country would lose this business as a result of a second term for Donald Trump? Yes, China would lose! Neither the left nor China would allow that. President Trump was proving that there were great days in store for America's future. Indeed, millions of Americans were experiencing better days. For decades, we Americans were aware of things that needed to be done for the improvement of America. We talked of things that needed to happen in order that America would ascend once again! Yet nothing happened! What irked the establishment, and especially the radical left, was the fact that it took less than four years for President Trump to make these significant changes that the establishment should have done decades ago! And they hated Donald Trump for his "America First" policies!

Four more years of Donald Trump might well doom the radical left to being buried in the trash dump of history. Trump had to go, either during his presidency or in 2021. There was no holding back. The tactic was to provide the American people with so much disinformation and lies that doubts about the president's integrity would arise. They preached the negative stories over and over and over. The doubts raised would result in enough discontent and questioning that President Trump would begin to lose support and votes. Also, by presenting the false narrative with an ongoing investigation, you could divert the public's attention away from the positive accomplishments being made by President Trump. They wanted to keep the public glued to the TV with the negative expectation that Trump would be proven to be a Russian asset in the White House. This was the patient Alinsky tactic that Alinsky's followers practiced from 2015 until 2021. It was disinformation. There is absolutely no evidence whatsoever that President Trump colluded with Russia. He was, I know, guilty of one major thing: He put America first! An "America First Policy" was something that neither the left nor China could allow to continue. They would lose power if there was another four years of President Donald J. Trump!

I just outlined the why and how of the totally false Russian collusion disinformation, used by the left, on President Donald J.

Trump. I would like to stop the discussion of Russian collusion at this point, but I cannot! The left accuses their opposition of activities that they themselves are guilty of and that they practice continuously. Please, evaluate the following paragraphs of factual information for comparison and contrast with all that you were told about the false charges made against President Trump and Russian collusion.

My word processing program still allows me freedom of speech. I intend to exercise that right, and I hope you will as well. May I reiterate what I heard the former governor of Arkansas, Rick Huckabee, say recently? I am paraphrasing, but his point was so well made. Basically, he said there was Russian collusion, but it was not with Donald Trump. The real Russian collusion was between Joe Biden and Vladimir Putin of Russia on the issue of the Russian Nord Stream 2 pipeline being built from Russia into Germany. Biden waived sanctions on the Russian company and the CEO that is overseeing the construction of the pipeline that will carry natural gas supplies into Europe. Guess who is a big buddy of the CEO in question. You got it, Vladimir Putin! You may be wondering, what is the problem with Biden waiving the sanctions?

The United States is the leader and the most powerful country of the NATO Alliance in Western Europe. NATO has been in existence for seventy years! The purpose of NATO has been to protect Western Europe from the enemy, Russia. Has Biden appeased Putin and the Germans with this action? What, I wonder, could be the effect of this event? The Russians now have leverage on the vital energy supplies of the Western European countries! Does that sound like a good idea to you?

It was the power of the United States that contributed to the downfall of the Soviet Union, and that in turn would allow for the reunification of Germany. The U.S. shielded Germany from the Soviets and Russia for decades. I challenge the Biden administration to point to just one historical fact that would suggest we can trust the Russians. As always, we must not paint with a broad brush. There are many morally good and brave Russians. But just as in any country, there are a select few who have no morals nor care for the welfare of their people and the country in which they live. They ascend to power for the purpose of gaining wealth for themselves. Can you imagine how much money Putin, his cronies, and Russia will make as a result of Biden's actions?

Please tell me how Biden's waiving of these sanctions against the company and the CEO responsible for the Russian Nord Stream 2 pipeline construction benefits the United States of America. Why would we put our NATO Allies in a position of dependency upon Putin for their energy necessities? What are the Germans thinking about? Does this action by Joe Biden conjure up any memories regarding his son, Hunter Biden? This action is counterproductive to the vital interests of the U.S. and NATO and is the action of hypocrites.

Do you remember the Biden executive order that cancelled the Keystone XL pipeline on January 20, 2021, only five months earlier than the lifting of the sanctions on the Russian Nord Stream 2 pipeline in May 2021? The Keystone XL pipeline would have transported some eight hundred thirty thousand barrels of oil, per day, from Canada to the U.S. Gulf coast refineries. There were some one thousand pipeline construction workers at the time Biden canceled the project. They lost their jobs. Reports suggest another ten thousand construction workers would have been hired to complete the project. Those Americans will not get the benefit of those high-paying American jobs because of President Joe Biden. Who knows how many peripheral jobs would have been created had the project been allowed to continue? Mr. President, do you know? And how many Russians will have construction jobs on the Russian Nord Stream 2 pipeline as a result of collusion by President Joe Biden with President Vladimir Putin? I am asking the question. As always, you can evaluate and make your own decisions.

The irony and the hypocrisy of these two actions of President Joe Biden, in the first six months of his presidency, is apparent to all who think and analyze. Environmentalists in the U.S. were overjoyed that the Keystone XL pipeline was cancelled! This was a great victory in the war against fossil fuels and for the preservation of the environment. Bring on the Green New Deal! But alas, the fossil fuel would be shipped by rail and trucks aboveground rather than in a sealed pipeline underground. Have you ever heard of train derailments? How about truck wrecks? I bet someone is smart enough to calculate the probability of pipeline leaks versus train derailments and truck wrecks. I must confess, I do not have such statistics. I do know that raw sewage leaves my home each day via a pipeline underground along the highway. I am unaware of any leaks, but I have seen numerous vehicle accidents along that highway. Also, I have seen train derailments in the vicinity. Perhaps you can use your skills to research who controls the trains that will now transport the fuel and make great profits. If you choose to do that research, I would encourage you to also determine who will benefit from the truck transportation of the fuel. Were the American people misled? There is another story of hypocrisy and irony in this story.

Mr. President, is a pipeline in our western states more harmful to the environment of the United States than a pipeline underground from Russia to Germany and throughout Western Europe? Why would you help Putin get a pipeline and cancel a pipeline that would transport fuel to the U.S. more cheaply from our ally, Canada? Why should Russia make great profits and transport natural gas more cheaply? Why would you increase the cost of energy for Americans at the pump? It costs more to ship by rail and truck than it does to deliver fuel via a pipeline, whether the pipeline is above or below-ground. The United States has less jobs than we should have, and the Russians now have more jobs than they should because of two decisions made by an American president. Based upon the total lack of any common sense or logical explanations as to why the president of the United States would make two such decisions, as the ones outlined above, I can only conclude there was Russian collusion. And Donald Trump was not involved either time. There is a glaring question that begs to be asked and answered.

Let us assume that in May of 2020 prior to the November 2020 election, President Donald J. Trump lifted the sanctions on the CEO and the company responsible for the construction of the Russian Nord Stream 2 pipeline. Based upon the facts you know regarding the false charges of Russian collusion against President Trump, what do you think the media would have said about Donald Trump and

Vladimir Putin? I think we all know what vitriol would have been endlessly voiced about President Trump right up to the time the last vote was cast or mysteriously found for counting.

Please, check the mainstream media for accounts of Biden's Russian collusion with Putin! The so-called media has rules for thee, but not for me. That is not journalism of a free and open press that serves as a watchdog for real collusion and corruption. The litmus test that all presidential decisions should pass prior to implementation should be one that is scrutinized with the query. Is this best for America? Was the lifting of these sanctions by the Biden administration best for America? You have the right and the duty to answer this question!

Do you realize that for the first time in seventy some years, the United States was energy independent? In fact, the U.S., under President Trump, was the world's greatest exporter of energy. What real American would not want that for America? Trillions of our dollars have been spent in the Middle East fighting wars. Thousands of American lives have been sacrificed, and many more thousands have been crippled physically and mentally. We were told that the U.S. and our allies could not afford for the wrong dictators to have absolute control of the world's energy sources of the Middle East. I accepted that premise, but I always said we should gain energy independence and save our treasure and blood from being spent on the sands of the Middle East. Surely, the U.S. could produce the energy we needed. Yet we did not produce that energy, and the blood and treasure we spent in the Middle East continued decade after decade. What a terrific price we have paid.

I realize there were, and there still remains, other national security interests for the U.S. in the Middle East, but we have been used! Donald Trump quickly removed the restraints on American energy production. The result was energy *independence* and lower prices for Americans. The fuel that drives our economy was less expensive, and all of America benefited. The U.S. became a net exporter of energy in a very short time period under the positive leadership of Donald Trump. Now that is an agenda of "America First" that I can support! How about you? Gas prices are now soaring since January of 2021.

Price at the pump has gone from $1.87 to over $3.00. Does anyone believe they will not continue to rise? The Green New Dealers, Russians, Chinese, and OPEC want the cost of fossil fuel energy, for America to rise! We are no longer the world's leading exporter of energy under the Biden administration. Which leadership do you prefer, Trump or Biden? Facts analyzed will tell the real story about how America was headed upward to new heights of prosperity and where we are now descending.

A Hostile Takeover: My Final Thoughts

There are elephants in the room, and they stand as questions that are going through millions of minds in 2021 as we approach 2022. Has the United States of America reached the zenith of our place in history and tilted so far to the left that we are starting to plummet in a downward spiral? Are we standing at the precipice and looking over into the darkness so many countries have fallen? Some will say these changes cannot be that bad. That is because they do not read history. Rest assured, there are many dark elements who want to see us fall into the inconsequential dark shadows of the world's stage.

While I do not have a crystal ball, I do have history to read that will provide an answer to the following big question. What will life in America be like if the radical left's agenda becomes the law of the land? That agenda is being implemented as I write. To answer this question, I have a modern-day example of comparison and contrast that should provide an answer and send chills through your heart because of where we may be heading with this socialist agenda.

There is a modern-day story of which we all need to be aware. Place a globe of the world or a flat world map on the table before you. Place your forefinger on the north pole and trace southward toward Washington, DC, 39 degrees north latitude by 77 degrees west longitude and pause there. Then proceed a little further south until your finger rests on the 38th parallel. From this point trace the 38th parallel eastward and you will pass just south of what used to be the Union of Soviet Socialist Republics (collapsed in early 1990s), move further eastward and you will trace over the People's Republic of China (Communist China), and continue eastward to the Korean peninsula on the 38th parallel and *stop*. Your forefinger rests on an international border, the border between North and South Korea.

This border exists due to the sacrifice of the South Korean people and UN forces, mostly American. That border had been established since the end of WWII. The communist dictator of North Korea, Kim Il Sung, got a blessing from the Communist Soviet premier, Joseph Stalin, and Chinese Communist, Mao Zedong, to attack South Korea on June 25, 1950. The war would last until 27 July 1953 and end where it started. Korea was the place the United States took a stand against communist aggression. The communists started a war as they sought to spread communism's power throughout the world. Communist aggression is responsible for the loss of millions of lives and the repression of billions more. Read the history; it does not lie. The communists have not yet taken the land south of the 38th parallel.

Straddle the 38th parallel, look north and you will see one world view of political economic governance that is in stark contrast with the view you get when you turn and look southward. Look north and you are looking at North Korea ruled by a communist totalitarian dictator who controls all land and the means of production and distribution to the citizens. Turn south and you see the Republic of South Korea, a democratic republic that allows for the direct election by the people of the chief executive. There are two other branches of government to divide power.

Neither I, or anyone else, has need of a crystal ball in order to see what could happen to the United States. All I have to do is take a look at the lack of freedom and destitution that is quite apparent in North Korea. Do not tell me that borders do not matter or that border security is not vital to the safety of a nation. It is the massed border security on the 38th parallel on the Korean peninsula that provides for the political freedoms, economic freedom, and success of South Korea. The 38th parallel's defensive fortifications, which are manned by both American and South Korean forces, is all that prevents communist aggression of North Korea from sweeping southward once again.

The communist totalitarian rule of North Korea stares across this invisible line at the South Korean Democracy and a mixed economy that has propelled South Korea to the tenth largest economy in the world. The South Korean economy is fifty-four times larger than the North Korean economy. Yes, I know that South Korea has twice the population of North Korea. Population is factored into the data bank on the site found at https://www.heritage.org/index/. Please, please, please go to this site! Once there, type in *South Korea* in the box "Find your country." When South Korea data comes up, look for another box that asks for you to type in another country so that the graph will plot both country's economic data side by side. Yes, you guessed it! I want you to compare North and South Korea. Also, at the bottom left of the graph, select the criteria that adds a comparison to the world average. From purely an economic standpoint, in which country would you want to live if you had to leave the United States? Any questions?

Here, on the 38th parallel, two very different ideologies share a common border, and the situation is quite precarious. Much is at stake along the 38th parallel just as it is inside the borders of the United States, at the American voting polls, and in the halls of congress in Washington. Take a look at the factual statistics that represent the failure of totalitarianism and socialism in North Korea versus the successes of the mixed economy in the South Korean democracy.

Go to the following URL site, https://www.theguardian.com/world/datablog/2013/apr/08/south-korea-v-north-korea-compared, for *the guardian's* presentation of the Datablog for statistical facts that compare North and South Korea on a wide range of economic topics. The facts are so stark in their contrast that they are a must read.

Go to the 2021 Index of Economic Freedom page found on URL site https://www.heritage.org/index/. Here you can type in the United States in the "Find your country" box and study a wide range of economic indicators. View the Index of Economic Freedom for North Korea, China, Venezuela, Cuba, or any country you want. Once you pick any country, there is an additional box that will allow you to compare that country with any other country along the lines of the 2021 Index of Economic Freedom indicators. The site provides you with a graph that plots the economic indicators from 1995 to 2021 side by side on the graph. You will find this a most telling comparison when you compare the United States of America to any socialist/communist country. Try it and form your own conclusions about what type of system you prefer to live in. There is no comparison! What is the left in our country selling? Whatever it is, I am not buying! Remember, when you view and compare the lack of economic freedoms and unalienable rights in those communist countries of socialism with our constitutional rights under the rule of law and free enterprise capitalism, you will be even more aghast.

According to the data presented on the site, https://www.statista.com/statistics/1035390/south-korea-gdp-comparison-with-north-korea/economy by Statista, South Korea's GDP, expressed in won, is almost fifty-four times greater than that of North Korea! The communists cannot feed themselves. Check their ranking on the Global Hunger Index. The North Korean's military spending, as a percentage of GDP, is 22.3 as compared to 2.8 in South Korea. The North's world ranking on economic indicators of freedom is 178th compared to twenty-fourth by the South. Infant mortality rate per one thousand live births is 26.21 in the North as compared to only 4.08 in the South. We could go on and on!

We have looked at Orwellian projections and the methods being employed by the left who are disciples of Saul Alinsky. We have compared our economic status to that of all of the failed socialist countries of the world. The basic freedoms and unalienable rights available to Americans as compared to the communist countries, well, there is no comparison as a zero score by the communists does not compute. Think it cannot happen to America? I bet the Cubans and Venezuelans did not believe it could happen in their countries either. I look at the rhetoric and the signs of the times and nothing makes sense.

So it appears to me that there is a plot and a plan that threatens what we have come to take for granted, our unalienable rights and economic freedom. I ask you to look at the platform of the left, listen to what they are saying, and make note of what they are doing as well as what they are not doing. When you think long and hard about these things, ask yourself if you want all power concentrated into one-party rule by the radical leftists. How you vote in 2022 is your business, but just know it is a crucial vote. Those who came before us possessed great wisdom, as demonstrated by the system they created that has worked pretty well for a very long time. I hope we do not cast votes that put our nation's opportunity for more success in jeopardy. I do not see any modern-day suggestion of governance that is as good as the one created in 1787!

Epilogue

Success is not final, failure is not fatal: it is
the courage to continue that counts.

—Winston S. Churchill

I chose to open this epilogue with Winston Churchill's quote because the wisdom of his quote provides individuals, groups, corporations, military forces, and nations with a north star of navigation on journeys that seek success in any endeavor. Whether you realize it or not, Americans have always lived, struggled, and thrived with the wisdom of such a famous quote. Americans have never rested upon their "laurels!" And if history teaches us anything, we know you can never afford to "rest upon your laurels." Americans, throughout our history, have experienced bitter defeats, but we refused to quit or to allow a defeat to identify who we are. Rather, we have chosen to succeed in spite of defeat.

Our foes, of the past and the present, have always been amazed by the fact that our warriors have not and do not believe that they can be beaten. Since Korea of the 1950s, it has been the politicians who are suspect! They have not been judicious when it comes to decisions of what battles to fight. And let me add that if you send Americans into harm's way, do not, and I repeat, do not tie their hands behind their back with ridiculous rules of engagement. The invincibility persona of our courageous fighters and their knowledge about what we fight for must be sustained. Failure is only fatal when you choose to quit! Thus far, we Americans have never quit upon the patriots and founding fathers who brought forth this glorious nation.

Today is the first day of the rest of America's history, and I am happy to say we are still here even though we are being tested. Therefore, we cannot fail the millions who have put their lives on the line, for well over two hundred years, to sustain this way of life. True Americans have always chosen to continue the fight because they value a way of life and governance that is unparalleled in the history of mankind.

My purpose for writing this book was to analyze the motivations and the significance of historical events that have shaped us as a nation. My goal was to make this presentation while comparing and contrasting the history of the past with the history we are now making. I felt that was necessary in order that we begin to carefully and faithfully take actions that will assure that the history of our future will be one that sustains all of the freedoms, values, and good traditions that resulted from the genius and courage of our founders. Will you take that challenge? I believe our founders are watching and listening! And I have benefited greatly by reading the thoughts of our founders as well as listening to my many friends who have read along as I write.

I wish to acknowledge the great help that I received from my friend, Charlie, both before and as I began the writing of this epilogue. Many of the points I make in this epilogue are the direct result of the late-night conversations he and I had on the phone and as we sat at his kitchen table. In fact, Charlie and I have had multiple midnight conversations regarding each section I have written. His interest, encouragement, and suggestions have been invaluable. Thanks, Charlie!

What the historians will write, about the future we choose to create, is dependent upon the actions you and I take, immediately, and continue into tomorrow and each day thereafter. We must attach a new urgency to the responsibilities of citizenry. If you appreciate your life, you cannot afford to be apolitical. Our country needs all of us to be politically proactive! We must not waste the lessons of history and let the radical left rob us of the heritage that has blessed us. It is through careful analysis of history, coupled with current events, that we are able to predict what is about to happen. Such knowledge can guide us to make the all-important decisions about what we must make happen for the salvation of our nation.

We older and younger people, who have enjoyed the great benefits of rule of law and the many opportunities afforded to us by our nation, do not want to die thinking that the great "American Dream," dies with us! To rest peacefully, we must do our duty that has been passed down by every generation since 1787. We must pass this torch of liberty on to our children and charge them with the responsibility of passing it on for all future generations to enjoy, defend, and to be duty-bound to pass liberty on to the next generation.

The following presentation about Churchill's leadership and philosophy for prosecuting WWII, along with a specific look at the 1940 Battle of Britain, will allow us to recount a time of desperation for an island nation and the world at large. As you read the following and reflect upon what you have read thus far, I hope you will analyze all of my writing with the following guiding question! How can the historical lessons brought forth in this book provide a north star for the United States in the twenty-first century?

"Success is not final, failure is not fatal: it is the courage to continue that counts." If ever there was a philosophy for assuring a long-termed successful endeavor for an individual or a country, I would rank this guidance at the top of my list. Winston S. Churchill was a leader extraordinaire! And Britain was lucky to have him during those dark hours of WWII. Britain stood alone against the onslaught of the Nazis during the Battle of Britain that began just after the "Miracle of Dunkirk."

Churchill and the British people stood defiantly when Hitler unleashed Hermann Goering's German Air Force, the Luftwaffe, on Great Britain. Make no mistake about it, Hitler wanted to destroy and enslave the British nation. The British, with "bulldog determination," achieved victory even though they were challenged by a most determined and vicious enemy.

I do not think I would have placed a bet on the British to win the "Battle of Britain." Nor were there many who believed that the rebels of 1775–76 could have defeated the most powerful nation in the eighteenth-century world. I believe it is plausible to think that neither should have won. Yet they did win, and it is important that we patriots of today emulate their persona and methods!

But in fact, there were some British in 1940 who apparently did not think they should try to win, and they favored seeking terms with Hitler. Can you imagine learned people being so naïve as to think you could negotiate with and trust Adolph Hitler? Do you believe that we can trust the Iranians, Russians, Chinese, North Koreans, or the radical left? I do not! (What worries me today is the fact that there are many Americans who do not realize the great danger we face. Many do not recognize that everything is at stake in this great political battle for the soul of America and the international battle we face abroad. We need serious patriot leaders for the perilous threats we face as a nation.)

And the proposition that Britain should consider seeking terms with Hitler was being voiced in 1940. You may recall that it was after the 1938 Munich appeasement of Hitler by Neville Chamberlain that Chamberlain waved a piece of paper and declared "Peace for Our Time." That was a short-lived illusion of a person who so desperately wanted to believe what could never have been. We all know how that worked out, and it should have served as proof positive that the only negotiation that Hitler could be forced to accept was a bayonet plunged into his throat. I can tell you this: Our enemies fear and respect only one thing, American strength and resolve. I do not see any of that in Washington, DC, today!

May I also say that there are many illusions being waved around for citizens who are not discerning, who do not question, or who are looking for the easy way and the free lunch. In the history of humanity, there has never been a free lunch, and there never will be such easy pickings. That thinking is an illusion that goes against the reality of natural law that all humanity is forever bound. These illusions are part of the "brainwashing" taking place in our public schools, private schools, and at the collegiate level of education. Sorry if you feel I have digressed, but there is much to say, and each part is a piece of a very large and complicated puzzle. Back to Churchill and Britain in 1940!

I would have bet a great deal of money that the British would not have won. But then I could not have known of the leadership ability and determination of the man who dared to have the courage to continue the fight and to never give in! Many foes in history have learned the hard way the British people are fighters.

> We shall go on to the end, we shall fight in France, we shall fight on the seas and oceans, we shall fight with growing confidence and growing strength in the air, we shall defend our Island, whatever the cost may be, we shall fight on the beaches, we shall fight on the landing grounds, we shall fight in the fields and in the streets, we shall fight in the hills; we shall never surrender.

Churchill made this determined and inspiring statement on June 4, 1940, at the House of Commons in spite of the fact that a few of his countrymen screamed for peace terms.

Churchill's philosophy, nature, and defiance were echoed throughout the world as a battle cry for victory. This battle cry served as a bold declaration that rallied both the citizens and the military forces of not only Britain but for Britain's future allies as well. His philosophy was second to none! The world and freedom benefited greatly by the defiance of the "island nation." The sacrifice and will of the British people under the leadership of Prime Minister Churchill resulted in Britain winning the Battle of Britain in the skies over the English Channel. I would be remiss if I did not speak of the wisdom of Franklin D. Roosevelt's "Lend Lease Program" that provided Britain with materials of war to continue the fight. There is much to appreciate and learn from this epic "Battle of Britain of 1940."

Before you read on, please, stop and reflect upon the entire story of this book. Read again the guiding question I presented to you. How can the following historical lesson and the entire book, for that matter, provide a north star for the United States in the twenty-first century?

Today, our country needs the fearless leadership of a man like Winston Churchill to lead us in the political battle to save America in the twenty-first century. We must adopt and use his philosophy. And just as importantly, our country needs an army of patriots who will stand up in debate and come forth at the 2022 and the 2024 elections. We need to take all of the like-minded people we can find with us when we go to the polling place to cast votes for the preservation of our freedom!

That means that you and I must use the democratic process and our free speech to save the democracy that has allowed us to flourish since 1787. This battle will be waged against a determined foe! To lose means that the United States will become unrecognizable and become a country that will fail economically and a country that cannot and will not stand up against the Iranians, Russians, Chinese, the North Koreans, or those from within who clearly hate what we are and are seeking to use our democracy and the so-called free press to destroy our system of governance, traditions, and values. Our enemies abroad want to see our economic system fail and our military might become unaffordable. They do not want to compete with free enterprise capitalism, the rightness of our moral standing, and they do not want to meet us on a desperate battlefield. They are using their surrogates they support and that we have elected to do the job of weakening and destroying this nation from within.

Much of the thrust of this book has been to put on display the perilous position that our nation now faces. Are we at the edge of a precipice and about to fall into a descending spiral like other nations that came before and eventually failed? I prefer to believe, and I must believe, that this nation is chock-full of brave patriots who have heard the "fire bell in the night" and who are rushing to preserve the land of the free. Remember the title of this book The Fight to Save American Freedom. And remember the subtitle, *November 3, 2020—The USA's Rush to Repeat the Darkest Failures of World History.* We need a leader who can put us back on that never-say-die ascendancy. A leader that we can follow who has the will to continue to climb the mountain toward the perfection of our creed, regardless of the number of times we will stumble.

You have made it, nearly, to the end of my book. Has this book made you uneasy, uncomfortable, or fearful about the future of the United States of America?

You may have now reached a conclusion, or not, that our country faces powerful forces from within and from antagonistic powers from around the world that plan to make "we the people" subservient to socialism, communism, and autocratic rule. They do not want to contend with the economic vitality and might of our economic system. The goal appears to be the destruction of our way of life and the freedoms we have enjoyed since the late eighteenth century. What are we to do in the aftermath of the November 3, 2020, presidential election?

The results of the 2020 election prompted me to title this book The Fight to Save American Freedom with the subtitle, *The USA's Rush to Repeat the Darkest Failures of World History.* We elected a president and vice president that are governing from a very far left perspective. That political position is antagonistic to everything that our nation has stood for, and it is destructive of our ability to sustain ourselves. They contradict themselves on a daily basis, but their goal remains the same!

Let me say this emphatically, "Never count the American people out!" But we cannot sit around and wait for someone else to fight the good fight. I believe, as did Thomas Paine when he wrote *The Crisis* in 1776. "These are the times that try men's souls." Thomas Paine was an ardent patriot for the American cause in 1776, and he wrote the following words:

> These are the times that try men's souls. The summer soldier and the sunshine patriot will, in this crisis, shrink from the service of their country; but he that stands by it now, deserves the love and thanks of man and woman. Tyranny, like hell, is not easily conquered; yet we have this consolation with us, that the harder the conflict, the more glorious the triumph. What we obtain too cheap, we esteem too lightly: it is dearness only that gives every thing its value. Heaven

> knows how to put a proper price upon its goods;
> and it would be strange indeed if so celestial an
> article as FREEDOM should not be highly rated.

I truly believe that we are in a crisis of our own! You may agree or not agree, but I feel this book has illustrated that point as being self-evident. The words of Thomas Paine were most appropriate in 1776, and in my opinion, they apply today. This crisis is so dire that I feel this is the time for a call for "all patriots on deck!" Americans have stumbled many times in our history when facing what seemed to be insurmountable challenges. We came back and fought on to the ultimate victory. We can do that again in 2022 and in 2024!

We cannot yield to these efforts to destroy our way of life. Think of all the sacrifices made by men and women who came before to create, build, secure, and sustain this nation. Can we, in good conscience, do any less than those who came before us? If you listen carefully and with quiet reflection, you will hear the desperate, encouraging screams coming forth from millions of graves where patriot heroes have been laid to rest every generation since Lexington and Concord, Massachusetts, in 1775. They implore us to "Fight on, never quit, victory is within your grasp, if you will but continue the fight!" You may feel that November 3, 2020, was a failure. If so, we all can take heart that failure is not final. It is the courage of Americans to continue that counts. We must stand strong just as the British did in the face of the Germans. We must stand strong just as those heroes of our "greatest generation" did when they stormed the beaches of Normandy on June 6, 1944. Never let it be said "We the people," the American patriots of the 2020s, were the people who failed to keep "old glory" waving over the "land of the free and the home of the brave!"

When you think of Biden-Harris and all of the radical left, I hope you think about the following:

1. our southern border;
2. a spending spree that will destroy our currency and our economic opportunities;

3.   the loss of energy independence;
4.   the increasing lack of law and order;
5.   the lack of a foreign policy that puts America first;
6.   the chaos of the Afghanistan withdrawal;
7.   Orwellian dystopia;
8.   socialism;
9.   the threat posed by China, Russia, North Korea, Iran, and terrorists around the world as well as the terrorists who are slipping across our border; and
10. I want you to recognize the need to vote in 2022 and 2024 so as to protect our children and grandchildren's future in the greatest nation of the world!

I titled this book *THE FIGHT TO SAVE AMERICAN FREEDOMS* with the hope that I might encourage millions of freedom-loving Americans to take up the fight against the radical agenda of Progressives who are destroying our way of life.

The statement made by the progressive democratic candidate for governor in Virginia, Terry McAuliffe, made freedom loving Americans furious. McAuliffe said, "I'm not going to let parents come into schools and actually take books out and make their own decisions. I don't think parents should be telling schools what they should teach." The defeat of McAuliffe is a repudiation of Critical Race Theory and Project 1619 curriculum instruction in public schools. The school house is not the place to confuse our children with some misplaced guilt about racism or the ridiculous proposition that there are multiple genders.

Public education should be controlled by the states. The bureaucrats in the departments of education in all fifty states need to understand that parents want schools to teach factual history, math, language arts, and science with greater vigor in order to improve student achievement. Parents will not stand for their children being indoctrinated and used for the purpose of advancing the false narratives of radicals.

On November 2, 2021 citizen patriots went to the voting booths and revolted against the insanity of progressives and the tyranny of autocrats! Votes cast in this revolt affirmed, once again, that democracy and our wonderful system of governance works when freedom-loving American patriots make their voices heard. We will not surrender our freedoms, we will not accept socialism, we will fight to secure our borders, and we will live free!

I am ecstatic about the results of the November 2, 2021 elections in Virginia, New Jersey, Pennsylvania, Ohio, and other states. Patriots in these states have taken the necessary first step to save America. It is up to all of us to carry this fight for freedom forward into the elections of 2022 and 2024! Patriots created this country, patriots have fought to sustain this wonderful nation, and patriots will win the fight to save this nation!

"Success is not final, failure is not fatal: it is the courage to continue that counts." Let this be the battle cry of patriots in America as we fight to protect this "Great American Triumph!"

P.S. Earlier, I promised to let you know my political history and who I am politically, though by now I am sure you know who I am at this time, but you may be surprised by my history. I first registered as a democrat. That was the party of my dad and his dad. When I went into business in North Carolina, I registered as a republican. By the time I sold my business and returned home to West Virginia in 2003, I was once again disillusioned, and I registered as an independent. I am, once again, a registered republican, but I am fiercely independent, and I will call out any who do not step forward to defend the constitution, stand for the national anthem, or pledge their allegiance to the greatest nation on earth, ever! She must be defended!

Thank you for reading!
Stan Duncan
August 2021

About the Author

Stan Duncan was chosen as the 2008 Preserve America History Teacher of the Year for West Virginia. This honor also placed him in competition for 2008 National History Teacher of the Year as part of the Gilder Lehrman Institute of American History in New York. The author taught United States history at three public high schools in Virginia and his home state of West Virginia during his twenty-six years of teaching. He holds a Master's Degree in Educational Leadership with a certification in Curriculum and Instruction. Stan was homeschooled by his mother for his first semester of formal education in 1957. In January of 1958, the author attended a one-room school in the Allegheny Mountains of southeastern West Virginia. Stan is the president of the Summers County West Virginia Public School Board in Hinton, West Virginia, where he resides with his wife, Donna.

CPSIA information can be obtained
at www.ICGtesting.com
Printed in the USA
BVHW080820240122
627015BV00001B/48